THE MERSEY ORPHAN

SHEILA RILEY

Boldwood

First published in Great Britain in 2019 by Boldwood Books Ltd.

This paperback edition first published in 2020.

1

Copyright © Sheila Riley, 2019

Cover Design by The Brewster Project

Cover Photography: Shutterstock

The moral right of Sheila Riley to be identified as the author of this work has been asserted in accordance with the Copyright, Designs and Patents Act 1988.

A CIP catalogue record for this book is available from the British Library.

Paperback ISBN: 978-1-83889-836-6

Ebook ISBN: 978-1-83889-321-7

Kindle ISBN: 978-1-83889-328-6

Audio CD ISBN: 978-1-83889-326-2

Digital audio download ISBN: 978-1-83889-327-9

Large Print ISBN: 978-1-83889-659-1

Boldwood Books Ltd.

23 Bowerdean Street, London, SW6 3TN

www.boldwoodbooks.com

This book is dedicated to that stoic generation who survived the dark days of war and its immediate aftermath. Heroes one and all.

1

SUMMER 1946

Nineteen-year-old Evie Kilgaren gathered her mane of honey-coloured hair into a loop of knicker elastic before taking a vase of heavy-scented lilies and freesias into the kitchen. The flowers were barely faded when she rescued them from the churchyard bin that morning.

Placing them in the centre of the table, she hoped their heady scent would mask the smell of damp that riddled every dwelling in the row of terraced houses opposite the canal and add a bit of joy to the place.

'Who's dead?' her mother, Rene, asked. Her scornful retort was proof she had already been at the gin and Evie's heart sank. She had wanted today to be special. Surely her dead father's birthday warranted a few flowers. Even if they were knock-offs from the church – at least she had made an effort, which was more than her mother had.

'I got them for Dad's...' Evie was silenced by the warning flash in her mother's dark eyes. A warning she had seen many times before. Rene gave a hefty sniff, her eyes squinting to focus, her brow wrinkled, and her olive skin flushed. Evie knew that when her mother had drunk enough 'mother's ruin', she could be the life and soul of any party or, by contrast, one over could make her contrary and argumentative.

'I thought they'd look nice on the table,' Evie answered lightly, quickly changing her answer to try and keep the peace. She should have known better than to mention her father in front of Leo Darnel, who'd moved in as their *lodger* six months ago and taken no time at all getting his feet under her mother's eiderdown. 'I found a vase in...' Her voice trailed off. Her mother wasn't listening. As usual, she'd disappeared into the parlour to darken her finely shaped eyebrows with soot from the unlit grate – make-up was still on ration – dolling herself up for her shift behind the bar of the Tram Tavern. The tavern was barely a stone's throw away on the other side of the narrow alleyway running alongside their house, so why her mother felt the need to dress to the nines was anybody's guess.

Out of the corner of her eye, Evie noticed a sudden movement from their lodger, who was standing near the range, which she had black-leaded that morning. Leo Darnel didn't like her and that was fine, because she didn't like him either.

He was a jumped-up spiv who tried to pass himself off as a respectable businessman. Respectable? He didn't know the meaning of the word, she thought, her eyes taking in the polished leather Chesterfield suite that cluttered the room and seemed out of place in a small backstreet terraced house.

'None of your utility stuff,' he'd said, pushing out his blubbery chest like a strutting pigeon. All the time he had a wonky eye on the bedroom door. He would do anything to keep her mother sweet and made it obvious every chance he got to show Evie she was in the way.

He'd been very quiet for the last few minutes, Evie realised. That wasn't like Darnel. He was up to something, she could tell.

He hadn't interrupted with a sarcastic comment as he usually did when she and her mother were having a tit-for-tat. His self-satisfied smirk stretched mean across thin lips as he hunched inside a crisp white shirt and peered at her.

His beady eyes looked her up and down as he chewed a spent matchstick at the corner of his mouth before turning back to the grate. His piggy eyes were engrossed in the rising flames of something he had thrown onto the fire. Her attention darted to the blaze casting dancing flares of light across the room.

'No!' Evie heard the gasp of horror and disbelief coming from her own lips. How could he be so callous? How could he? As he stepped back with arms outstretched like he was showing off a new sofa, Evie could see exactly what he had done.

'You burned them!' Evie cried, hurrying over to the range, pushing Darnel out of her way and grabbing the brass fire tongs from the companion set on the hearth, desperate to save at least some of the valuable night-school work.

Two years of concentrated learning to prove she was just as good as all the rest – reduced to ashes in moments. Thrusting the tongs into the flames again and again was hopeless Her valuable notes disintegrated.

'Mam, look! Look what he's done!' Her blue eyes blazed as hotly as the flames licking up the chimney.

'You are not the only one who can crawl out of the gutter? Mr High-and-mighty!' Evie was breathless when her burst of anger erupted, watching the flames envelope her books, turning the curling pages to ash. She balled her work-worn hands, roughly red through cleaning up after other people and pummelled his chest. Why? She caught his mocking eyes turn to flint before being dealt a quick backhander that made her head spin.

Her nostrils, which only moments before had been filled with the sweet fragrance of summer freesias and Mansion polish, were now congested with blood as traitorous tears rolled down her cheek. Evie dashed them away with the pad of her hand, ashamed and angry because he was privy to her vulnerability. Her pale blue eyes dashed from the range to her mother, who was now standing in the doorway shaking painted nails.

'That evil bastard burned my exercise books. They had all my notes in them – two years' work gone up in smoke!' She had scrimped and saved every penny for the books from her measly wages, earned from skivvying in the offices of Beamers Electricals.

'Who're you calling a bastard?' Darnel was not the biggest or strongest man she had come across, but was no less intimidating. Leaning into her face, his carefully enunciated words through nicotine-stained teeth dared her to retaliate. 'You had better watch your mouth, my girl.'

'I am not *your girl*.' Evie spat the words. '*My* father would've made ten of you!' *If his ship hadn't impeded a German torpedo back in 1943*, she thought. 'If he was here now there'd be no need for a jumped-up racketeering lodger.'

'I pay the rent in this house,' Darnel's voice was low and menacing. 'An' if you don't watch that attitude, you'll be out on your ear!'

'And you reckon you'll be the one to do it?' Evie knew she was skating on thin ice challenging Darnel. He had no compunction about hitting her, although never when her mother was around and always with the threat that if she opened her mouth, he would make life very difficult for them. But he had slipped up this time. Her mother could see what a snake he really was and would throw him out for sure.

'Don't backchat Leo,' her mother said. 'He's been very generous to us.'

Surely her mother wasn't going to side with this so-called

businessman, who was as slippery as a wet fish and operated his crooked empire under the radar of the local constabulary from their front parlour. 'Oh, well, in that case,' Evie answered with a withering sarcasm that could match her mother's. Rarely stooping to the lowest level of communication, she felt this occasion called for it.

Her mother coveted the money he brought in, blinded by the gifts he plied her with, no questions asked. It became apparent to Evie her mother would not allow anybody to spoil their cosy set-up. Not even her own daughter.

'He's good to you. That's all that counts, isn't it, Ma?' Evie detected a flinch in her mother's posture. Rene liked to think she was still vibrant and desirable, there was no room in her life for words like *Ma.* 'I've studied hard to get qualifications that could get me out of this bombed-out dump – I'm doing my final exam tomorrow.'

'Surely your friends will lend you their notes if you ask. What about Susie?' her mother said, blowing her nails dry while Darnel hovered in the background. Evie let out a snort of derision, recalling the taunts of her lifelong nemesis, Susie Blackthorn. Evie trusted her own sound knowledge, before she would ask that scatterbrain.

'I don't have friends.' Evie shot her mother a meaningful glance. She had been discouraged from making friends to look after her young brother and sister before they were evacuated to Ireland seven years ago. Then the war came, along with the Yanks, her mam's favourite servicemen... Evie had locked herself in her room to avoid them while the good people of Reckoner's Row tut-tutted their disapproval. 'You wouldn't even let me go to Ireland with Jack and Lucy – I was a twelve- year old child who had to stay home because her mother couldn't face being alone.'

'That's not the reason and you know it,' Her mam glared at

her, silently warning her not to say another word. Rene suddenly changed the tone of her voice when Evie remained silent.

'Surely there's someone you can ask. Honestly, you make a mountain out of an ant hill!'

'I'm not like you, Ma, I don't *ask people* – I prepare, I study, I get the job done under my own steam!' Evie knew her mother had no hesitation in asking for anything. *Splash the cash, make things better for poor Rene!*

'You're too bloody independent, that's your trouble,' Rene said, gingerly pulling out a straight-backed chair so she didn't smudge her nails.

'I shouldn't need to ask anybody, Mam. I've worked hard on those notes, and he knows it.' Evie knew Darnel wanted her out. 'Will someone sit the exam for me if I ask nicely, too?'

'Don't be sarky,' Rene said applying another coat of Cutex nail polish in Young Red to her bullet-shaped talons while Darnel poked the ashes of two years' work through the glowing coals. 'You've got a job. Why can't you be satisfied?'

'I don't want to clean up other people's mess for the rest of my life, Mam.' Evie had skivvied all her life and yearned for something better. She wanted to be like the girls who dressed smartly in twinset and pearls. 'I don't want to be the dogsbody doing everybody's bidding.' Evie's eyes blazed. 'I am more than a skivvy.'

'You've got a very high opinion of yourself,' Darnel sneered. Evie refused to respond to his arrogant put-down. A reply would provoke him into the row he wanted. She continued as if he hadn't spoken.

'Can't you see not every girl wants to depend on a man, Mam? I don't want the same kind of life you've had.' She would not fall prey to the first man who showed any interest. 'What thanks do the women 'round here get for cooking, cleaning and popping out babies until they have nothing left to give?' She wanted to be independent, successful. 'I want to be someone.'

'You'll be someone in Ford cemetery if you give me any more lip.' The threat rolled off Darnel's tongue like spit off a hot iron and Evie knew he could put fear into most people, but he didn't scare her anymore.

'I know your little secrets,' she said with a nod of her head to strengthen the hidden threat of betrayal, satisfied her words hit home when she noted a flicker of alarm. 'I know you hide your contraband in our cellar, and as God is my judge,' she continued, strong in the knowledge she had found his Achilles heel, 'I will see my day of you, Leo Darnel. But I won't have to sink to your level to do it.'

'You arrogant bitch.' He raised his hand to strike her again, but Evie was quick to get out of his path causing his hand to flounder in mid-air. Even though his earlier heavy-handed slap had caused her nose to pop, Evie would not back down to this contemptable man any longer.

She looked to her mam to see if she would intervene and when Rene did nothing, Evie shook her head in disbelief. It had come to something when even her own mother wouldn't defend her.

'Is there a chance you will bring Jack and Lucy home, soon?' Evie turned her impotent fury onto her mother. 'Or have you forgotten you've got a fourteen-year-old son and a ten-year old daughter? Maybe, they don't count – until they're earning – is that it, Mam?' She wanted to hurt her mother in the same way she was hurt.

'Tell her to mind her own bloody business, Rene.' His belligerent tone told Evie she had the upper hand and it gave her courage to speak her mind.

'You're nothing but a coward who refused to fight for his country, not like my brave father – a real hero.'

'Hardly, from what I've heard,' Darnel answered scathingly. But Evie ignored his remark. His words were worthless to her.

'You're nothing but a conniving conchie who spent the war years hiding in attics and cellars.' He'd built up his crooked empire when good men went to fight and, as a regular in the local tavern where her mother worked, she wouldn't be surprised if he'd had Rene wrapped around his little finger even then. 'You wouldn't be so quick to take the high ground if our Jack was here.'

'A fourteen-year-old kid?' Darnel sneered, 'I'm shaking in me boots.'

Jack might be fourteen, but he was as strong as an ox. Working on a farm in Ireland, he and Lucy ate good fresh food. Evacuation had done her siblings the world of good. They were the picture of glowing health, the last time she managed to visit. But this was their home, where they belonged, and she missed them so much it hurt.

'We were doing fine until you showed up.' Her angry eyes were transfixed on the crimson spray of blood on Darnel's singlet and Evie realised she had gone too far, when he lowered his head. All the while his eyes were fixed on hers. Circling her. Never letting her near the door. Flinty-eyed, he was like a bull ready to charge. The only question was – when? She could just make out her mother hovering to the side...would she come to her aid if need be?

The tight grip of his hand around her throat was swift and forced her lips into an O of humiliation. In the process the back of his hand clipped her lip and another spray of blood splashed his white shirt. Evie heard a small gasp coming from her mother, sitting near the open sash window.

'Leave her alone, Leo!' Rene's tone sounded calm to the

untrained ear, but Evie knew better. Her heart pounded fiercely. Mam would throw him out this time, surely? But it soon became apparent that Rene would do no such thing when her tone suggested she would only contain the situation. 'She didn't mean anything by it. Did you, Evie, love...? Tell him.'

For those few moments after she admitted knowing where he kept his contraband, Evie thought she had won the battle, but it was quite clear victory had slipped from her grasp.

'I mean it, Rene – if she doesn't belt up...' He didn't paint a picture, elaboration wasn't his style, but his vice-like grip said enough. Evie sensed her mother's agitation but doubted she would intervene. Darnel got away with murder where Mam was concerned. Loosening his grip, Evie slumped, rubbing her throat, fighting back the tears.

'Go see if our dinner's ready, love.' Rene relaxed visibly, screwing the top back on the bottle of nail varnish. 'My mouth's watering, thinking about that lovely piece of silverside Leo brought in.' Why did her mam always have to chivvy him out of a bad mood?

'This lot round here would give their eyes for a decent joint of beef.' Darnel said pushing out his pigeon chest and stretching to his full five feet nine inches. Rene was glad she didn't have to intervene. He had the means to deliver expensive, albeit knocked-off, meat when some of the neighbours couldn't even afford spam

'We've had steak twice this week, aren't we the lucky ones?' she said, humouring him.

'Black-market meat isn't something to brag about,' Evie said under her breath, feeling her stomach tighten in disgust when her mother gave him a look that held a promise.

'I'm too good to you.' Darnel's cocky reply gave him a swagger. 'You had nothing when I came here, and now look...' His stubby, ring-covered fingers spread to encompass the ox-blood leather suite, the dining table with four ladder-backed chairs that matched the mahogany sideboard – her mam's pride and joy.

'I would have the whole street in to show off my posh new furniture,' Rene said. 'There's not many who can afford silk drapes.'

Not just curtains? Evie thought with venom. Her mother loved the idea she was 'on the up' as she called it. There had always been an element of *them and us* where her mam and the neighbours were concerned.

'I'm not allowing the great unwashed over my threshold,' Darnel growled, checking himself out in the mirror over the fireplace.

Since when did it become your threshold? Evie thought, but didn't voice her question, knowing he would only kick off on her again. Great unwashed indeed!

The people who lived around here might not have much, but they had their pride and they did their best with what little they had. Darnel had grown rich on their hunger for anything that would relieve their grim existence in this bomb-scarred port, and never failed to remind them of his ability to come up with expensive goods still on ration.

'I was expecting a delivery, and it isn't where it should be,' said Darnel. Evie's eyes trailed to the cellar door and then to the fire before the penny dropped. She knew why he'd burned her books now. Darnel was vindictive. Her suspicions were confirmed with his next words. 'You refused to take in the delivery, didn't you?' It wasn't really a question, Evie knew. It was an accusation. More likely, the reason he burned the valuable work she had strived so hard to produce. His delivery was obviously contraband. Booze. Cigarettes. Ration books. The valuables he hid down in their cellar could put him in Walton gaol for years. Stuff that people who worked all the hours God sent could not enjoy unless they had the readies – because money was the only language Darnel understood.

'Nobody called today, and nothing was delivered.' She lifted a defiant chin, wanting nothing to do with any of his dodgy black-market schemes. She couldn't trust herself to look at him – if she did, she might crack him over the head with the brass tongs she still had in her hand.

'I'll put a left hook on that chin if you don't lower it,' Darnel warned and Evie, knowing he meant every word, turned to her mother who gave a slight warning shake of her head.

'Come and keep me company at the table, Leo.' Her mam was sitting at the table by the open sash window, fanning herself with the *News of the World*, and her eyes darted a silent warning. 'Let's have the wireless on, listen to *Family Favourites*.'

'You don't want to see him for what he is, do you, Mam?' Evie's shaking voice was barely above a whisper. Everybody knew Darnel was a crook who enticed people with his money. Then cowed them into dependency. *Well not me, Mam. Not me.* She would rather spit in his eye. But that would mean sinking to his level. And it would be a cold day in hell before she sank that low.

'Evie...' Her mother's green eyes were pleading, but Evie had a stubborn streak.

'You expect me to back down to this bully?' Evie said as she headed to the kitchen door. Darnel took the seat near her mother and dashed away a buzzing bluebottle. She flinched, causing a satisfied grin from Darnel and a slow shake of her mother's head. His amusement was plain to see when he pulled a fat cigar from a silver case.

Flash bastard... Evie thought. She'd seen men with families who had to work every hour in grease and grime, bad weather and worse. They shared match-thin hand-rolled cigarettes on a pin, just to get that one last puff. Cigars, an unheard-of luxury, were beyond the prospects of dock and factory workers who occupied Reckoner's Row's line of neat terraced houses.

'We don't need a lodger, Mam.' Evie's voice became a high-pitched squeak. 'You've got the job in the pub, and as soon as I've finished my course, I can hang up my mop bucket and get a secretarial job at Beamers. They pay decent money and my tutor said she'll give me a good reference.'

Having worked as an office cleaner at the electrical works since she left school at fourteen, Evie longed to climb the ranks to office clerk. To better herself. To save the money to bring her siblings home from Ireland. And to hell with Leo Darnel!

Her mother's eyes implored her to be quiet as Darnel picked up the Sunday newspaper and rustled it noisily, drowning out the wireless and the heartfelt messages to families of soldiers still serving abroad. Evie swallowed angry tears of injustice that threatened to spill onto her bruised cheek. The spiv would have to go before the authorities came sniffing around and they all ended up on the street. Hurrying out to the scullery, Evie's tears fell on to the huge piece of meat he had supplied the day before

Preparing the tray, which her mother had borrowed from the Tram Tavern and had conveniently forgotten to take back, she heard him passing through on his way to the lavatory down the yard. This was her last chance to try and talk some sense into her mother. Quickly, she filled the tray and elbowing the door open, she hurried back into the kitchen.

'Mam,' she pleaded, brushing away the tears once more, 'we can't go on like this, walking on eggshells when he's around. Talking in hushed voices when he's resting his eyes.'

'What have I told you about that mouth of yours running away with itself?' Her mother's eyes darkened, and Evie felt a cold hand turn her racing heart to ice. She was beaten. Her mother was onto a good thing and would not let Darnel go in a hurry.

What's the use? she thought. Mam was hardly going to take her side over his. But Evie knew she must try and make her see sense, for both their sakes. 'Are you going to let him treat us like dirt under his shoe?' she asked, banging the tray so hard on the table it made the cups rattle and upending the salt cellar.

'You're not saying that when you're eating the good food he brings in,' Rene countered, absent-mindedly throwing spilled salt over her shoulder. 'You get on my nerves, the pair of you.'

'What's got you spooked, Mam?' Evie asked, plucking the skin on her fingers, sensing her mother was holding something back. 'You don't usually give in to him so easily.'

'Leave it, Evie,' Rene warned. 'There are some things I can't talk about... things you wouldn't understand.'

'By God, he's got you well trained, Mam.' Evie slowly shook her head – something wasn't right. Rene Kilgaren wasn't the kind of woman who scared easily, and certainly not by the likes of Darnel. No, Evie suspected her mother had something more troubling on her mind. Why else would she be so blasé about the way the spiv treated her eldest daughter?

'This has nothing to do with Leo,' Rene answered. 'All I can say is, ask no questions and I won't have to lie.' Rene's face, still handsome if somewhat lived-in, was now pinched with worry. Evie recognised the expression. She had seen that look often when Da had been home on leave too long and they had no money.

'He needs locking up, Mam,' Evie said. 'He's as crooked as his own front teeth.'

'He's got a good heart,' Rene answered. Out of habit she pinched the lit end of a half-smoked cigarette, putting the remains on the mantelpiece next to the clock for later. Evie knew her mother was trying to distract her from asking too many questions when she raised the volume on the wireless. 'Did you forget

Leo bought this wireless, when you were singing along to Vera Lynne?'

'If he paid for that wireless, I'll eat me hat,' Evie snorted. 'If he's so generous, why won't he let you have the money to bring Jack and Lucy back? This is their home, too, remember.' Rene picked up the cigarette she had just extinguished and re-lit it. Evie could tell she was nervous for some strange reason.

'I can't bring them home just yet – and I do want to, believe me.'

'Throw him out, then.' Evie countered, hands on hips.

'I can't, I need his rent money – and never you mind what for,' Rene said quickly. They were so engrossed in their exchange they didn't hear the back door quietly close. Then, more quietly Rene said, 'Evie, if anything ever happens to me, just remember, I could not burden you with the ugly truth.'

'I will never trust him,' Evie said imagining her mother was still talking about Darnel. 'I've seen his runners taking the betting slips from hard-up housewives, traipsing down back alleys, rummaging in their pinny pockets for an extra penny or two. If they haven't got the cash, he lets them have the bet on trust – with a huge interest charge thrown in for good measure!'

'It's up to them if they fancy a flutter,' Rene defended Darnel. 'He doesn't put a gun to their heads. Anyway, it's not him I'm talking about.'

'Then who?' Evie asked angrily.

'That's enough, Evie.' But Evie wasn't listening. She was getting into her stride.

'Why is he lodging in a dockside backstreet when he can afford all these luxuries? What about his smart house in Formby, by the sea?'

'He's got to be here, near his work.' Rene knew he could not bear to sever all ties with the busy port he grew up in. Nor could he bear the wife he'd left behind.

'It's no use trying to get through to you, Mam, not when you're in this mood.' She would never throw Darnel out. The expensive presents he brought home kept her sweet.

'Evie...' There was a note of caution in her mother's tone that told Evie she should say no more. Women who made men look small around the tough, dockside streets did not go unpunished.

'He's the lodger. He's got no right...' The slightest nod of her mother's head was a warning that reduced Evie to silence. All her life she'd been told to keep her eyes open and her mouth shut. Say nothing. No matter what she saw.

But should I? Evie thought rebelliously. This man was nothing to her and she didn't want to stick around to see him rule her mother with fine things... An easy life was seductive to a woman who had nothing, she supposed, but she didn't have to stay around to see it.

'You wanna watch that mouth of yours, girl.' Darnel's voice accelerated Evie's heartbeat immediately and she spun around. How much had he heard?

Enough, if that grim expression on his face was anything to go by. She would have to brazen it out, even though her legs didn't feel strong enough to hold her.

'And why do I have to watch what I say?' she countered, picking up the boiling hot earthenware teapot. If he lifted one finger to her again, he would regret it for the rest of his life.

'Go and see Connie.' Her mother, sounding defeated, lowered her head and stared at the floor. Her voice was barely audible as she added, 'She's got a spare room.'

'But Mam...' Darnel's firm grip on her arm silenced Evie. The action told her he had won. He had got his way. Stunned by her mother's betrayal, Evie glared at both of them, repulsed.

'Evie.' Her mam didn't look at her. 'There's a small suitcase on top of the wardrobe.' Her mother's conquered tone spoke volumes, her words a sharp slap.

Devastated, Evie took the stairs two at a time. Her own mother had disowned her. Even as she bundled up what few possessions she owned, Evie willed her mother to come into the small back bedroom and tell her it was all a misunderstanding. But she didn't.

'Keep your bloody suitcase, Mam,' Evie said to herself as she filled a pillowcase with her few measly belongings. 'You never know when you might need it.' She would see her day of both of them. 'I've been looking after myself for years, it makes no difference now.' Wondering how a mother could choose a man over her own kids, she didn't look back at the sparsely furnished bedroom before slamming the door shut behind her.

'I wouldn't stay here if you paid me,' Evie shouted as she reached the bottom of the stairs. Nor would she beg Connie for a room. Evie would find a place of her own. 'When he tires of you and you haven't got someone fetching and carrying for you, it will serve you bloody well right, Mam!' Her fiery words carried through the closed kitchen door as Evie hurried down the narrow lobby. Grabbing the brass doorknob she had polished that morning she gave the front door of the three-up three-down redbrick terraced house a hefty slam.

The narrow street was teeming with noisy kids. Boys in short trousers were swapping bits of shrapnel left over from the war, while young daredevils cooled off by diving from the bridge into the grotty canal. Every front door was open, except theirs. Darnel didn't like fresh air – or neighbours calling in for a natter. Breathing in the dusty heat, she couldn't recall the last time their front door stayed open until bedtime, like everybody else's.

* * *

'Evie, your nose is bleeding!' Danny Harris, hurrying down the steps leading to the bridge, stopped when he got to Evie's gate. He leaned on the granite post of the gate she had just opened and his deep authoritative voice gave Evie cause to cover her face with her hands. Film-star handsome and tall as a door, Danny was a sergeant in the King's Own, and the last person she wanted to see right now.

Feeling bedraggled, she noticed his indomitable mother, whose thick leg-o'-mutton arms were tightly folded across a stately bosom, keeping watch from her front gate. It was common knowledge Ada Harris thought her family were a cut above the Kilgarens and she made no secret of her disdain.

'Ten out of ten for observation, soldier.' Evie's feeling of irritation turned to humiliation as she fumbled for her handkerchief, while trying to ignore Leo Darnel's voice carrying down the lobby and through the closed front door. His furious expletives were proof he hadn't yet finished this fight.

'Here, let me help,' Danny said, putting down the heavy-looking kitbag that had been slung over his shoulder as if it weighed nothing. Evie felt a rising panic. She didn't want Danny mixed up in her fight. Breathing hard, she straightened her back, lifted her chin and said the hardest words she could muster.

'You can mind your own bloody business and keep walking.' Her words, spoken with plausible conviction, dampened the pitying expression that flittered across his handsome features and gave Danny no choice but to back off, probably believing she meant every syllable. Evie's blue eyes were wide with fear.

'Fair enough,' he said amiably, 'if that's how you feel.' Picking up his kitbag, he gave her a smart salute before making his way down the street towards his disapproving mother. Evie knew that

Ada Harris would not condone her precious oldest son fraternising with a common skivvy. Even though Ada was a cleaner in the Tram Tavern next door, she described herself as the housekeeper.

Watching his retreat, Evie brushed a strawberry-blonde curl from her pretty freckled face as a ship's horn gave a low moan in the nearby dockyard. It sounded just how she felt.

There must be something better than this, she thought, momentarily distracted by Leo Darnel's cronies huddled in the shadow of the bridge playing an illegal game of pitch and toss. The waterfront was crammed with people scratching an existence and making do, but she didn't want that.

She wanted to make something of herself. Depend on nobody. She would not emulate her mother or live off the corrupt earnings of a villain. Before she closed the gate at the end of the short, tiled path, the front door opened and was slammed shut again, her mother's voice loud and piercing – as if she was struggling to keep the argument contained.

But Evie knew that was not going to happen when the door suddenly flung open with such force it bounced off the lobby wall. She had no time to flee as Darnel launched himself down the path. His strong hand gripped her long fair hair that had escaped the doubled loop of knicker elastic, forcing her head back onto her shoulders. The pain slicing through Evie's head and neck was nothing compared to the sudden thundering slap that caught her side-on.

'Go to Connie,' her mother hissed, trying to hold Darnel back 'She'll see you right!'

2

'Isn't someone going to help that poor mare?' Connie Sharp, pulling pints behind the bar of the Tram Tavern, could hear the desperation in Evie Kilgaren's voice over the din of Sunday afternoon drinkers.

'If it's not my missus,' said a man gazing into his pint, 'then, it's not my concern.'

Connie thrust a pint of dark mild beer on to the bar in front of him and rang the loud clanging bell.

'Ten minutes for you lot to drink up and bugger off home,' she called in a voice that brooked no argument. Working a dockside pub, she had to be tough, but fair. The drinker's attitude did not surprise Connie. She knew that local men, suited and booted, wanted to enjoy their pint in peace after a hard week's graft on the docks, and did not involve themselves in another man's argument. Lifting the counter flap after serving the last customer, she slipped from behind the bar, dropping it with a bang behind her.

'Sharp by name and sharp by nature, that one,' said a bent-nosed stevedore through a fog of Old Holborn. 'I wouldn't leave her ten bob short in her wages, that's for sure.'

Connie shot him a dagger of disapproval, but he didn't care as he downed the dregs of his beer.

'Mind your manners, you!' Connie said, her marine-coloured eyes blazing as she stormed across the chequered floor and headed towards the window. With innate certainty borne of growing up in this tough port where noise, dirt and poverty were a fact of life, local lore dictated people keep their noses out of another man's business. And for the same reason they expected nobody to poke their snout into matters that did not concern them. But Connie didn't think like that.

'I'm dying of thirst over here,' someone called, rapping the bar with a silver shilling.

'Then die quietly.' Connie threw the words over her shoulder. 'The bell went for the last orders of the afternoon ten minutes ago – so when you've snuffed it, I'll send for your Aggie to come and cart you off.' It was a good thing the pub closed at three each day, otherwise this lot would carry on drinking 'til they had no money left to spend. She was sure they had hollow legs, these tough, hard-working dock workers who barracked and bantered without malice – well, most of them, anyway.

Unlikely as it sometimes seemed, she knew this was a close-knit community who had fought a war together. They'd lost loved ones, their homes, and even their children – some departing to long years of evacuation, others to eternity.

Nursing in Italy during the war, Connie knew enemy raids on the nearby docks and railways had almost brought Merseyside to its knees, especially this dockside area of North Liverpool where the life force of the country's existence ebbed and flowed every single day.

But the local community of stout-hearted women whose husbands had gone to war staved off starvation and bowed to nobody – not even the enemy. They were not beaten then, and looking out of the window, Connie could tell by the sound of their robust jeers they weren't broken now either.

'Why would Rene give house-room to that spiv? Leave her be, you bully!' a neighbour yelled from her front door, obviously alerted by the disorder outside the tavern. 'You wouldn't hit her if she had her father behind her!' The women of Reckoner's Row were gathered at the bottom of the bridge near the tavern watching the commotion with interest, although keeping a respectable distance.

'That mother of hers is no better than she oughta be, neither!' Ada Harris called, scurrying up the street in carpet slippers so as not to miss anything. *There's no show without punch*, Connie thought, watching the tavern cleaner join the gossiping swarm. The women, clannish through shared hardship and misfortune, were less inclined than the menfolk to keep their opinions to themselves. But Connie knew they'd give their old man a blow by blow account over Sunday dinner, whether his nibs liked it or not.

'They're going at it hammer and tongs...' Ten-year-old Bobby Harris had stopped collecting the glasses, a little job he did on Saturday and Sunday afternoon to help Connie and for pocket money. He was on tiptoes looking out of the window, craning his neck to get a better view. He winced when he saw Evie being dragged out into the street by her long, sand-coloured hair.

'Evie's giving as good as she gets, but she's no match for the spiv.' Everybody in Reckoner's Row called Leo Darnel 'the spiv' – although never to his face.

'I bet a pound to a pinch of horseshit, Rene comes into work with another shiner,' Connie said, peering over Bobby's head to get a better view. Her concern was growing as she added, 'it's not like Evie to get into an argument in the street, and certainly not with the spiv.' Pushing up the net curtain to get a better view, she ignored Bobby dragging a wooden crate. 'Rene jumped out of the frying pan and into the fire when she took up with that crook! You'd think she would have more sense.'

Connie never imagined the barmaid would take up with the spiv after suffering that bloody husband of hers. Frank Kilgaren – an outside angel if ever there was one – was a tyrant in his own home. He'd done Rene a huge favour when he got himself blown up in the Atlantic. But Leo Darnel was notorious for dealing in the black market and other nefarious activities. His arrogance sickened Connie, who knew he had Rene just where he wanted her, hiding his contraband in Rene's house while his own house in Formby near the posh seaside resort of Southport was squeaky clean. He wouldn't shit on his own doorstep, Connie thought, skewering him with an unflinching glare, but he didn't mind sullying Rene's. The man was a thug who could silence the bar just by walking into it.

'Ma said he's Rene's lodger,' the boy said, and Connie's dark eyes rolled heavenwards.

'Some might call him that, Bobby.' Connie's voice betrayed the revulsion she felt. Since Frank's ship went down, Rene was like a caged bird set free.

'It's Evie I feel sorry for,' Connie said. 'That girl hasn't had it easy. Maybe it's just as well the younger two are still in Ireland.' Although not one to judge, thirty-year-old Connie had standards. Rene's riotous revelry was the talk of the street. After Frank copped it, visiting servicemen were often late-night visitors, especially during the war.

Bobby clambered aboard the upturned crate and rested his chin on the wooden sill to get a better view of the crowd outside. The women of Reckoner's Row, like cooing pigeons, huddled near the wooden railings lining the Leeds to Liverpool canal lambasting the sweaty man.

'He's lost the buttons off his shirt and his vest is splattered with blood!' Bobby exclaimed, wriggling on the crate, certain he had a splinter in his knee.

'But whose blood is it?' Connie wondered out loud. She dug her nails into the palm of her hands, wishing she were a man who could knock seven bells out of the spiv when he lunged at the pretty girl in a torn dress. Connie noticed Evie was too quick for him and had the good sense to step out of his way.

Moving from the window, Connie slowed her pace at the door and watched as Rene hurled herself down the narrow path of the redbrick terraced house. Her bare feet slapping the rust-coloured tiles as she lunged into the tangle of arms. Dragging Darnel's hands from her daughter's waist-length hair, Rene stumbled into an untidy heap when Darnel pushed her away and Connie tensed.

Gasping for breath, Rene scrambled to her feet, pushing back the bottle-blonde hair sticking to her damp face and dragged her daughter out of harm's reach.

'That poor girl...' Connie said, pressing her lips into a stiff straight line, aware that on a sweltering day like today every door in the single row of jerry-built terraced houses would be open. The boy should not be witness to such a carry-on, she thought. He should be home eating his dinner. Bobby was the youngest of Ada Harris' three kids – *an accident,* Ada called him even within his earshot – and they lived at the other end of Reckoner's Row next to the small bridge and the debris.

'Bobby, did I just hear your mam calling you?' Sometimes, this wasn't the place for a ten-year-old boy to spend his time. He should be down on the debris with the rest of the kids playing football or cricket. The debris was the space where the two houses adjoining his own home had been blown up during the war. Luckily, Bobby had been evacuated and his family were in the air-raid shelter. His older brother Danny fighting on the beaches at Dunkirk had also had a lucky escape while Ada's only daughter, Grace, was a stewardess on an ocean-going liner. All in all, Ada Harris and her family led a charmed life, but the same could not be said for Evie Kilgaren.

'I don't want to go home, I'd rather stay here, with you,' Bobby said, his cheerful face turning a shade of pink under the usual muck that accumulated during his normal day, and Connie ruffled his unruly mop of dark hair.

'If I know anything, Ada will have your guts for violin strings if you're late for your Sunday dinner,' she warned.

'Mam's got our Danny to talk to – he's home on leave so she's not interested in what I get up to.' Bobby was still looking out of the window, and his candid observation pulled on Connie's heartstrings. She sighed. The boy might be right, Ada was besotted with her oldest son and told anybody who would listen how proud she was of his bravery during the war.

'Who needs a war when you've got this on your own doorstep,' Bobby said as if privy to her thoughts, his eyes glistening with excitement. 'I love a good scrap, don't you, Connie?'

'No, Bobby, I do not.' Her voice was sharper than intended. 'Especially when it involves poor Evie. She doesn't deserve to be treated that way, no kid does.' Sickened by events outside, the oppressive heat was making her unusually irritable and Bobby turned, his face a crumpled frown.

'Didn't you want kids of your own, then?' he asked with child-like innocence.

'Don't you tire of asking questions?' Connie asked, returning to her duties and whipping up the beer-stained bar towels. She lashed them into the sink with such force the water splashed over the bar. Of course she wanted children of her own. But that joy was not to be. So, there was no use fretting about it.

'Why don't you go and get your dinner and stop mithering me?' The pub had been busy since she opened up until closing time, and she was looking forward to putting her aching feet up for a few hours before the night shift. Although, she doubted she would get much peace.

Mim, her mother, would want every tiny detail of the fracas, even though she had the advantage of a front-row view from behind the lace curtains in their living room upstairs.

After a few moments, Connie realised she had unsettled Bobby with her hasty retort, and she felt a pang of remorse for being so short with him. He wasn't a bad kid, he just got up to mischief when left to his own devices. But what ten-year-old didn't?

'I'm sure you must be starving,' she said, her voice softening, 'a growing lad like you?' She relaxed when his sudden cheeky grin let her know they were pals again. Having given up hope of having children of her own, she often treated Bobby like the son she never had – and he took full advantage of her kind heart.

'D'you know everyone round 'ere, Connie?' Bobby asked.

'Aye, Bobby, I'm like the fixtures and fittings,' she answered, drying another glass and putting it on the shelf above the bar.

'Didn't you want to get married?' His forthright manner never ceased to raise an eyebrow. 'I mean, you're not *that* old – I'm sure someone would have you!'

'I'm fine the way I am, thank you.' Connie busied herself putting glasses behind the bar, so he couldn't see the smile turning up the corners of her generous lips. A former nurse, she had served in France and Italy during the war and Bobby was always asking questions about her time there.

She thrilled Bobby with stories about the heroic deeds of the brave servicemen, although remaining deeply private about her own war – especially to Mim. Her mother didn't need to know about the secrets that had cost her the nursing career she loved.

Being the type of woman who didn't think too deeply about things she had no control over, Mim wouldn't understand why she couldn't face returning to nursing after Italy. So, when Mim said she'd had enough working days behind this bar, Connie took over the reins.

Wiping a damp sheen from her brow, Connie pushed the thoughts of those terrible Italian days from her mind, realising too much time had been ruined by things she had no power to change.

Sighing, she weaved an escaped russet tendril back into the victory roll that haloed her head and as Bobby approached the bar with more empty glasses, she forced a practised smile.

'You've got nice eyes, Connie,' he said. 'They change colour when you smile.' Tilting his head to one side his expression was quizzical. 'Are they green or blue?'

'They're sky-blue pink,' Connie answered with skilful nonchalance, repeating the phrase her mother often used when she was a child. 'Sometimes they even turn red when I get angry.' She made a playful lunge towards him, flicking a damp tea towel, laughing when Bobby curled his skinny body to protect himself, his delight echoing through the empty bar.

'I like it when you're in a happy mood,' he said unfurling, and taking advantage of her good humour to straighten a box of Smith's crisps under the counter with keen-eyed precision.

'You look... well, you know... younger,' he said, stepping back to make sure the half-filled box was just the way it should be.

'I doubt that,' Connie raised a cynical eyebrow. She suspected Bobby's angelic face and easy compliments would make him a heartbreaker like his older brother Danny one day.

'You do it a lot, you know?' he said, straightening the packets inside the box.

'Do what a lot?' Connie stopped what she was doing and eyed him with light-hearted suspicion. She was being soft-soaped and surmised Bobby wanted a packet of crisps. She nodded to the box and he eagerly helped himself.

'Smile, you smile all the time...' he said, taking his snack and resuming his place by the window, looking down the row, waiting for something else to happen. 'Everybody's friend, that's you, Connie'.

'Aye, if you say so, Bobby.' Connie sighed, watching him open the twist of navy- blue waxed paper from inside the bag of crisps and dipping his finger into the salt. He turned his face towards her, and she laughed when his right eye bunched and his mouth stretched into a shuddering grimace.

'That'll teach you not to eat salt.' Connie said, rinsing soapy water from her hands. Bobby was quiet for a while, crunching away, his mind on other things. Then a couple of moments later he surprised and delighted Connie when he suddenly said, 'I wish you were my mam, Connie, you'd make a great mam,' he said. 'My mam won't let me do nothing.'

'Your mam won't let you do *anything*,' Connie corrected him, folding bar towels.

'That's what I said,' he answered, engrossed in sprinkling more salt onto his crisps while Connie swallowed the tight knot in her throat. Bobby didn't know he had just paid her the biggest compliment. But it was no use wondering, longing to know what it would be like to have a child of her own. That time had passed.

'You don't half say some daft things, Bobby.' Connie said after taking a calming deep breath, but she realised he wasn't listening anymore.

'Connie, come and see!' Bobby's tone was urgent, their

previous conversation forgotten. 'They're at it again... The spiv's just clocked her one.' The crate he perched on wobbled, his impotent anger clear as day. 'I wish I was big, like our Danny – I'd give him what for!'

Connie rushed from behind the bar and this time she headed straight to the open door to see the throng of irate neighbours gathered like clucking hens. Her heart pounding and her mouth dry, Connie hoped one of the gambling men would intervene, but none of them did. They wouldn't take a chance of getting on the wrong side of Leo Darnel. A mortal foe among those who crossed him, the spiv was holding Rene at arm's length while grabbing hold of Evie.

'You show her who's boss, Leo,' one of his followers called, stooping low in the mouth of the jigger, playing an illicit game of pitch and toss. 'Put 'er in 'er place!'

'You want to mind your own business,' Connie told the gambler. 'I've heard you're not slow in running from your wife's rolling pin.' The other gamblers and a few women roared with laughter while Connie, shrewd as a hunting cat, eyed Darnel's every move. Her heart went out to the poor girl who had become a source of entertainment for the local kids who ceased their afternoon games to gawp at the carry-on from number two. Connie itched to set Evie free.

'I think she's had enough.' Connie's voice was loud, and firm enough for all to hear. The way Evie was being treated sickened her. Darnel let go of both women and rolled up his sleeves, enjoying the sport as Connie met his contemptuous gaze without fear.

'I said, enough!' There was a hint of menace in her voice.

'This is a private matter, Connie.' Rene sounded apologetic, standing with arms outstretched between her daughter and her fancy man. Connie knew Rene was a proud woman whose dignity was tested only when there was a man around. But for all that, Connie liked her and counted her as a friend and confidant.

'It doesn't look private, Rene.' Connie edged forward. 'You could sell tickets.'

'Mind your own,' Darnel sneered, ignoring the calls from the increasing throng of concerned women.

'I'll show you whose business it is, shall I?' Connie answered, turning her attention back to Rene who looked quite dishevelled after her tussle with Darnel. 'You ought to be ashamed, brawling in the street, making a show of yourself.' Connie kept a close eye on Darnel's balled fists, watching him bob and weave like a boxer limbering up for the big fight after Evie wrenched her arm from his grip.

Gobshite! Having lived in the dockland all her life and owing Darnel nothing, Connie had no fear of the black-marketeer. 'You need to put those fists in your pocket, where they'll do no harm.' Connie's voice was clear in the sultry summer heat. 'If you lay one more finger on that poor girl, I'll have the Jacks on you.' She knew Leo Darnel had a healthy regard for staying under the radar of the local constabulary. 'You might terrify the poor mare, but you don't scare me!'

'You nosey ould bag!' Darnel spat, causing globules of white-foam saliva to spurt from his mean lips and cling to his shoestring moustache. Connie shuddered in disgust and walked towards Evie. She would be safer in the tavern. But she didn't manage to reach the stricken young girl.

'You wanna watch your manners, Darnel!' The male voice issued a warning and Connie's head whipped around. Her heart lifted when she saw Danny Harris sprint up the street, heading straight for the spiv.

No seven stone weakling that's for sure. Connie could see the army had built Danny up like a centurion, and he was more than a match for Darnel. She smiled when local women in their brightly coloured, turbaned headscarves nudged each other and nodded to Danny.

'Not so cocky now, Mr Darnel,' one woman shouted. Faced with Danny, and in his haste to retreat behind the door of number two, Darnel pushed Evie with such force she staggered and fell onto the cobbled road. Then, grabbing Rene by the arm, he dragged her into the house behind him, slamming the front door with a bang.

Evie looked dazed and unsteady when Danny scooped her into his arms. The satisfied housewives of Reckoner's Row nodded their approval, although Evie, her blouse ripped and her matted hair streaked with her own blood, didn't look happy at being rescued.

'Put me down, right now,' she demanded, and Connie could see the pink tinge under her splash of freckles, Evie's acute embarrassment obvious. 'Let go of me before I scratch yer bloody eyes out!' Danny did as he was told, lightly lowering her to the cobbles.

'Off you go and get your dinner, Bobby. There's a good lad,' Connie told the boy. The sideshow was over. The onlookers were dispersing to their own houses to chew the afternoon's shenanigans over with their roast dinner. Connie knew, no matter how hot the weather or how light their purse, the women of Reckoner's Row always put on a hearty Sunday dinner.

Bobby did not conceal his disappointment when Connie ushered him to the bar to collect his cap. He suspected their Danny had a soft spot for Evie, and reckoned he'd let Darnel go because he had his mind on something other than fighting with a lowlife in the middle of the street.

'Connie, can I go swimming in the Cut?' Bobby asked, haphazardly pushing his cap onto his head.

'Ask your mam,' Connie answered, returning to her chores while an embarrassed Evie scolded Danny outside.

'Mam won't let me she says it's too dangerous,' Bobby answered, putting the last glass on the bar.

'So, what makes you think I'll let you?' Connie asked, taking it and washing it in soapy water.

'You've got a soft heart, me mam hasn't,' he replied, and his remark made Connie's stomach flip, but even so she refused to be drawn into Bobbie's emotional blackmail.

'I'm not so soft-hearted, because I'm saying the same,' Connie answered. 'You can't swim in the canal because it's filthy. You'll catch something nasty.' That's what she would have said to her own child, too – if she had one.

Taking in a lungful of stifling air, Connie knew it was pointless thinking that way, knowing she was never likely to have one. Not anymore.

'I'll go for me dinner, then,' Bobby said, loping off, hands in pockets. He kicked an empty cigarette packet, vaguely aware his big brother, Sergeant Danny Harris, impeccable in the uniform of the Kings Fusiliers, was being berated by Evie Kilgaren for interfering.

Serves him right.

* * *

'Your nose is bleeding again.' Danny said, holding out a handkerchief. Evie looked up through hair that now resembled rats' tails and wiped her bloody nose with the back of her hand.

'Well spotted. Ten out of ten for observation.' Using the only weapon in her armoury, she attacked with her tongue as a form of defence. Her cutting retort hid a lifetime's belief she was not worthy of a brave man's handkerchief. *Please walk away*, a voice in her head pleaded as she dabbed the blood from her face, knowing she should thank him. But she couldn't. Danny Harris could have his pick of any girl he wanted, while she looked like she'd just gone two rounds with a grizzly bear.

Averting her gaze, Evie ignored his outstretched hand, and fumbled in her pocket for the ripped remnant of a candy-striped bed sheet – her handkerchief. Trust Danny to be the one to come to her defence, she thought, blowing her nose.

'Don't do that, you'll get two black eyes,' Danny said, looking concerned.

'So you're a doctor as well as a hero?' Evie said drily, in no mood for pleasantries. *Our kind don't mix with the likes of the Harrises, Evie.* The pearl of her mother's addled wisdom popped into her head. But, Evie thought, she might just be right on this one.

The Harris family went to early mass on Sundays. Evie had seen Ada singing her loudest in the front pew, knowing her own mother was sleeping off the night before. They paid their rent on time, and the rent man was always using them as an example of what good tenants should be. Not like her mother who used to hide behind the sofa on rent day.

Danny's family didn't have raucous Saturday hooleys when the tavern closed for the night. Nor did they sing 'til all hours, waking the rest of the row, or fight in the street after a Sunday afternoon drinking session... Tears of humiliation welled in Evie's eyes, trickling down her cheeks and she rubbed them away with her knuckles.

'Evie...? Please let me help you,' Danny said, sounding genuine enough. But she didn't want his help. She wanted the ground to open up and swallow her, knowing this latest episode of the Kilgarens' lowlife would be the talk of the place for days. Her teeth clenched tightly together when, to her utter shame, she realised the contents of the pillowcase were strewn all over the filthy road.

Her underclothes, nothing special to look at in the first place, looked like rags in the gutter and her one and only under-slip was dangling from the canal railings. Bending to pick up her discarded belongings from the gutter, Evie could hardly see for tears blurring her vision. But, keeping her head down, she made sure Danny and the other nosey buggers didn't see them.

Returning her few bits of clothing to the dusty pillowcase gave her an opportunity to gather herself together. Then, without warning, her legs collapsed under her. She tried to stand. But, like a newborn foal, the effort took its toll on her legs, and in the end, she was forced to allow Danny to help her from the gutter.

Straightening, she held her head high, refusing defeat. But the gesture made her light-headed and she staggered, the canal undulating, the cobbles swimming before her eyes. She felt Danny's arm around her waist, keeping her safe, and she was grateful for the security it gave her.

'Here, let me help you.' Danny's concern was a sharp reminder of her dilemma and made her feel suddenly helpless. Swallowing hard, she lifted her head. Agonisingly mortified, Evie wished she didn't like Danny as much as she did. And she wished he was anywhere but here, standing so close, trying to make things better – when nothing could ever do that.

'You can mind your own business,' she said, pushing his hand away. 'I can look out for meself!'

'I'm sure you can, under normal circumstances... I've got no doubt about that,' Danny said in that deep soothing voice while nodding to Connie, who was now standing in the doorway of the Tavern. He knew the girl needed help but wouldn't accept it from him. She needed a woman's touch. A sympathetic ear.

Who better than Connie Sharp, an ex-nurse who was always

on hand when a baby was being born or a body needed laying out – not to mention the bits of life in between.

'Connie will help you,' he said, relieved when Evie allowed him to help her to the door of the Tavern without much fuss. 'Will you see to her, please, Connie?'

'Aye, lad,' Connie said, putting her arm around Evie's waist and taking her weight from Danny. 'Come on, Evie, love. Come inside away from prying eyes.' Helping the girl into the cooler confines of the bar, Connie was aware of the blazing anger in Danny's eyes as he grabbed a chair when her legs could no longer hold her up. He headed towards the door.

Unaware of Danny's impotent fury, Evie gave a gentle whimper. She hadn't had much experience socialising with neighbours on account of her mother building an invisible but effective 'them-and-us' wall around her all her life.

Handing Evie a glass of cold lemonade and a clean handkerchief to wipe the blood from her tearstained face, Connie's heart ached for the poor girl who didn't deserve the life she led.

'I suppose we're the talk of the street – again.' Evie, chancing a smile, winced through a swollen lip.

'You won't be the last,' Connie said putting her own glass of lemonade on the table. 'The things I hear behind that bar would make your hair curl.' She pulled out a chair and sat opposite Evie. 'I have to pretend I've got me deaf ones on. The customers forget I'm only a few feet away.'

'Thanks, Connie...' Evie said taking a tentative sip of her cold drink. 'I don't know what I'd have done without you.'

'Give over,' Connie said, feeling sorry for the kid who'd never had it easy. 'My halo's slipped more than once.' There was a moment's silence and then Connie asked, 'What are you going to do?'

'I know of some lodgings, there's a room going spare on the other side of the canal.'

'You can stay with me and Mim, you know,' Connie said watching Evie nod her gratitude. 'We'd love to have you!'

'Thanks for the offer, Connie...' She shook her head. 'But I've got to get away from Darnel, he's bloody evil.'

'Are you sure?' Connie asked, and Evie nodded. 'You know your situation better than anybody, but the offer of a room at the Tavern will always be there if you change your mind.'

'I know, Connie, and don't think I'm not grateful, because I am —' Evie squeezed the older woman's hand '—but I'm getting away from Reckoner's Row. And, it will be a cold day in hell before I ever come back again.

3

JANUARY 1947

'Jaysus, room! You're colder than a whore's heart!' Evie gasped. She
had left Reckoner's Row six months ago and had not heard a peep
from her mother since moving into the attic room of this Victo-
rian redbrick lodging house on the other side of the canal.

With its leaking roof and neighbours who liked to keep themselves to themselves, Evie still preferred living here to sharing the
same house as Darnel, even when the weather took an arctic turn
and her windows were cloudy with ice on the inside as well
as out.

Grabbing her coat that was spread over her bed, Evie put it on
and shivered as iciness seeped into her bones. Little puffs of
opaque air left her lips and hung in the freezing atmosphere. She
instantly regretted the vulgar swearword she had used. They were
Darnel's words.

She did not want to think of the crooked spiv who had robbed
her of her mother and forced her to find lodgings in this dilapi-
dated, bomb-damaged house where nobody gave her the time of
day. But it was the best she could get.

Air raids had devastated Bootle, Kirkdale and Liverpool

because of the proximity to the docks – so the area didn't have much in the way of decent accommodation since enemy raids had blitzed most of it. She was lucky to find lodgings at all, especially near her workplace.

But, for the first time since her mother had taken up with Leo Darnel, Evie could sleep without fear of him skulking along the landing in the dead of night and lurking outside her bedroom. She didn't fear this dark, austere room. Even though the three-storey house stank of damp and the landlady was as cold as poverty, her lonely attic room was preferable to living with fear and dread. Her solitude was a small price to pay for peace of mind.

Shivering, Evie pushed back the grey net curtains that, no matter how many times she washed them, never looked clean, and winced as the cold damp air wrapped around her like a hoar-frost shroud. She would have to leave soon for her shift at Beamers. She quickly found her shoes before rummaging around the bedside table for the box of matches. Glad of the money she had managed to save, Evie considered the bitter weather that had closed more businesses than the Luftwaffe did during the war. She was determined to bring Jack and Lucy back from Ireland, and when she did they were going to need all the help they could get.

She held a lit match to the mesh gas mantle and the eking gas gave a feeble plop, lighting only the immediate area of the sparse room and failing to reach the far corners. Peering through the gloom, she could barely see the narrow iron bed she had just left, or the straight-backed chair that supported a rickety table and counted herself lucky to have a single gas ring attached to a rubber hose, so she could make herself a cup of tea and bring scant warmth to the icy room.

Looking in the coal scuttle, she saw it was half-full and

decided she would save it until she came home, later. Miss Blythe the landlady, allowed her tenants one bucket of coal a day and Evie knew it didn't go far in this weather. But still, she was glad of the roof over her head.

She scraped a web of lace-patterned ice from the inside of the window's glass with a chipped thumb nail and could clearly see her old home across the grey meandering spine of the canal that split the narrow streets of back-to-back terraced houses.

On the far side was her past. The place she once called home. Things hadn't always been so bad in Reckoner's Row. When her father was alive things had been different. Da took care of everything. He would never have allowed Mam to enter a public house, let alone work in one.

The news that was being relayed from a wireless on the floor below brought a welcome voice. Mrs Travers who lived downstairs was stone deaf, and her wireless was always turned up to full blast. Other boarders complained about the din, but Evie loved listening to the BBC Light Programme, finding the cost of a wireless of her own prohibitive. She liked listening to the presenter's chatter.

Though she was lonely here, the sound of another voice, even in another room, meant she was not alone. The thought gave her comfort and stopped her thinking of the mother who abandoned her just as easily as she abandoned her siblings.

'Here is the five-o'clock news...' Evie stood still. 'Worsening weather has closed many businesses across the country...'

'Don't I know it,' she said out loud. There were rumours going around Beamers that the whole staff could be laid off before the end of the week through lack of fuel caused by the severe weather.

Along with her wages, Evie knew she would also lose the chance to practise her typing skills before the office staff arrived every morning, and she had worked so hard on the home study course she had seen advertised in the Picture Post.

'*... major roads and country byways are impassable. Trains are disrupted or stranded in heavy snow and people are advised not to make unnecessary journeys...*'

'It's best you stay indoors, Tom,' she said, opening the door and letting in her landlady's ginger cat who had been scratching at her door for a saucer of milk. He stank the house out, but at least he gave her a chance to hear her own voice. Smearing her hands with green soap, Evie rubbed vigorously to get rid of the disinfectant smell still lingering from her last shift at Beamers, but when she turned on the single copper tap, the knocking and banging loudly told her the pipe was frozen. Looking longingly at her empty cup on the wooden drainboard, Evie couldn't even make a hot cup of tea to warm her.

'You could have saved me from all this, Mam,' she said aloud, pulling up the collar of the coat, 'but you didn't...'

* * *

* * *

More than once she had stayed behind to help Susie with her filing and had even typed up a few letters when Miss Hawkins, the office manager, was busy elsewhere. It gave her much needed practice of office work and she found the work enjoyable and so easy.

Evie needed a better-paid job to bring her brother and sister home. A cleaner's job was never going to allow her to do that. Also, if Susie Blackthorn could become an office clerk, Evie thought with a flourish of determination, she could too.

Her heart thundering in her chest, Evie neatly folded the

letter in the same way she had seen the other clerks doing it, reverently placing it inside a business envelope before licking and sealing it. Evie knew she would never be so deceitful if there was any other way. But she was desperate to bring Jack and Lucy back from Ireland and she needed more money to do so.

A hubbub of growing voices told her the office staff would be here any minute. Quickly, she scribbled the name and address of head office in perfect copperplate handwriting. Then, rising from the desk, Evie pushed the résumé into the outgoing post tray, dragging the cover over the typewriter while her eyes swept the office, taking in her earlier work. Everything was as it should be.

I've dusted the wooden filing cabinet. Desks are polished. Floor is mopped...

She didn't mind doing the office jobs the others loathed. It broke the monotony of cleaning, brewing tea for the office staff and running errands. The chores meant she was useful and gave her a good excuse to hang back when her working day was over, instead of going home to a cold room.

Keeping busy was as natural as breathing and helped smother unhappy memories. The panstick-smeared mirror over the fireplace. Spilled nail varnish on the tablecloth. A knocked-off brandy glass cradled in the palm of her mother's hand while ruby-red lips pulled smoke from ever-present cigarettes.

Evie tried to ignore disturbing memories of GI *uncles* who brought precious gifts of nylon stockings and candy. But her mother's looks had eventually faded, leaving her to the loathsome attention of the notorious spiv.

'We would have been happy when the kids came home, Mam,' she whispered, 'but you chose him...' She jumped when the office manager entered the office, followed by a breathless Susie Blackthorn, who was obviously late – again.

'Talking to yourself, Evie?' Susie rolled her mascaraed eyes. 'You can get locked up in the mad house for that.'

Evie! You're just plain Evie Kilgaren. Don't get above yourself with any fancy ideas. Her mother's words echoed in her head and that familiar wave of uncertainty washed over her.

The solitary, buff-coloured envelope was conspicuous in the outgoing mail tray, but she could not retrieve it. Then the never-ending doubt crept in. *Was she good enough to call herself an office clerk?*

'Have you been here all night, Miss Kilgaren?' Miss Hawkins quipped, causing Evie to smile nervously.

'I finished ages ago, I was waiting to see if you had any news of office vacancies.'

'I wish I could bring you good news...' Miss Hawkins put the files on her desk and Evie automatically tidied them away.

'Grovelling won't get you anywhere.' Susie said. 'Cleaners don't get promoted to office clerks.'

The notion of becoming somebody who could be as professional as Miss Hawkins seemed ridiculous now. The home study course a pipedream, to distract her from her constant companion, crippling loneliness. But something forbade her to pick up the letter she had placed in the out-going mail tray. She didn't want to be *plain Evie*. She wanted to be *somebody*.

'I won't do any more than I get paid for. I'm nobody's fool.' Susie said.

'It keeps me going, and there's less chance of hypothermia.'

'Get you, with your hypo-thingy!' Susie scoffed. 'You should have kept your *new* coat on.' Susie eyed the woollen monstrosity hanging in humiliating solitude behind the office door, away from Miss Hawkins smart camel coat and Susie's showy beaver lamb draped over the wooden coat stand. 'It's big enough to keep us all warm.'

'It's decent quality,' Evie never allowed Susie to see how deeply her snide remarks hurt.

'It looks older than God's sister,' Susie replied. 'I wouldn't be seen dead in it.'

Evie picked up her mop bucket.

'Stay for a moment longer, Evie.' Miss Hawkins' voice was grim.

'What have you been up to Evie?' Susie's sly eyes gleamed. 'Been caught pinching Aunt Sally's disinfectant? Is it put-your-coat-on-time for you?'

Evie's heart skipped a beat when she remembered her letter in the outgoing post tray. Stealing was a sackable offence. She had used company paper *and* an envelope. *Oh, Lord!* Evie gasped.

'Enough of that, Miss Blackthorn!' Miss Hawkins face was set in a frown. 'We must all put our coat on. We are being laid off. Beamers must close. Fuel shortages.'

Evie felt her heart slump. No work meant no pay.

'This latest snap of arctic weather is having a devastating effect on the whole country.' Evie repeated the news she heard on the wireless.

'Proper little ray of glad tidings, aren't you, Evie.' Susie's usually pouty red lips were even more so. 'It's like the war never ended... how are we supposed to manage, money-wise, without a job?'

Miss Hawkins handed out small brown wage packets. Evie knew if she wasn't earning, she would have to dip into her hard-earned savings to pay the rent on her lodgings.

'It appears you finally got your wish to stay home out of the cold weather, Miss Blackthorn,' Miss Hawkins told her. 'Mr Beamer held out for as long as possible—'

'Got his pound of flesh out of us, more like,' Susie interrupted, tidying her desk. 'This office is so cold, rigor mortis is setting in.'

'That's enough, Susie,' Miss Hawkins checked the clerk with a disapproving glare. 'We will contact you when business resumes.'

'I could have another office job by then,' Susie answered peevishly.

'I doubt it.' Miss Hawkins tone was caustic. 'You kept your position here only by the skin of your teeth. I would say simple filing is about your metier.'

'What's a metier?' the other girl asked, too affronted to mind her manners.

'Vocation,' Evie answered, determined not to smile.

'Swallowed a dictionary, have we?' Susie's expression was livid in its glowering delivery as Evie went to put the tools of her trade into the store cupboard. Businesses were closing all over the country. What chance did an office cleaner have if good clerks would be so easy to come by?

4

Unbeknown to Evie, her siblings had been back home since early January. Jack's lanky strides made slow progress down the cobbled street, hampered by the paper-thin layer of smooth rubber covering the soles of his size nines. Placing an uncertain foot on each glassy step leading up to the bridge, he muttered to himself.

'Don't slip, Jack.' Not daring to lose concentration, he placed his other foot on the step, urging himself onward, his freezing hands gripping the homemade trolley which, out of necessity, he'd cobbled together from a rough much-sought-after wooden pallet and four pram wheels rescued from the canal before it froze over. It had only one buckled wheel.

The trolley-cart was a godsend for collecting precious scraps to burn, not having a single lump of coal in the house and no prospects of getting any. Looking around, it seemed there were many who had the same idea. The proof was in missing wooden railings, torn down for kindling.

His blue eyes were drawn to the glow of the full moon mirrored on the surface of the frozen canal and he marvelled at its haunting beauty. A dreamer, Jack was fascinated by the trapped detritus bulging from the ice, longing to capture it in precious charcoals Aunt Brigit gave him for Christmas, before he and Lucy were so abruptly put on a boat home.

'One day...' he said, determined. He knew he didn't have the funds for the materials unless he found himself a proper job instead of foraging, the life he had led since returning. If coal was plentiful, they still could not afford to buy any.

He yearned for cosy nights around the turf fire, drawing the majestic horses he had been lucky enough to work with on the farm. Jack knew he'd been away too long to call this place home. So much had changed. He spoke differently. Even the voices in his head had a Celtic lilt.

However, Lucy had taken to the narrow backstreets immediately, making friends with that young snapper, Bobby Harris. She loved the busyness of the port town, the smoky smell of soot-covered buildings, the foghorns on the river. Agile as anything, she flitted through bomb-damaged streets like a gazelle...

A razor wind bit into his naked ankles and fresh-falling snow seeped into his shabby galoshes. It was time to shift himself. Artistic urges were an impossible dream. Lads like him worked on the grimy docks, in the ear-splitting factories or the back-breaking warehouses that lined the Mersey. They didn't paint.

Creativity and imagination were not deemed possible for a backstreet boy whose gauzy illustrations captured the tranquillity he longed for. He had dreams and ambitions. Living, not just existing...

'Kill the dream, Jack, you eejit!' His words hovered on the freezing night air as he pulled up the frayed collar of his jacket. He had to move on before he froze to the spot. The winter cough that had kept Lucy indoors for the last couple of days would not last forever. She would be out skating on that ice if he wasn't there to stop her.

What was the use of worrying, it was never worthwhile. His soft whistle penetrated the silence as he crunched through the snow, his young sister's pinched expression urging him on. Digging cold rough hands deep into his pockets he lowered his head against the sudden onslaught of icy hail that stung his face and neck. Jack recalled Ma's words when she came to fetch him and Lucy off the boat from Ireland. She'd promised better days ahead.

She lied.

* * *

Connie popped two hot water bottles into her bed. They would take the chill off, and the bed would be nice and cosy by the time she finished serving behind the bar. It was on nights like this that she missed Rene Kilgaren. The bar was quiet of late because of the bad weather and the night seemed endless with nobody to talk to.

'I'll bring you your favourite nightcap, Mim,' Connie called from her bedroom on the same landing. 'By some miracle, we got a delivery today,'

She pencilled her dark brows before applying mascara to her long lashes. A touch of rouge brought a rosy glow on a cold winter's night and complemented the hunter's bow of red lipstick. A quick spray of sugared water to her upswept coronet of russet curls completed the glamorous film-star look she was aiming for.

'You remind me of me when I was your age...' Mim said when Connie went into the living room. Still handsome in her late fifties, her mother would not have looked out of place in a Rube-nesque painting. Mim had been landlady of the Tram Tavern since she and Connie's late father, Bert, married thirty years ago. A bolting dray horse tragically killed Bert, the life and soul of any party, during an air raid. 'We didn't close the tavern doors once, during the war – did I tell you?'

'Only a few times, Mim.' Everybody, including Connie, called her mother Mim. 'Shall I bring you a nice tot of rum to go with your Guinness?'

'Don't put yourself out on my account... but it does help me sleep since your father left.' Mim refused to say he was dead. If she said the words, it meant his demise was permanent. Final. He was never coming back.

'I know.' Connie thought to herself that if Mim didn't nod off after tea and snore her way through the news, she might sleep a lot better when she went to bed. But she would never begrudge her mother anything. Mim had worked long and hard enough in that bar downstairs to deserve anything she wanted. In the mirror, she saw Mim rubbing her stomach.

'Are you all right, Mim?' Connie asked, worried that her mother was in pain.

'It's just my hated hyena. It's been playing up all day.' Mim got up and walked over to the window.

'Shall I fetch you a little magnesia?' Connie's mother had self-diagnosed a hernia. Connie, a qualified nurse, suspected the loosening of her mother's corset would immediately solve her problem. However, Mim would not allow her 'bits to jiggle' in public. It would not be decent, she had said many times. A daughter of the Edwardian Age, Mim felt she must be securely held together at all times.

'I'll get the doctor out if you're no better tomorrow,' Connie said, knowing her mother was a fit as a flea. She was not in the least surprised when Mim shook her head and said, 'There'll be no need for doctors, thank you very much! You can see to me.'

Every day some imagined ailment tormented Mim, convincing her she was not long for this world. 'What's the use of wasting half a crown on that old quack when I know exactly what's wrong with me?'

Connie rolled her eyes. Yesterday Mim suspected she had double pneumonia, with quinsy thrown in for good measure, although she insisted on taking it all in her sainted stride and did her best to let every customer know how much of a martyr she truly was. Connie, fed up of listening, had laced her tea with a generous tot of rum and Mim was as chirpy as a canary after that.

'I'll be closing early tonight,' Connie said, knowing the foul weather was keeping most men indoors. That, and the lack of work.

'Don't forget the tot of rum for my hyena!' Mim called when Connie opened the door leading down to the bar. 'Did you hear me?' Mim's strident tone contradicted her prognostic near-death condition.

'Yes, Mim, I heard you!' Connie shouted back. *The whole bloody street heard you*. She pulled the bar door a few times, releasing it from the twisted frame, a legacy of those terrifying nights when the Luftwaffe got too close for comfort. Although she wasn't here when it happened, she was thankful to the people of Reckoner's Row who pulled together when Mim was on her own.

Forget the war, Connie told herself. *It's over. Done with. Time to move on...*

Unlocking the bar door and taking a quick peep outside, she shivered. The tranquil street was lit only by a shimmering full moon and was unusually quiet. The children of the Row were indoors, tucked up in their tidy terraced houses. None were skating on the frozen canal or throwing snowballs at each other.

The bridge at the top of the fifteen stone steps outside the tavern was also quiet. Usually busy with horse-drawn carts carrying goods to or from the docks, the steep bridge was too slippery for the horse's hooves to grip the cobbles. Local women scattered ashes from their dead fires that morning, but it had made little difference to the thick layer of ice as lorry wheels slid from one side of the bridge to the other. Some drivers had looked for different, flatter routes, but most were prevented by snow-blocked roads.

'Mind how you go,' Connie called to a neighbour venturing from the warmth of her fireside.

'It's cold enough to freeze your thoughts,' the woman said, hurrying, head down, towards the chip shop. Connie quickly came back indoors and banged the door shut. It had taken all her powers of persuasion to convince her mother she would not stay open later than was absolutely necessary. And yes, she would listen to her favourite mystery wireless programme, *The Man in Black*, later. Mim didn't like listening alone and said how fortunate she was to have her daughter safely home, pulling pints instead of shrapnel.

Don't think of the war, Connie silently scolded herself, poking the fire in the bar. *Those days are gone*. She forced her thoughts towards another newer worry. Falling trade and lack of beer would soon force her to reduce the Tavern's opening hours, until the weather took a turn for the better. There were still a hardy few who huddled around the pub fire, mainly to save using their own precious coal. But making a gill of beer last all night did not pay enough to keep the place running. Something would have to be done. However, contrary to her mother's advice, Connie was determined not to go by way of the black market. Straight and true. That's how she liked to run her business. That way, she was sure of a good night's sleep and could open her door to anybody.

5

The following evening, Connie hurried back to the tavern after picking up the wintergreen liniment for Mim's arthritic knee. Although it was just turned five o'clock, the street was dark, lit only by the full moon that illuminated the icy, glass-like strips on the pavement made by little buggers who dared not go skating on the frozen canal. Connie shivered when she looked towards the canal to see the adventurous, older kids risking life and limb knowing they'd be in for a walloping from their mothers if they were caught skating on it. The thought made her heart dip.

What must it be like, to be a mother? A curse for the worry of keeping your offspring fed and safe? Certainly. Especially around the docks, where temptation to get into mischief was around every soot-covered corner.

Children, the most important of blessings, had been denied her. Becoming a bride and a widow on the same day saw to that. *Don't think of it now.*

Blocking out the events of that terrible day was impossible, and it was easier to say nothing than to go into every small forensic detail her mother would demand to hear. As for losing the child... conceived out of wedlock... Mim wouldn't be able to cope with the knowledge her daughter was an ordinary human being who could fall in love, just like everybody else.

The only person she'd told about that awful day was Rene Kilgaren. Tough as old boots, nothing shocked her, and she had a way of getting information without even asking questions. Having been through her share of worry and heartache until she lost her husband at sea, it was the most natural thing for Connie to share her biggest secret.

Rene hadn't been at work for over a week. Connie had knocked on the permanently closed front door a few times but got no answer, even though she was sure there was somebody inside.

Deep in thought, her attention was caught by someone peering through Rene's parlour window at the top of the street next door to the tavern. She was too far down the street to identify this nosey bugger, whose face was sandwiched between both hands to get a better view through the window.

Halfway up Reckoner's Row, Connie wondered if she should call out.

Connie's breathing quickened, her heart pumping in her throat. There was nobody around. The deserted street was silent. Every front door closed. Rene had thrown Darnel out on Boxing Day after discovering he was a bit too friendly with a woman from Beamer Terrace. Maybe he was crawling back, looking for Rene's forgiveness? But this fella looked too tall for Darnel.

'Here! What you up to?' Connie's voice rang out and hung in the icy air. 'Come away from there!' He turned to face her. His features were hidden behind a dark balaclava, in the diminished glow of the nearby gas-lamp. He didn't move, but watched her unhurried footsteps make their way up the street.

You don't half pick your time to get brave, Connie. She found it hard to breathe as the frantic thump, thump, thump of her heart drummed in her ears. Slipping her tongue over her parched lips she looked around for something to give her courage, knowing a jar of wintergreen would not have the same impact as a stick. No, something heavier. A house brick. Just a half-set. She only wanted to frighten him – not kill the bugger!

'I'll call a bobby!' Her voice, as good as any weapon, caused a few curtains to twitch, but did little to quell her anxiety. Two front doors opened, and she saw the peeping Tom take flight. Disappearing down the narrow alleyway between Rene's house and the tavern.

'Are you all right there, Connie?' Ada Harris, called from her front door. And for the first time, Connie was glad her nosey neighbour had come to see what the commotion was about.

'Yes thanks, Mrs Harris,' Connie's voice, even to her own ears sounded too cheerful, and she waved as she made her way up the rest of Reckoner's Row. She would call in on Rene later. Clutching the wintergreen, she was glad she hadn't had to use it as a deterrent.

* * *

Stealing a glance over his shoulder to make sure the coast was clear, Jack headed towards the dockyard to collect the wood he had hidden earlier. It was teatime, and the delicious smell of cooking permeated the frosty air making his stomach growl.

Trying hard to ignore his yearning stomach, Jack kept to the shadows of the prefabricated warehouses that had replaced the striking redbrick buildings destroyed during the war. He knew every inch of the dock road, with its narrow streets of back-to-back houses and its public houses on every other corner.

When he and Lucy reached Clarence Dock after Christmas, Jack understood how protected he and Lucy had been during the war and he recalled how his chest swelled back in Ireland when he stood up and told the whole class that this was his hometown.

The sight of rubble, where family homes had once stood, shocked him to the core, bringing home to him how much better off they had been in Ireland. Devastated houses. Ruined businesses. Like broken teeth against the backdrop of the River Mersey, they were still visible. His heart ached, remembering the pre-war streets. This wasn't the same port he had left as a seven-year old. How could it be?

The enemy had tried to wipe its buildings and people off the face of the earth, because of its proximity to the docks. The seven-mile plateau of granite and sandstone wet docks along the northern shoreline were fronted by warehouses filled with hardware, railway parts, casks of ale, muslin-wrapped cheese, pottery, iron, food of every description, meat from as far away as New Zealand. The Ganges and the Saint Lawrence were the Mersey's tributaries and most of the world's imports were handled in the port.

Threading his way through the port's interconnecting alleys and streets that filtered down to the docklands that kept cargoes on the move, he understood why this was one of the most important and dangerous places on earth to live during the war, as goods were shifted from the waterfront to the bustling storehouses and factories across Britain.

Liverpool, the maritime giant, the pinnacle of the food chain, sensitive to the insecurities of the world's plight, was a colossal threat to enemy triumph. Jack could clearly see the result of the order to destroy the port by any means possible. He knew local men who had done their bit, came home expecting a land fit for heroes and returned to shattered streets ribbing the backbone of the River Mersey.

Memories of the good food he enjoyed back in Ireland made him salivate. After being so well fed and looked after, the severe conditions horrified him when they came back here to little short of nothing, and it was getting worse day by day. *Encouraging the export drive*, the papers said, as poor families lived from hand to mouth. It wasn't right. Victors were coming home to much less than they were promised. *The whole bloody country's banjaxed*, he thought.

Jack was aware a dire housing shortage forced people to share a house with family, or friends or even neighbours. He worried that people would cotton on to the fact his mother had done a bunk and that number two was now occupied by a lad of fourteen and his ten-year-old sister. They'd inform the landlord who would turf him and Lucy out on their arse. Where would they end up? Lucy would be taken away!

Jack trudged on through the snow, his feet soaking wet. He would not let anybody take his little sister, no matter how bloody annoying she could be. They had been together since the day she was born.

Jack's footsteps crunched through the snow. He could hear his blood pumping through his veins. The dock road was silent. He had never seen this area so still, with tarpaulin covered wagons lining the granite walls, unable to get through snow-blocked roads.

Grateful for the canopy of darkness, he pushed through a space in the wooden railings bordering the yards along the docks, suspecting some had been pinched to keep the home fires burning.

Wary of the lightly sleeping bobby sheltering from the sub-zero elements in his little hut, or wagon drivers tucked up inside their vehicles, filled with precious cargo, a magnet for unscrupulous ne'er-do-wells who would neither work nor want, Jack hurried towards the docks.

Slipping his wraith-like body through the narrow space between locked storage sheds, Jack prayed that nobody had discovered his stash of kindling. Since the army had been stood down from port duty after the war, this part of the dock was an Aladdin's Cave of merchandise, which locals would never get their hands on – unless the spivs got there first.

Darting through the scrapyard hills of iron and steel towering above him, he cut through timber yards full of Canadian lumber that ebbed and flowed on great ships every day.

When he heard the noise, his head turned on a swivel. His heartbeat accelerated from one to sixty in the time it took to blink. The sound came from the clank of chains hitting the side of a small boat along the dock wall, and he let out a slow, shivering sigh, his fear mixing with the smell of oil and pitch and timber.

Dropping the thin rope that steered his cart, he blew warm air into his frozen fingers, surveying the area before making his next move. Catching sight of a great black mound he realised, on closer inspection, it was coal. Just sitting there. As high as a house. A few precious nuggets for Lucy would mean the difference between health or hell.

Some might fall onto the back of his cart if, accidentally on purpose, he slipped and happened to knock the black hill, dislodging a few big pieces... He wasn't greedy.

Surveying the abandoned dockyard, he held a silent, one-sided conversation with a higher being. Lucy's need was greater than his, he reasoned. She was only little. A wee thing. Not nearly as robust as he was. A little bit of coal would go a long way to ease her suffering and had nothing whatsoever to do with his need to thaw his frozen bones.

Farm labouring in Ireland made him fortunate enough to enjoy good health and strength from an early age, no matter how thin his appearance. But Lucy was another matter... Jack gave the hill a tentative nudge with his cart, stretching his elasticated scruples at the thought of a blazing fire when a few black cobs slid onto the homemade trolley. He would only take enough to get them through. To what though? Mam hadn't been home for days.

Picking up some big pieces he put them on the cart. Needs must, and nobody would miss a few measly lumps. Looking over his shoulder, he would have to be nippy. If he got caught, they were both done for.

When Jack heard another noise, he ignored it. He would be out of here in no time. Then he heard voices. Angry voices. His body tightened. Ready to flee. He held his breath...

'I'm telling you, old man, open it or you'll be sorry!'

'I'm having no part in it, and that's that!' Jack recognised the voice of his neighbour, Mr Harris. The watchman lived a few doors down, and thrilled Jack as a young'un, with tales of how his toes rotted off in the mud-filled trenches of Passchendaele.

Mr Harris had been an Air Raid Precautions warden during the last war and Jack recalled the old man telling him he was unhindered by having half a foot missing when he dragged dead bodies out of burning buildings. He had seen enough dreadful sights to be afraid of no one.

'Here, what d'you think you're doing with that thing?' Mr Harris said. 'You can't pull a gun out on people!'

A gun! Fear like a line of marching ants trickled down Jack's back when he heard the low tangle of voices squabbling, not ten yards away. As their anger escalated, Jack lost focus and he slipped. Digging his heels into the deep snow, his flailing hands caught hold of a thick chain protruding from the dock wall and his body stopped with a jerk almost pulling his arm out of its socket. Holding his shoulder, he dared not cry out in pain.

Don't move, Jack! He was certain the voice inside his head was trembling. His foot gave way, and he slipped some more. The coal shifted. Some of it rolled. Conspicuously black against the virginal snow. The squabbling stopped. Jack held his breath...

'Rats?' the old man said further down the quay when he heard the coal hill shift, invading his heightened senses. The put-put-putting of the lorry's engine filled the air with the smell of petrol.

'It didn't sound like no rat to me,' another, unfamiliar voice said. 'It'd have to be bloody strong to move a big hill of coal.'

'Open the door, old man, or else...' The sound of metal chains and the squeal of rusty hinges did nothing to mask the threat in the gunman's voice.

Don't open the door, Mr Harris! the voice inside Jack's head cried while he remained silent. He peered through the falling snow, which wasn't heavy enough to block out the dark silhouettes moving about under the flicker of dipped headlights. The opening of the warehouse doors widened, and a flat-backed lorry edged inside.

Jack knew he had to get out of here, before his eyes saw something he would regret. A bundle of driftwood and a few cobs of coal were never so dangerous to come by. Edging back, with his one good arm he grabbed the thin rope and started to move the cart.

Maybe the weight of combustibles caused the cartwheels to squeak, Jack wasn't sure, but he knew one thing – he had made a right pig's ear of collecting his swag. The first chance he got he was legging it! But not without the wood. From the corner of his eye he noticed two men jumping down from the lorry. His curiosity got the better of him and he paused.

One man followed the truck into the warehouse, while another backed the old watchman inside with the nose of his gun. This wasn't just any warehouse robbery, Jack thought. This was big! And he wanted no part. The less he knew the better. He had to think of Lucy.

But what about Mr Harris? He couldn't just leave him. He wanted to let him know he would get help. But that was impossible. The law would want to know what he was doing on the dock. Jack swallowed hard. What if they locked him up for pilfering? But what if the old man got hurt – or worse? That fella had a gun! Jack knew he couldn't live with the guilt if anything happened to Mr Harris. But what about Lucy?

From the narrow beam of the villain's torchlight, Jack could see wooden crates stacked high. Booze. Cigarettes. There would be a glut of contraband on the streets tomorrow, he thought, and turning on a swivel he lost his balance completely, upsetting the hill of coal. The rumbling avalanche went on forever, or so it seemed. When it subsided there was a dense silence so thick, Jack didn't dare breathe.

'A rat, I told ya!' Mr Harris' words betrayed an uncertain tremor. 'They don't like being disturbed – a bit like meself.'

'That was no rat, I tell you,' Jack heard the man say, as he reached inside his pocket, lifted his arm and—

'Put that away you bloody fool,' said a man with a Celtic accent. 'You'll bring the law!'

'Stealing from the King's dockyard's a hanging offence, ya know,' Mr Harris added with some authority.

'It's arson on the King's dock that sets you swinging, old man' said the Celtic lilt and as Jack tried to keep every muscle, every sinew, every screaming nerve still he caught a glimpse of the man with the gun. 'You'd better not have warned the authorities!' The Celtic lilt took on a threatening tone, and Jack heard a dull thud.

A groan, and then there was silence after Mr Harris hit the deck.

Jack realised the gasp that filled the freezing air came from his own trembling lips. He must get help for Mr Harris. Dragging the cart, he hurried towards the main road.

'Hey you!' An angry voice carried on the freezing night air as the bright light of a torch beam gave Jack a momentary glimpse of the gunman. A loud crack split the air and his leg seized. Jack panicked, wincing when his leg refused to budge. It grew heavy, then collapsed like a stack of cards beneath him. *Jesus wept!* He groaned, drawing back his lips, and his eyes rolled when painful spasms seared through the muscle at the top of his leg. Gripping his thigh, he could feel the warm wetness trickle through his fingers. He daren't look.

But it was difficult to avoid seeing the dark red splashes peppering the pristine snow. His heart leapt to his throat. He had to get out of here. Get help. Easing his hand from his leg, Jack's stomach sank when he caught sight of his blood-covered palm.

Holy Mother… he shot me! His breathing was ragged. *Stay calm! Breathe. Nice and slow… Shit!* Scrabbling to find his trouser pocket, Jack's trembling fingers hindered him. Eventually managing to locate the grubby piece of ripped sheet he used as a handkerchief, he pushed it against his thigh and dragged himself towards the cart. He must get off the dock. Back to the main road.

Ignoring the vivid red trail that followed him, Jack concentrated on moving his leaden muscles. What if they came looking for him? He stumbled. Fear catapulted the breath from his dry lips. Every nerve in his body was screaming. Exhausted, he neared the dock road, scrambling and faltering, he tripped as something warm and heavy pushed against him, urging him onto the cart. Lifting his head, Jack looked into the biggest, darkest eyes he had ever seen. Unafraid, he heaved great gulps of air, glad he'd made it this far. A man in a black balaclava was looking down at him and he was relieved. At least he would not die alone. Pain ripped through his leg as Jack slumped onto the wooden cart. The light of the moon faded as he sank into oblivion.

6

Evie couldn't think straight as she finished her last shift and left Beamers. Rushing through the darkness, she was pushed along the street by a bitter wind. She pulled her collar as high as it would go against the sudden strafing of icy hailstones attacking the unprotected areas of her face.

If she had known she would be laid off, she would not have bought the coat, because she would need her precious savings now more than ever. With little chance of another job until the weather improved, she must watch the pennies.

'Evie...! Evie...! Hold up!'

'Please, no!' she whispered recognising the deep disciplined tones of Sergeant Danny Harris. Panic zinged through her body and hit her ribs like a wrecking ball. She hadn't seen him since that awful day last summer when he'd rescued her from the gutter, and even now, the shame of it still made her cringe.

Pretending she hadn't heard, Evie hurried on. But in the thick snow that levelled the road and the pavement, she lost her footing on the edge of the kerb. Her arms and legs windmilled in mid-air. Too late, she realised she could not save herself and landed in an undignified heap in the middle of the snow-covered road. Danny, beside her in seconds, helped her to her feet. Evie had never wanted to disappear so deep into the snow as she did now. Lifting her to her feet like a rag doll, reminding her of the humiliating afternoon last summer.

'Thinking of taking it up as a hobby?' Evie's humiliation clipped her words.

'I don't understand.' Danny's dark brows pleated. 'Taking what up as a hobby?' Evie wondered if he was being gallant or just plain dense and shook her head, trying to rid herself of the shameful memory.

'Nothing, it doesn't matter.' He didn't remember. And why should he? She would not be worth a second thought to a man as good-looking as Danny Harris, who, like a much-needed cream bun, was delicious but out of reach.

Oh, the shame! Evie thought, ignoring the throbbing pain in her backside. If he had been anybody else, she wouldn't have minded half so much. But Danny Harris! *What a bloody mortification.*

'Are you all right?' His eyes seemed full of concern. Or maybe it was pity, Evie couldn't tell as warm clouds of opaque air escaped his confident smile and showed straight white teeth. 'I was calling you.'

'I didn't hear you,' Evie answered, knowing she looked like something the cat dragged in, while he looked handsome and smart in his impeccable army overcoat.

'You must have your deaf ones on,' he said, brushing snow from her ugly coat. 'Are you injured?'

Just my pride and dignity, she thought, but she said, 'I'm fine, really.' Pushing his hand away she concentrated on dusting the rest of the snow from her coat, trying to hide her obvious embarrassment. 'Cold, isn't it?' she said, immediately cringing at her own stupid remark.

'So cold when I opened the wardrobe my shirt was wearing my coat,' Danny said, and they both laughed. Evie relaxed a little. He really was a gentleman. Not brash or showy like he had every right to be, but funny and friendly. She could see that now. Then he did something she couldn't have dreamed of.

He took her cold hands in his and cocooned the swollen digits. Breathing warm air into his huge cupped hands, she felt the delicious warmth seep into her fingers.

'You're freezing,' he said, massaging life back into her hands and once more, shame made her insides shrivel. Her fingernails were ragged, her hands red-raw and rough through scrubbing and polishing. Trying to pull away to hide her ugly hands in her pockets, Evie realised she couldn't. Danny was too strong. To her amazement, he stripped off his gloves, and eased Evie's hands inside.

'I'm fine,' she claimed, 'I'll be home soon. And I don't want to sound ungrateful, but these are far too big.' He was being kind and she was castigating him. She resented being treated like a charity case. She knew people had looked down on her all her life. She was never quite as good, or clever, or pretty as other girls. She did not have the confidence to push herself.

Even when the Susie Blackthorns of this world waded in and stole her thunder, she did not have the self-confidence to stand up and be counted. Accepting her lot in life: the underdog, the doormat. Pulling the fingertip of the glove, she felt the icy draught invade the luxurious warmth. Danny stopped her from removing the gloves by tucking the overhanging tips inside the woollen fingers.

'There, nice and snug. Protected from this nasty weather...'

'Cold enough to freeze the balls off a pawnshop!' a passing

docker said, with his hands dug into his pockets, he huddled deep inside a heavy donkey-jacket, an oily flat cap covering his eyes.

'Language, Squire,' Danny said, issuing a mild rebuke. 'A lady's present.'

'Beg pardon, miss,' said the workman, heading down the row, and Evie experienced a rare glow of warmth. Nobody had ever called her a lady before.

'I thought you'd left the row for good,' Danny said as they walked.

'I have,' she answered. 'Do you make a habit of lending your gloves to people?' She tried to keep her voice steady.

'You're not people, you're a neighbour in distress.'

Just a neighbour. Keeping a safe distance. It was something she was good at. Her solitude kept her safe from the ridicule her mother's antics had heaped upon her. But she had to admit, Danny was one of the kindest people she knew.

'Still in the army, then?' she cringed inside. It was obvious he was still in the forces.

'I'm being demobbed next Friday.' Friendly and always chirpy, Danny was popular with everybody.

'So, you'll be home for good, then?' Evie was glad he couldn't hear her thudding heartbeat pumping a little faster. She could bump into him anytime, and even though she liked Danny, Evie would never dare let him know. Men as handsome and ambitious would not look twice at a skivvy like her. The thought made her determined to do something with her appearance.

'I got my heavy-goods licence in the army, and saved some brass... I want to start my own business.' His cerulean gaze tugged her heart. 'I can't face work on the docks, like me dad.'

'Good for you.' Evie was genuinely pleased for him. Not one to poke her nose into other people's business, she had no need to ask questions. Danny volunteered information like they were old friends.

'I'm going to buy a wagon.' He seemed to light up as he talked. 'Go into the haulage business. Drive the open roads. Be as free as a bird...' Evie's smile widened. She felt honoured he was telling her all this.

'It's good to have ambition, it warms the blood – at least that's what Miss Hawkins says.'

'Miss Hawkins?' Danny asked, his voice sounding genuinely interested. For the first time in her life, Evie was chatting to him like it was the most natural thing in the world. Who'd have thought Danny Harris would be interested in what she was doing with her life? She had ambitions too, she told him, feeling it suddenly very important he should know she had no intention of staying in the backstreets for the rest of her life.

'I got my certificates for secretarial work and bookkeeping – so if you ever need someone to keep track of your empire, you know where I am.' Her bright smile hid a crippling mortification. Did she just ask Danny Harris for a job? *The shame of it*!

'Well, you need something to look forward to, that's for sure,' Danny responded with a nod of encouragement, 'although I won't be building any empires for a while.' A lengthy pause hung in the air when neither could think of anything to say. But the silence was broken by the high-pitched honeyed tones of Susie Blackthorn's voice.

'Danny!' Susie's telephone voice, the one she used when talking to clients, reverberated through Evie's skull like the crash of cymbals. Evie watched Susie approach coyly, knowing it was all phoney and exaggerated for Danny's benefit. Susie hugged the fur collar of her beaver-lamb coat close and speared him with a little-girl-lost look from under thick, black lashes. This wasn't the same spiteful cat Evie had known since her schooldays, when Susie had taunted her for being the daughter of the town drunk.

The tangible reaction burned her gullet, it caused her heart to pound, it made her clench her teeth and she wished Susie Blackthorn would fall on the ice. Not to hurt herself, obviously. But to look foolish – and to wipe that pillar-box red smile off her smug, over-made-up face. Evie experienced an emotion she had never felt before. Evie recognised the feeling immediately. She had witnessed it first-hand and ignored it. *So, this is what jealousy feels like.*

Evie felt her spirits sink to the snow-covered cobbles, as she watched Susie cross the street with the élan of a film star, and could not shake off that familiar feeling of being utterly irrelevant.

'Danny,' Susie purred, giving him a kiss on the cheek, leaving a perfect impression of two full red lips. 'When did you get home? Did you get my letters? Your last was so short.'

Having been elbowed out of position, Evie recognised the pervading scent of the cheap cologne Susie wore, which reminded her of the gin her mother drank. Standing in the snow, the icy wetness seeping into her shoes, she watched Danny's reaction. She couldn't read his expression. Was he uncomfortable with Susie's over-friendly greeting, or did that pink tinge on his neck signify unexpected pleasure in the siren's kiss? Two minutes ago, she and Danny were having a friendly conversation, Evie recalled. Now, he couldn't even look at her.

'Well, I'd best be off.' Evie said with forced indifference, nodding to Danny who barely said goodbye. A few steps further, Evie caught Susie's unguarded words quite clearly.

'That one's got delusions.' Susie's voice was full of scorn. 'Well, once a skivvy always a skivvy, I say... Her, a bookkeeper.

Can you believe it? She'd be like a jam puff in a beef stew. The cheek of her!'

'That's enough of that kind of talk, Susie,' Danny said without a hint of warmth.

Evie didn't catch Danny's further reaction as she lowered her head and scurried as fast as the icy ground would allow, smarting from Susie's barbed comments. Her mother had been right, Evie thought. She did have ideas above her station. Her swirling thoughts matched the blizzard that surrounded her. Mam had told her not to get above herself. The fall could be painful. But why should she be satisfied with nothing? Living hand to mouth in a freezing garret. There had to be more to life than this.

7

The smell of grease, oil and bitumen mixed with the salty tang of the River Mersey, provoked memories of the past as Evie headed towards the lonely attic room, which she refused to call home. Still reeling from Susie's catty remarks, she was careful not to slip again and bring attention to herself. One humiliation a day was enough – two was just plain greedy.

A foghorn on the river sounded as melancholy as she felt, and bittersweet memories of days long gone trespassed on her thoughts. The tug of Jack's little hand clutching her skirt on the quayside. Drying his tear-soaked face with kisses. Persuading him everything would be fine – even though she knew nothing of the kind. Lucy's chubby arms hugging her neck as her exhausted little body heaved an avalanche of sobs, her red face blotchy. The pleading fear in her young dark eyes had haunted Evie ever since...

Shh, baby... Evie could still hear the unforgivably soothing words that came out of her mouth as she sent her darling sister to a strange place with people she didn't even know. *I'll come and fetch you both soon and bring you home.* That one promise still shamed her.

'You were only a child of twelve-years-old,' Reason said.

'But you lied,' Integrity answered.

Evie was helpless when her mother pulled baby Lucy from her arms and handed both children to a maiden aunt boarding the ship to Ireland.

'There's not much to bring you back home to, except rations and rubble,' she said, to nobody in particular

If she had a backbone, she should go straight around to Reckoner's Row and demand her mother bring her children back to where they belonged. But Evie knew the milk of human kindness had soured in her mother's breast when she took up with the spiv. It would do no good to fight it out. Although not one to give up easily, she knew Mam had no intentions of bringing Jack and Lucy home while he was in residence.

However, when she'd saved up enough to bring them home, Evie vowed Jack and Lucy would have nothing to do with their uncaring mother. She was determined her siblings would not be subjected to the tyranny she had suffered in Reckoner's Row.

Jack's fourteen now, she thought. *He'll be old enough to leave school next summer. Young Lucy won't even remember this place.*

* * *

Jack was aware he was moving down the cobbled road of Reckoner's Row. The pain... such evil pain screamed through his leg with every bump. He could hear the squeaking wheels of his cart and slowly opened his eyes even though he longed to sleep. The man dragging the cart was asking him questions.

Do you see Evie these days...? Jack couldn't answer. He hadn't seen Evie since he and Lucy had come home. He didn't know where she was.

How's little Lucy? Questions. Questions. So many bloody questions... Lucy was a worry.

His eyes fluttered when the cart stopped outside his own home, and he caught sight of his rescuer disappearing down the narrow alleyway that locals called *the jigger.* Jack raised his hand that had gripped his aching leg. It was covered in blood. The street began to spin.

Evie? Where was Evie? Stay awake, Jack...

* * *

The icy weather kept many indoors and the underpass had become an alarming, vicious, howling wind trap, reminding her of the unceasing racket of the munitions factory. Evie kept her head down. Hurrying to her lodgings, she recalled her selfish attitude during the war, of being grateful the enemy raids targeted the bottom end of the street closest to the docks, leaving the top end alone

Apart from the wind, the tunnel was silent. Hugging the wall, Evie concentrated on keeping her balance along the slippery ground, wondering if she had enough savings. She certainly had time to look after Jack and Lucy, now she had been laid off. Her mother wouldn't. She never could... She'd have to keep Jack out of Darnel's way.

She usually felt safe in the teeming port streets but tonight was different. The raging wind, wailing through the tunnel like a discommoded banshee didn't help matters. The darkest part of her journey was almost upon her.

Edging along the ice-covered wall, she knew even the brave did not venture through here after dark, and when she saw a fleeting shadow slip behind an overflowing dustbin her heart spun out of control. Maybe it would have been better to take the long way around, she thought. And she would have taken the longer route if she hadn't fallen and been helped out of the gutter by Danny Harris. Again!

A crescendo of noise triggered by the clattering of a galvanised bin lid ripped through the tunnel and Evie stopped. Terror fizzed through her body as she tried to make sense of the din. Looking over her shoulder, her eyes met a wall of inky gloom. A few steps forward and she would be outside. But that was where the noise came from.

Determination forced her to put one foot in front of the other. Her darting eyes searched for the source, and she jumped when a mangy-looking cat sprang into her path.

Evie took in a shuddering lungful of chilly air, to calm her ragged breathing.

`Just a bloody moggy!' she gasped. Her words sounded remote as they bounced back along the domed wall. Pulling up the collar of her coat, as much to feel the security of the material as for its warmth, Evie moved forward...

Every hair on her body stood to attention when the male voice, thick with menace, came at Evie from the place she was heading towards. She recognised it immediately.

The sneering tone of Leo Darnel caused her stomach to tighten. She had to keep her wits about her. Darnel would take her down in an instant if she dropped her guard. As he did, that day last summer.

Then he was in front of her. Looming over her. Dark and intimidating. Blocking her exit. But she was stronger now. Evie must keep telling herself that. The knowledge spurred her on. Drawing herself to her full five feet and four inches, she squared up to him, ignoring her quivering insides.

'Hello Evie,' he said in that smarmy voice he saved for his black-market customers, as he slithered up towards her. The smell of carbolic soap and cheap cigars hung like a threat on the frosty air. She tried to push him away. But Darnel was solid, immoveable. With rising terror, she feared he would stop at nothing to get what he wanted.

'You caused me no end of trouble...' All niceties had seeped from his voice. Darnel's guttural voice, brutal in its intensity, echoed in the tunnel. Evie froze as he pushed his hand across her mouth. The leather ridge of his gloves dug into her lip. Panic fizzed behind her eyes; she could not breathe.

'Ain't you the daring one,' he said. His voice came in low, menacing bursts. 'Not like that mother of yours. Now there's a woman who knows her place.'

Evie found strength from Lord knew where and bit through the leather glove. Whipping his hand away, it boomeranged back to hit her face with such force her eyes danced. But she was not beaten yet. She wouldn't let this thug see he rattled her, like he did her mother.

'You keep away from me,' Evie said with as much determination as she could muster, but even to her own ears the tremble in her voice was obvious.

'If you show willing, you could be an asset to my business dealings...' Darnel said, 'I recall you were always eager to please, happy to help out...'

'Not you,' Evie cut in, her anger rising. She wanted nothing to do with his shady dealings. 'I'll make something of myself and see my day of the likes of you.' She shook her head free of his grip.

'You need to watch yourself,' Darnel warned. 'If you want to stay safe, that is.'

'What d'you mean?' Evie sounded braver than she felt. 'Are

you threatening me?' She was sure he would get back at her any way he could and knowing Darnel as she did, anything was possible. But she would show no fear. *Brazen it out, girl,* a voice inside her head urged. *Don't show him you're scared – that's what he wants.*

'What the eye don't see, and all that...' Darnel pushed himself into her and Evie closed her eyes tight, trying to block out memories of the awful past when his eyes would roam her body, making her feel ill at ease, soiled.

'Are you all right there, lassie?' a concerned voice echoed from the mouth of the tunnel. Evie felt her legs turn to aspic. *Thank you!* She offered a silent, relief-fuelled prayer of gratitude.

'Evening, squire,' Darnel said moving back, allowing Evie to break free. As she did, Evie raised her knee, thrusting it with force into the spiv's groin. Darnel doubled up.

'You'll be bleeding sorry you did that!' he gasped, his eyes wide with shock. But Evie didn't hang around long enough to see it. She sped towards the exit of the tunnel and gasping, she said, 'He cornered me, Mister.' Evie had never been more glad of an intervention. 'I'm only defending meself.'

'You appear to have the perfect deterrent, lassie.' His voice, full of admiration, made her feel safe. 'He had it coming, from what I could see.' Evie could not see the features of her saviour. His head and face covered with a dark balaclava, like so many men in these arctic conditions, but she was glad he arrived when he did. Looking over her shoulder she could see Darnel still doubled up, seeming to hold up the redbrick wall trying to get his breath back. 'Thanks, Mister,' she said, counting her blessings, although certain this would not be the end of the matter.

8

Connie had just finished serving Leo Darnel when the stranger came into the tavern and clicked his fingers for service. She had never seen this one before, she thought, her back to the bar, viewing his arrival through the mirrored tiles behind the cash-till. She would have remembered. A dockside Gregory Peck. He moved across the floor to the far end of the bar like he owned the place.

There was always one. She sighed. But, no matter. She would still call for last orders in ten minutes! She picked up a pint glass and began to polish it, ignoring the click of his fingers.

Connie would never answer to the click of a man's fingers. Even if this handsome one was dressed in an expensive cashmere overcoat and trilby hat. He was not a sailor, that was for sure – those clothes were not the attire of your average matelot, and definitely not those of a local docker.

* * *

Standing at the far end of the bar, rolling a half crown through his fingers, Angus McCrea knew the barmaid was aware of him. If he'd learned anything about these places, where the close-knit community had an innate wariness of strangers, he was certain every person in the smoky bar had him in the periphery of their vision, even if they didn't look at him.

His every move was being scrutinised, contemplated, even muttered over. Which might seem surprising, considering the tavern was so close to the dock road. Popular with sailors from all over the world. But that was the precise reason the regular conversation receded to a low hum and he was being given the once-over.

Clicking his fingers again, he grew curious when the barmaid ignored him, and he lifted his head to look at her. A tailored black dress skimmed her voluptuous curves, and her fiery Titian curls were swept up very becomingly into that familiar Betty Grable style that he had seen painted on the cockpit of American P-51 Mustang Bombers.

'Excuse me, is anybody serving here?' his deep Scottish inflection carried along the dark mahogany bar, and he watched the barmaid place the glass she had been polishing on the shelf. She answered with a silent, direct gaze.

'Did you not hear me the first time?' Angus asked when she approached him.

'I heard a finger click.' Connie said, looking at his hands while stretching to retrieve another glass. 'And just so you know, my love, if you want me to serve you, then you should never do that – or you'll go thirsty.'

Angus nodded, chastised. Her captivating smile could tame even the most savage beast, he thought.

'I'm sorry. Terrible habit,' Angus answered. It had been a long time since anybody dared tell him what to do.

'That's better, Mr...?' Connie dazzled him with her ruby red smile, her teeth film-star white.

'McCrae,' he said, 'but you can call me Angus, Mrs...?'

'Miss,' Connie said, wiggling the naked third finger of her left hand, 'but you can call me Connie – everybody around here does.'

'Pleased to meet you, Connie. May I have a pint of your best bitter, please?' He was glad he'd called in now.

'Charmed, I'm sure.' Connie, pulling the pump, poured his pint and looked up as the door of the bar opened. The cold wind blew in two Irish men singing loud rebel songs.

'Well, if it isn't Leo Darnel,' one said, his arms wide open and so drunk he was zig-zagging the floor to the bar.

'Can I help you, pal?' Darnel, who did not look as if he wanted company, put down his pint.

'I'm not your pal.' The Irishman's words were low, deliberate and laced with menace; a spark of recognition in Darnel's eyes dimmed to a hard, unwavering stare.

'Are you looking for something?' Darnel asked, undaunted. 'A thick lip, maybe?'

A rush of mirthless laughter came from the lips of the other Irishman, and the din of conversation died, filling the bar with an uneasy silence.

'Play nice, boys,' Connie warned. She knew Darnel was not a man to be crossed. Some had tried – but never twice. 'We don't need a floor show, thank you very much.'

She spoke as she delivered the pint to Angus. In one clean movement she took his money and cleared the bar of any weaponry, beer bottles and empty glasses before she had even reached the till.

'No trouble here, Missus.' The Irishman's lined, weather-beaten face stretched into a slow smile. 'No trouble at all.'

'Then piss off!' Darnel forced the words past the fat cigar clenched between his nicotine stained teeth. The Irishman, in the process of walking away, turned back to have the last word.

'Keep your eyes and your ears open, Mister Darnel...' he said, tapping the side of his nose.

'What time does the singer come on?' Angus asked dryly, giving Connie a practised grin. He didn't expect an answer as he watched the exchange between the rivals with interest. Maybe he should stick around.

'You wouldn't believe this place has been quiet, because of the bad weather and blackouts, and except for the habitual stragglers sitting around the fire, business has been slack.' Her smile, as bright as any seasoned performer, hid her relief as the Irishmen were now leaving the tavern. 'These lot are here raising a glass for an old docker who fell down a hatch and broke his neck.'

Ringing the bell for last orders, Connie was determined not to put more coal on the dying fire as she had done the night before. The minute she re-fuelled the grate the buggers went home. What a bloody waste that was!

'Last night they sat with a measly bottle of stout, making it last all night to save their own coal – but what can you do?' she asked. To keep warm, she had washed every glass, aunt-sallied the floor, windolene'd the mirrors behind the bar until they sparkled, there was nothing left to do, except read the book she borrowed from the library. 'But one good thing came of it,' she told Angus. 'When they buggered off home, I caught the late murder mystery on the wireless.'

Angus smiled at her positive attitude and in the short time since he discovered Connie Sharp shared the same planet he did, he knew, if ever he was looking for a woman to occupy his lonely hours, she would be the one.

'Can I get you anything else, love?' Connie noted his shock of dark hair flecked with silver around the temples. Not that she was looking, mind. It was just an observation.

'A room?' He smiled, putting his trilby hat on the polished bar.

'I beg your pardon?' The warmth of his twinkling eyes softened his chiselled features, but Connie was not in the mood to be soft-soaped tonight. 'You'd better not be getting fresh with me.' She wanted an early night, her feet were aching, and she had done the afternoon shift on her own. The bar had been busy this afternoon, because the dockers had a strike meeting for better pay and fewer hours before raising a toast to their lost mate. The usual.

'Can you tell me if there are any lodgings round about, lassie?'

'I doubt it,' Connie said knowing the area had lost a huge percentage of housing during the May Blitz of 1941 when Merseyside was bombed to devastation. 'And it's a long time since I was a lassie, but I'll take the compliment. Now, for the last time, can I get you anything?' Like the rest of the country, she too desperately needed cheering up.

'I'll have a wee dram of single malt, if you please,' he said. And Connie realised it wasn't just his Scottish accent that told her he was a stranger in these parts. It was unusual for anybody to come into the tavern and ask for a single malt, because it was almost impossible to come by – unless you knew the right people, and in a dock road public house it was easier than not. However, her natural suspicions regarding strangers told her to be on her guard.

'I haven't had single malt since Churchill wore a siren suit.' She wasn't lying. The good stuff, which she never drank, was kept locked away for trusted customers only. The ones who kept her mother in the fine things, which other people could never afford.

'Ahh,' he grinned. 'It was worth a try. In that case, I'll have another pint of your best bitter.'

'A pint of best, coming right up.' Connie pulled the pump with practised ease. What did he mean by *it was worth a try*, she wondered?

Looking under her thick dark lashes, she poured the last pint and noticed his eyes sweep the room, taking all in.

Ma Green was tickling an out-of-tune melody on the upright piano and she saw the grimace he did nothing to hide.

'They come in here to torment my ears and hog my fire,' Connie said as the old woman and a group of likeminded pals were strangling the popular wartime version of 'Roll out the barrel'.

'She couldn't hold a note in a bucket,' he said.

'You think?' Connie felt protective of her regular clientele. 'Well, let me tell you, she was singing on the stage of The Metropole, before someone blew it up.'

'I can see how that would nae do much good for her voice.' Angus knew he'd said the wrong thing when Connie scowled at his flippant remark.

Who did he think he was?

'You don't even know her,' Connie snapped. 'The poor mare lives alone in a cold, half-furnished room – and glad to have it. Her family were all blitzed. This place is her lifeline.'

'I'm sorry.' Angus looked contrite. 'I didn't mean to offend anybody.'

'You haven't,' Connie replied with a mischievous glint in her marine coloured eyes. 'She'd have the eyes out of your head and take up residence, if she thought she could.'

'You mean it's not true?' Angus gave a theatrical sigh, looking relieved.

'Oh, it's true enough,' Connie nodded, 'but like I say, it doesn't do to make snap assumptions – there's always a story.'

'I consider myself reprimanded.' Angus smiled, relieved as he raised his glass. 'Will you have a drink with me?'

'I'd have a port and lemon if we had any port – or any lemons, come to that.' She gave him a quizzical look when he threw his head back and laughed; that joke was so old it had whiskers. 'I'll have a drop of mother's ruin, if you don't mind. I can always get my hands on a bottle of gin.'

'Be my guest,' Angus said, and as the bar cleared of drinkers, they were chatting away like old friends.

'I'm not casting aspersions,' Angus explained, nodding to the singing revellers. 'It was just an observation.'

'Have a lot of observations, do you?' Connie asked, still on her guard.

'Old habits,' Angus answered. Some things were not up for discussion.

This one had something about him. Something she couldn't put her finger on.

'I don't suppose there's any chance of a room here?' Angus asked.

'Here, are you taking advantage? One gin doesn't reap favours, you know.'

'Och, as if I dare,' he said in a good-natured tone. 'Perish the thought.'

'Don't talk about perishing, either,' Connie said with a shiver. 'The whole country's fed up trying to make do, and then we've got this awful weather.' The fire would last another half an hour, she supposed. 'Considering the war ended over a year ago, there's still a lack of everything.'

'What happened to the *land fit for heroes*?' he asked, watching every departing customer.

'We should frame that saying, hang it on the board and throw bloody darts at it!' Connie laughed, and the sound awoke something inside him he thought lost forever.

'We should,' Angus said.

'Listen to me harping on.' She gave a little laugh, covering her confusion at the lingering touch of his fingers as he handed over the money. It had been a long time since anybody, except young Bobby Harris, took her hand and held it longer than was necessary. 'I'm turning into a right old moaning Minnie.'

'Been here long?' Angus asked, putting his pint of bitter on the bar.

'All evening,' Connie answered. He was getting no information from her.

'I mean working here,' Angus smiled giving her his full attention – and a knowing look.

'Born and raised here.' She didn't mind talking about herself but found it wise not to discuss her clientele. 'Apart from nursing overseas during the war, I've been here all my life.'

'A nurse?' Angus looked impressed. 'What made you give it up to work behind the bar?'

'I'm the landlady.' Connie's blunt reply was a clear sign she was cautious of his direct manner. 'And I don't talk about my war work.'

'Fair enough,' Angus said, changing the subject. 'So, do you know of any lodgings going begging?'

'There aren't many lodgings, owing to the Luftwaffe gate-crashing the party,' she answered. 'Most of the properties in this area were damaged or destroyed.'

'I need nothing fancy,' Angus said, 'just somewhere to lay my weary head after a day in the office.' She noted his clean nails. His hands did not have the usual rough segs that patterned the hands of local men who worked the docks and factories.

'Is there room at the inn?' Angus ventured. This place would be ideal for his line of work.

'We sell beer, cigarettes and spirits, if we're lucky enough to get a delivery,' Connie said, 'but we don't rent rooms.'

'That's a shame...' He looked disappointed and against all her instincts, Connie, a sucker for a sob story, felt a little sorry for him when he said, 'I have a room for tonight, but I have to be out in the morning.'

Connie wiped the clean bar again. She had nothing against light conversation but was having nothing to do with lingering looks. Where did he think he was? Casablanca? He offered a warm smile that would give her a lift in other circumstances. But she hadn't just come over on a banana boat. She knew when a customer was giving her a load of old flannel.

Looking at the clock behind her, she realised the radio play she had been waiting to hear would start in half an hour. Angus, following her eyes to the clock, knew if he would persuade her to rent him a room, he didn't have much time to do it.

If she was to rent him a room, Connie knew she would have to consult Mim first. Not that she needed her mother's permission, but if sulking was an Olympic sport, Mim would win gold. 'I'm housetrained. Clean. Tidy. Handy with a hammer.' Angus watched her expression change. She looked deep in thought, raising his hopes.

Works in an office, Connie thought. No dirt and grime clinging to his clothes. A clean job. A collar and tie job. 'Your wife?'

'I'm a widower,' Angus said, and she nodded.

'I'm prepared to pay well above the going rate, for the area,' Angus said, 'and the convenience, you understand?'

This would be a perfect opportunity to make extra cash. The pub was limping, because the men were laid off. There were a few unoccupied rooms upstairs that, during the war, were rented out to foreign sailors, it was a shame to let them go to waste when they were furnished for someone who would be out at work all day.

'A hot meal and a bed for the night, you say?' Connie asked. He looked respectable, and it would be nice to have a man about the place again. 'Can you supply references Mr McCrea?' It surprised her when he reached inside his pocket and took out a slim brown envelope. 'Our rooms are clean, comfortable, well-furnished and, above all, this is a respectable house.' She stressed the last part.

'I'm sure.' Angus said, watching Connie. This would be the ideal place to stay. On top of the docks. A good view of surrounding streets he would be free to observe with alacrity.

'I will show these references to Mim – my mother. She owns the place, I'm just the dogsbody with the licence.' Connie knew her mother would not let go of the reigns if she could help it.

'I will call tomorrow morning, if that's all right. Is eight-thirty too early?'

'Not at all.' Something about him impressed Connie.

'In that case I will bid you good night and look forward to seeing you tomorrow.' Angus finished his beer and made his way to the door with a *cheerio* to the stragglers.

'He looked nice enough,' said Ma Green as she put on her scarf and prepared to go home.

'His name's Angus McCrea,' Connie said, staring at the closing door. 'He's got work on the docks – looking for lodgings.'

'If that smile across his clock is anything to go by, my girl,' Ma Green said with a mischievous grin, 'I'd say he's looking for more than that.'

'I don't know what you're implying.' Connie feigned astonishment, and even to her own ears the remark sounded lame. But one thing was for sure, the only interest she had in Angus McCrea was his rent money.

'Go on,' Ma chuckled, pulling up her collar. 'You can't kid me.'

'Be off with you, old woman,' Connie laughed, 'I've got a date with Valentine Dyall.'

'I forgot *The Man in Black* was on tonight,' Ma said, hurrying out and into the snow. 'See you tomorrer, girl.'

'Aye, Ma... Mind how you go.' Connie said, watching her climb the lethal-looking steps to the bridge. As she turned to go back inside, she saw a suspicious-looking mound outside Rene Kilgaren's house...

It moved. And as her eyes grew accustomed to the hazy light of a cloudy full moon, she realised the mound was a body. A man, motionless, sprawled between the pavement and Rene Kilgaren's tiled path. Screwing her eyes, Connie peered a little harder and saw the figure wasn't a man. He was just a boy – and the copious amount of something dark seeping from his body told her he was in serious trouble.

9

Connie didn't need her medical qualifications to see the kid was in trouble. If the blood trailing onto the snow-covered pavement was anything to go by, his injuries were serious. Hurrying, she went to see what she could do.

'Are you all right?' Connie asked, kneeling in the snow patting the cheek of the unconscious youngster, and was just able to make out a face she had not seen for many long years. As he began to stir, his eyes were full of terror.

'Jack? Jack, is that you?' Connie hadn't seen the lad since he was knee-high to a grasshopper. But there was no mistaking those blue Kilgaren eyes.

'I've had an accident...' Jack gasped, his words petering out as he tried to rise. Connie knew she had to work fast. She had to get him up off the cold tiles and into the house.

'Lean on me, Jack,' she said, hooking his arms around her neck and levered him to a standing position, her medical training kicking in. 'That's it, Jack, you can do it... Put all your weight on me. Now straighten your back... That's it... Good lad. Do you have a key?'

'Inside the letter box.' His voice was barely audible, as if the effort to make himself heard was too much. Leaning forward, Connie lifted the long black knocker and put her hand inside the letterbox to retrieve the key hanging on a piece of string.

'Who'd that be?' Caution in the child's lilt was plain to hear behind the closed door. Connie looked through the letterbox. Jack must have lost consciousness before he was able to alert Lucy. It was pitch black behind the front door. No wonder the child was terrified.

'Lucy, don't be scared... It's me, Connie! I work in the tavern next door, is your mam in?' Connie's tone was gentle, given the child's cautious demeanour. She doubted Lucy remembered her or Reckoner's Row. She had been so young when she was sent to Ireland.

'Jack said I mustn't open the door 'til he comes home,' Lucy called.

'Don't worry, he's here with me,' Connie assured her, while Jack was getting heavier by the moment. If the child didn't open the door soon there was a danger of them both ending up on the icy pathway.

'Why won't he speak?' Lucy sounded unsure. 'It's dark in here. I'm frightened.' The child had been left alone. Connie's irritation grew. On a night like this, Lucy should be tucked up in bed, safe and warm.

'It's all right, Lucy.' Jack barely lifted his voice above a whisper. 'Open the door.'

'I can fix the light.' Connie assumed the gas money had run out and she was glad when the door swung open. Edging out, the child lifted her hands to her lips and gave a little yelp of concern.

'Holy Mother, Jack, what happened?' Lucy gasped as Connie helped her brother into the house. 'Jack, you're bleeding! Shall I fetch water...? I'll get a chair! Oh Jack...'

Guided only by the light of the full moon through the small window over the front door, Connie helped Jack along the narrow lobby into the kitchen. Finding a straight-backed chair was not so straightforward in the room's darkness.

'It will be easier to manoeuvre you from here,' Connie said when her foot hit the leg of the chair and she sat Jack down. She shivered, unable to ignore the intense cold that made the air damp on her skin.

'Did you get us the wood, Jack?' Lucy's gentle inflection sounded hopeful. 'I can get a good blaze going in no time.'

'There are a few sticks on the cart,' Jack gasped. 'Not many, though.'

'When will your mother be back?' Connie called from the lobby, putting pennies into the meter. When she came back to the kitchen to light the gas mantle, the boy's ill-fitting clothes were soaked in his own blood.

'Ma won't be long,' Jack answered, too quickly for Connie's liking.

The shabby room was a stark contrast to the last time she saw it when Rene invited her in for a drink after work last Christmas. She remembered complimenting Rene on her polished, red leather three-piece suite, and stunning mahogany sideboard that matched the dining table. Now there was just an old rickety dinner table covered in newspaper, three mismatched straight-backed chairs and a sofa that was bursting at the seams.

'Are you all right, Lucy?' Connie was worried, the child was obviously freezing. When did she last eat? How long had she been on her own? Evie didn't live here any longer, and who could blame her. The girl had a bellyful of her mother's lodger and had moved into a room on the other side of the canal. It wasn't much, but at least Evie was out of danger from Leo Darnel.

By the look of this desperate situation she suspected Rene

had been gone a while. She hadn't been in the tavern since Christmas, but Connie knew it wasn't unusual for Rene to go off somewhere that took her or Darnel's fancy. Since her husband's ship copped it in the Atlantic, Rene was a free agent. Able to up sticks on a whim. But she'd imagined the barmaid would have changed her ways when the kids came home from evacuation. *None of us are saints*, she thought.

'Right, let's have a look at your leg,' Connie said, using the no-nonsense, all-knowing tone she adopted with injured soldiers. It put them at ease, knowing they could concede control to someone more knowledgeable. And, if ever there was a time for her nurse training to kick in, it was now.

Because if she was not mistaken, something other than a slip on the ice had caused a wound as severe as this. Connie found a pencil and a piece of paper and she scribbled something down.

'I want you to take this note around to Evie in Beamer Terrace,' she told Lucy. 'Knock on the door and wait for an answer. Can you do that for me?' Lucy nodded, thrilled she was being given the privilege of responsibility.

'Jack treats me like a baby,' Lucy confided in a whispery voice, 'but I'm all growed up! I'll be there and back in no time.' Shoving the note between her teeth, the child pulled on her coat, already halfway down the narrow passageway.

'Do you know where it is?' Connie, glad of the child's enthusiasm, sighed when Lucy shook her head. It was late, and she should probably go herself, but that wound could not be left much longer. Connie had no choice but to send the child. 'It's over the bridge. Turn left when you go out of here, climb to the top of the stone steps, careful not to fall... and it's the second street along, across the debris'

Lucy, whippet-quick, was halfway up the bridge before she

had even finished speaking. 'Right, let me put the kettle on for hot water, then I'll have a proper look at that leg.'

'Sure... It's not'n.' Jack didn't want to see what state his leg was in, but didn't have the strength to argue, 'Ma will be along any minute...' That said, Jack afforded himself the luxury of putting his head on the table knowing Miss Sharp would take over...

Wasn't it a good thing that man was passing along the dock road when he needed him... Sure, everybody should have a good shepherd. *That's what he called himself. A good shep...* but his thoughts got no further as Jack drifted into oblivion.

Connie could see that in this sad situation, Jack and Lucy needed all the help they could get. Yet, concentrating on their plight, she had failed to see the lone figure watching the child scurrying through the snow-covered street...

* * *

'I haven't had your ruddy coal,' Miss Skinner said when Evie ran-tanned on her landlady's door.

'Well, somebody has,' Evie answered, noticing the old woman's sparrow-thin legs were a mottled red, like she'd been sitting close to a blazing fire all day. She knew the measly ration of coal Miss Skinner eked out was not a strong enough blaze to cause those kinds of markings.

'You young ones are so generous with yourselves. Everybody must get their fair share.'

'I had half a bucket of coal when I left this morning.' Her coal had dwindled before while she was out, but now the whole lot had disappeared!

'I'm not sure I like your tone,' the landlady said, pulling her baggy cardigan over deflated bosoms. 'You've used your ration, and now you're hoping I'll take pity and give you more.'

'I have not used my ration!' Evie felt anger strangle her words, making them high-pitched and barely audible.

'Don't upset yourself, dearie.' Miss Skinner's words were as sickly sweet. 'It's human nature to want a bit more in this weather, I know you're not accusing anybody.'

'I am accusing somebody!' Evie was nobody's fool. The days of taking the flak for somebody else's wrongdoings were over. Defending herself had never come easy. But she knew that somewhere, deep down, there was a girl with the strength and the courage of a lioness.

'We'll say no more about it,' Miss Skinner said, and Evie felt that it was pointless to argue. She had no proof. She watched Miss Skinner shuffle across the faded linoleum to her own rooms. All she had to do was dig down deep enough to find her inner lioness.

Miss Skinner nodded to the three-legged table balanced under the coin-operated telephone on the wall, and said, 'you've a letter... No stamp... Came through the letter box.' Then she slammed her door shut.

'Shrivelled old witch,' Evie whispered, marching down the passageway. If she had somewhere else to go, she would be out of here like a shot. Although curiosity tempered her irritation when she saw Connie's neat handwriting on the unstamped envelope addressed to *Miss Kilgaren*. Ripping it open, Evie's eyes ping-ponged the single sheet of blue lined paper, and as she read the words, an icy chill ran through her that had nothing to do with the freezing weather...

Evie placed one tentative foot in front of the other, reluctant to hurry on the icy ground which was so slippery she feared a broken bone. Steadying herself, she put a freezing hand to the rough redbrick wall. Her shallow breaths came in short bursts, her thumping heart pulsating in her throat. It was dark, and lonely. Nobody in their right mind would be out on a night like this. Skittering rodents negotiated the gutter, slipping down the grid when a feral jigger rat followed, on the prowl for food...

Evie continued, ignoring her fear, urged on by anger at her mother for not letting her know that Jack and Lucy were home. If she met Darnel now, she would smash his face in, she was so angry. Her mother had done another flit, obviously having no intentions of changing her selfish ways.

Did the woman have no shame?

Mam couldn't help herself when men came calling. Taking off when a new 'uncle' showed his face. It was nothing new. It didn't matter what country the servicemen were from or that she could not understand some of them. Working in a dock road alehouse she met every nationality, every colour and creed. But if he had the readies, Mam had a whale of a time.

'We could all be dead tomorrow,' she'd say during the war. Squinting away the smoke from the cigarette hanging from her ruby coloured lips, enhancing her thick dark lashes with boot polish or soot when she didn't have a sugar-daddy to supply her with black-market make-up. Responsibility had never been important to Mam after Da copped it. He was the one who took care of business. Keeping Mam in line, he used to say.

When Darnel came along, Mam thought she'd hit the jackpot and off she went again. Evie remembered the nights when the enemy planes came over, strafing the street with bullets and incendiary bombs. She tried to bury her fear of the cellar and suffered the air raids alone. It became a regular ordeal. But it was no use complaining. Mam was having a fine old time...

Marching through the snow she was careful not to slip, hoping her mother didn't show just yet. Because Evie was boiling mad. And once her mother's ills were revealed, they could never be secreted away again.

The tantalising smell coming from the chip shop made her doubtful her siblings had eaten much of late if her memory served her well, remembering the familiar hunger when her mother would retreat to be picked up by servicemen with deep pockets and shallow principles.

Well, I intend to keep Jack and Lucy from having that kind of life, she thought, ordering fish and chips with the money from her last weekly wage. And if her mother wanted a fight, she could have one!

* * *

'Come in,' Connie breathed, standing back, letting Evie through the front door. Evie shivered. The place seemed more drab than when she left it. The smell of old tobacco and fried food clung to the walls and floors.

'What's happened?' Evie asked, surprised it was her mother's employer who opened the door. Connie put a finger to her lips, to let Evie know she must keep her voice down.

'There's been an... no, not an accident, there's been an incident – and Jack got caught up in it.' Connie whispered.

'What kind of incident. Where's me mam?' Evie felt her heart sink. She knew the answer before she asked the question. 'She's done a flit again, hasn't she?'

'It looks like it,' Connie agreed, knowing Rene had up and left many times in the past.

'When did they get back home?' There were so many questions she needed answers to. But first she had to see her brother and sister. It had been so long since she had seen them. However, this was not the way she imagined they would be reunited.

'Jack has been...' Connie could not bring herself to terrify the living daylights out of poor Evie, by telling her that her beloved brother had been shot. 'He's been hurt. I don't know how it happened. All I know is, Jack was in the wrong place at the wrong time. And there may be consequences.'

'What kind of consequences? Connie, just tell me what's going on,' Evie hissed, not waiting for an answer as she made her way towards the kitchen door. But Connie stopped her.

'I'll tell you everything later, but for now, I have to warn you, Jack has a gunshot wound to his leg.'

'A what?' Evie felt her stomach turn. She must have misheard. People didn't go around shooting young lads.

'Most people saw enough guns in the war to last a lifetime,' Connie answered. 'He isn't saying much. Shock, I suppose, he will need careful monitoring.'

Evie nodded, letting Connie know she understood, but for some strange reason she couldn't utter one word.

'It's a flesh wound,' Connie was saying, and Evie wished she would stop talking and let her see Jack and Lucy. They'd been gone too long. She needed to be with them.

'It hasn't hit the bone – and I should know, I've seen enough of them. Although I've cleaned and dressed it, the wound needs suturing so I'm going to speak to a doctor I know, he is very discreet.'

'What do you mean, discreet? Why would he have to be discreet?' Evie was growing impatient with all this cloak and dagger nonsense. 'I need to see Jack and Lucy – you do what you have to do.' The wireless was playing the theme tune for the popular thriller series *Dick Barton* and Evie thought it apt in light of the news.

'Yes, go and reacquaint yourselves while I go and fetch the doctor.' Connie lowered her voice. 'And don't worry, the police won't hear anything from me.'

'What?!' Evie's eyes widened in shock. She hadn't given a thought to the police. They should have been the first people she thought of, given Jack's injury, but she knew people usually sorted out their own troubles before bringing the law into it. Especially people like Leo Darnel.

'There's no fuel in the house, and the poor mites are freezing. I'll go and get a bucket of coal – by all accounts Jack was on the dock looking for something to burn when this happened.' Connie said.

'He was on the dock? And they've got no heating! This is getting worse by the minute.'

'Don't worry, we get a coal allowance from the brewery, so I won't let them go short.'

'That's not what I meant,' Evie should be grateful for Connie's help and this was not the time to look a gift horse in the mouth, but her concern for Jack and Lucy caused her to forget her manners. On opening the kitchen door, she knew the sorry sight that met her would stay with her for a very long time to come. She gasped when she stepped into the miserable hovel that had once been her home. This was nothing like the place she had left behind last summer.

'It's colder in here than it is outside,' she said when she saw there was no fire in the range, only the charred remains of something burned to keep the life in her siblings. And judging by the look of her ten-year-old sister, it had barely done the trick.

'Evie!' Lucy squealed with delight, wrapping herself around her big sister like an octopus, all skinny arms and legs. Her tangle of rust-coloured frizz looked like it hadn't seen a comb in months. 'I kept all of your beautiful letters and the gorgeous lace hankies you sent me.' Lucy's voice sounded like the Irish nuns who taught her at school, crystal clear and tinkly like a bell. 'Oh Evie, we have missed you so much.'

'I've missed you both, too, poppet.' Holding her at arm's length, Evie could see the healthy glow of Lucy's freckled complexion, which she gained in the clean fresh air of the Irish countryside, had faded. Now it was a dull grey like dried pastry, as if she hadn't had a wash – although, her dark eyes, so like Mam's, still sparkled.

Evie's eyes darted to Jack, her brow furrowing when she saw him sitting on the sofa, his long leg propped up on the straight-back chair.

'Hiya, Sis,' he said with a lopsided grin, wincing when he moved. 'Sorry I can't get up and do the same as Lucy.' Evie's false laugh did little to ease the pinched expression on her face. His inflection, although not as strong as Lucy's still had a Celtic lilt.

'You stay there, Jack,' Evie said, shivering in the dim light of the cold room. 'Don't you move – we've got all the time in the world to catch up.' She relinquished the heat of the chippy parcels from inside her coat and offered one to Jack.

'You must eat, keep your strength up,' Evie told her brother.

'Well, if I can't eat much, they'll certainly keep my hands warm.' He took it, albeit reluctantly and managed a wan smile when she placed the steaming parcel of food in his hands. Sitting at the bare kitchen table that might once have been beautiful but was now unpolished, scarred and clearly showed the crusty remains of something unrecognisable, Lucy could not take her eyes off the steaming food parcels.

'Why didn't someone let me know you were home?' Evie asked, unwrapping the newspaper for Lucy. 'I was in lodgings across the canal, didn't Mam tell you?' Questions tumbled from her lips as the child eagerly took the food and they ate their supper. Evie had yearned to see her siblings and here they were, as if they had never been separated at all.

As she watched Lucy devour her food, she noticed Jack wasn't so keen and she wondered how long it had been since they last ate a hot meal. Though, she wasn't going to go into all of that just yet. There was much more important things to sort out, and Lucy had much to tell.

'Mam said it was best we stayed in.' Lucy couldn't get the words out fast enough. 'Then we found out she'd pawned our good clothes, all we had left were these tatty old things.' Lucy's freckled nose wrinkled in scorn. Evie shook her head sadly; nothing her mother did would surprise her after this.

'Where's all the good furniture gone?' Evie asked and the two youngsters shrugged.

'Two men came and put it all on a flat-backed wagon.'

'Pawned or re-possessed?' Evie asked, recognising the ragged sofa, so faded she could not make out its original colour and spilling its horse-hair innards. The mismatched chairs – one was bottle-green, the other – not so shabby – was dark burgundy and pushed up hard against the gas cupboard. Her father's chair. This furniture had been dumped in the unused parlour when Darnel came to stay, replaced with the fancy furniture he brought. But Evie had little time to delve when Lucy wanted her attention.

'I've been sick too, but I'm better now,' Lucy said as Evie noted the dark shadows, stark against the insipid pallor of her skin. She, too, needed building up.

'I'm here now,' Evie said, taking off her coat. 'I'll put everything right.' How? She didn't know, but somehow they would muddle through. She would do the best she could for them although, with no money coming in and just her savings to live on, Lucy wouldn't be dressed in velvet anytime soon. But as she wrapped her coat around Jack's trembling body, Evie was sure that anything she could do would be better than the way they had been living lately.

'I am so thrilled that you are both home.' Certainly, she was. 'It's all I've wanted for the last seven years!' Evie swallowed hard, hating herself for the unruly thoughts running amok in her head. What about her plans for the future?

Her dream of bettering herself. Getting a good job. Maybe even becoming an office manager like Miss Hawkins! Getting out of the backstreets and moving to a place where the air was clean, where there were green fields and flowers...

'You're here, Evie, that's all that matters,' Jack said, wrapping Evie's capacious woollen coat around his thin shoulders. Young Lucy gripped Evie's hand as she went out to the dark scullery, and Evie sighed... It had been a dream. It looked like this was her reality now.

'Don't worry, poppet, I'll sort it all out. I'm not going anywhere.' Evie's words sounded more confident than she felt.

They were home. That is all that mattered. Now she must make them secure and do all she could to help them.

'May God forgive you, Mam,' Evie whispered, 'because I never will,' She made them a cup of hot tea from the rations she had brought with her, and when they were all together in the austere kitchen, she asked the question.

'Where's Mam, Jack? How long has she been gone this time?' Evie's voice was soothing, and he closed his eyes, not speaking. He looked truly defeated and her heart went out to him. It couldn't have been easy coming back to this deprivation after the good things he had grown used to in Ireland. Food. Fresh air. A loving family who cared...

A knock at the door sent her scurrying.

'Where's the patient?' a doctor in his fifties asked succinctly, 'Connie has told me the situation.'

Jack winced as the doctor, a man of few words, expertly tended the gaping wound in Jack's leg. Whether it was shock or mounting pain that twisted her brother's features, Evie wasn't sure. But either way, he was in good hands. Thankfully, she had the money to pay for his services.

'I had hoped Mam would settle down once she had these two back home.' Evie's voice was thick with contempt, knowing her mother was fond of dock road nightlife. Nothing had changed, it seemed. 'If I know her, she'll be in some dock road pub, warming herself and filling her belly with gin.'

'Darnel was in the tavern earlier,' Connie told Evie after the doctor had left. She picked up the bowl of soiled dressings and wrapped them in newspaper to burn when they managed to get a fire going. 'Mind you, he didn't look like he was in the mood for questions.'

'How could any mother do this to her kids?' Evie asked, and Connie shrugged.

Having been denied the privilege of rearing children of her own, she couldn't understand it either. She knew Rene had thrown Darnel out after Christmas, but Connie didn't ask questions, feeling it was better not to know.

'Don't judge her too harshly,' Connie told Evie. 'Your mam's been having a hard time since she gave Darnel his marching orders.'

'There's nothing new there.' Evie answered. 'She attracts spivs, conmen and losers like iron filings to a magnet.'

'She's soft-hearted. That's her trouble. She caves in when she hears a sob story.'

'She said she had to meet someone,' Jack said, too weary to appreciate the attention from these two competent women who were fussing and fixing the place as they busied themselves. Evie had got a blaze going in the grate and Connie was busy washing the bowls in the kitchen. 'I think she went to see what's-his-name, Leo Darnel.'

Evie felt her heart miss a beat. He'd given her the impression he no longer came anywhere near Reckoner's Row. But he was a born liar. Connie had served him in the Tram Tavern.

'We never met him,' Jack managed to say as the doctor gave him an injection in his thigh. 'He'd gone by the time we got home.'

'None of them stick around for long,' Evie whispered to herself. 'He was here longer than most of the lodgers Mam brought home.'

'She said she needed to see a man about some money,' Jack explained in the Celtic lilt he gained after seven years away. 'She said tomorrow would be a better day.'

'She's been saying that for as long as I can remember, Jack.' Evie felt the sting of angry tears. 'Do you know what, it never bloody is.' Frustration tinged her voice. She was annoyed with herself for not being here when she was most needed. 'You should have come for me.'

'We could have asked the neighbours where you'd gone, but Ma said not to,' Jack said. 'She said you were better off out of it.'

'Out of what?' Evie asked and Jack shrugged, his eyes growing heavy.

Connie, efficient as ever, took the soiled linen out to the scullery and said nothing. It was happening again, she thought. Rene was a great worker, better than most, but when it came to difficult situations, she was nigh on useless. Evie was the one who had always been a mother to Jack and Lucy and cleared up her mother's mess.

'Worry over,' Connie's doctor friend said, suturing the gash. 'There's no bullet in there, although the bugger gouged a deep trench in your thigh muscle.'

Evie was grateful Connie hadn't insisted on calling in the authorities as she might, being a nurse and all that. Jack could have got into serious trouble with the police if he had been found trespassing on the dock. Even if it was only to collect a bit of driftwood.

'I'll make sure he stays out of trouble from now on,' Evie whispered out of her brother's earshot. The older woman had been a real help but, still wary of outsiders, Evie informed her she would take over for now. She needed to find out what happened before Jack started answering questions from the authorities.

'This might sting a little.' The doctor's comforting tone lulled Jack, but moments later his body was rigid. Evie could tell by the distorted grimace on her brother's face that the pain must be excruciating.

'Jesus, Mary and Joseph!' Jack gasped, covering his eyes with his hand and gripping the side of the chair. 'Sting a little? It nearly took me effing leg off! Sorry about the language.'

'The saline will help it heal quicker,' Connie said with authority when he wiped tears from his eyes, watching as the doctor finished tending his leg.

'Jesus! That hurt like the coals of hell!' Jack said when he could speak. 'How can it be good for you if it hurts like that?'

'If that is all, I will leave him in your capable hands, Connie. Any problems, do let me know.'

'How did this happen, Jack? You haven't answered my question.' Connie was binding Jack's thigh with bandages that the doctor had brought with him

'Is it any wonder!' Jack was reluctant to tell her everything. However, it didn't take long for Connie to coax him. She did it in such an open-minded, cunning way.

'Don't worry, I won't be hot-footing it to the authorities,' Connie said. 'You were looking after your sister, the only way you knew how.'

'I'm like a tiddler in a goldfish bowl,' Jack said when Lucy peered over Connie's capable shoulder.

'Can I have a little peep at your wound, Jack?' Lucy asked, enthralled.

'Maybe tomorrow, Lucy,' Connie said kindly. 'We don't want your cocoa to get cold now do we?' Lucy shook her head,

'I hope tomorrow comes soon,' Lucy said with an angelic smile. 'I can't wait to see Jack's stitches.' The more gruesome the better. 'Not that I'm glad you're injured and in pain,' she explained, 'but I'm not squeamish about blood.'

Jack rolled his eyes to the ceiling. Growing up on a farm affected some people that way, he thought. 'She's the only kid I know who would cut a worm in half, so it had someone to play with.'

'I beg your pardon?' Connie asked puckering a confused brow. Jack looked to his young sister and then back to Connie.

'Someone told Lucy if you cut a worm in half you get two worms, so she did. Just so the ugly thing had a playmate. I ask yer!' Jack grinned when Connie threw her head back and laughed until tears ran down her cheeks.

'I have heard nothing so funny in all my days – cutting a worm in half so it has a playmate,' she wiped the tears from her eyes with the pad of her hand. 'Precious!'

'Are you sure the bullet didn't go right in? It feels like it did,' Jack asked, certain he had been mortally wounded.

'Trust me,' Connie said, watching Evie and Lucy clearing away the water and soiled lint, 'you would never have made it to Reckoner's Row if the bullet had gone right through.' She was horrified somebody had opened fire on a fourteen-year-old boy. But she would say nothing. News travelled faster than lightening around the dockside, and some people would put two and two together and come up with five, adding a bit on for good measure.

'I can deal with cleaning and dressings every day and the doctor said he will call in if need be – he's a good friend, I've known him for years, he's doing this as a favour to me,' she told Evie.

'But surely we should tell the police?' Evie said. 'Whoever did this must be punished.'

'We don't know what we're dealing with, here,' Connie said gravely. 'Your mother knew some very dodgy people – who knows what they are capable of if Jack can identify them.'

'Leo Darnel?' Evie asked, but Connie didn't acknowledge the question.

'I'm only next door if you need anything.' Connie's tone belied the gravity of the situation, but Evie soon cottoned on when the former nurse whispered, 'He's going to need careful monitoring. It may only be a flesh wound, but I've seen enough of these injuries to know they need careful handling to reduce the risk of infection.'

Putting a steadying hand on Evie's arm she realised the girl was shaking. 'Doctor Johns is very discreet. Whoever did this is hardly an altar-boy. I think Jack got caught up in something that didn't concern him. But until we know, it's better to keep the authorities out of it.' Connie's tone was low so Lucy couldn't hear.

'What's that supposed to mean?' Evie asked defensively, remembering Darnel's warning. Her fears grew from a minor vortex and ripped through her body like a tornado.

'All I'm saying is, if we take Jack to the infirmary, there will be many questions. Some would even delve into his mother's absence.'

'I'll make sure they're well looked after from now on,' Evie said, understanding the situation more clearly and knowing she would have to put her secretarial ambitions on hold for the fore-seeable future. 'I can do without the complications. But I need to know what happened when...' Evie stopped when Connie put her hand on her arm.

'Jack needs to rest and heal,' she said knowing Evie had even more concerns to worry about. Keeping her family safe being the most important of all.

11

'Let's go out here where we can talk,' Connie said, leading Evie to the back kitchen. Evie shivered. The place smelled of her mother's 4711 cologne and fried food. She hadn't noticed before.

'What's happened?' Evie asked, and Connie put a finger to her lips to let Evie know she must keep her voice down.

'I think Jack stumbled on something that wasn't his place to see. There's been another warehouse robbery tonight and old Sid Harris was caught up in the middle of it,' Connie whispered.

'Is he all right?' Evie asked, her heart sinking. 'He's not...?'

'No, not dead, but certainly shook up by the sound of it,' Connie said. Rene knew people who were mixed up in stuff that could be dangerous for all the family. Why else would she flit for this long?

'For all of your sakes, let's hope this isn't a consequence of Darnel's business dealings.'

Evie knew Darnel had his finger in a lot of sticky pies, which was why her mother didn't ingratiate herself with neighbours. Mam used to say they were a shower of nosey beggars who minded everybody else's business but their own – but Connie was different. Her mam liked Connie.

'This isn't the wild west, Connie.' Evie said, 'people don't go around carrying guns.'

'Not even in the wild north-west.' Connie's stab at humour went straight over Evie's head she was so worried.

'I'll check Jack's settled.' He was sleeping on the couch and would stay there for the time being. 'I'm not one to interfere, so let me know if I overstep the mark,' Connie said. 'I nursed injured soldiers in Italy during the war, so I can get a bit bossy.' Evie smiled. Mam never spoke about her employer, so Evie knew little about her. But she seemed like a decent sort.

'I've seen injuries like this many times,' Connie said, 'and little can be done, except keep it clean and infection-free. Fortunately, I can pop in each day and keep an eye on how well his injury is doing. If that's alright with you. It saves awkward questions.'

'I understand,' Evie said, wary of the authorities. Mam was always telling her to keep away from the powers-that-be and tell them nothing.

'Don't worry about it now,' Connie said. 'Take time to get to know your family again. Questions will be answered later.'

'I only have one more,' Evie whispered. 'How bad is his leg?'

'He'll live,' Connie said, sidestepping her question, 'but he was lucky.'

'That's the first time I've heard being shot is lucky,' Evie answered. 'But I'll stay until Mam gets back home.'

'It's good to see you again, Evie,' Connie said. 'I must get back to Mim.'

'Just let me know what needs to be done, and I'll do it.' Evie's confident tone was in complete contrast to the helplessness she felt. But her pride would not allow her to ask for any more help than was necessary.

'Don't worry,' Connie put a reassuring hand on Evie's arm. 'Nobody will hear about this from me.' Evie breathed a sigh of relief. She was grateful it was Connie who had found Jack and not one of the other neighbours in Reckoner's Row. Ada Harris especially.

'I didn't mean to sound ungrateful.' Evie's voice softened knowing she shouldn't be so quick to judge. 'People make snap decisions about other people... I didn't mean to...'

'Think nothing of it,' Connie said heading out to the front door. 'I won't take no for an answer.'

* * *

Evie woke early the next morning. She was amazed at the change in her brother and sister since she last saw them. She lit a fire in the hearth and put the kettle on to boil, leaving Lucy to sleep until she had some tea and toast ready for her breakfast.

They had a lot to catch up on. Jack was a long streak who looked like a good feed would do him the world of good, Lucy also. If she had her mother here now, she would tell her exactly what she thought of her for letting this happen. But Evie knew she had to stay calm. Be strong. Not let them see she was just as terrified as they must be.

'I've kept all of your letters,' Lucy said thickly, hardly awake as she headed for the warmth of the fire she sat on the mat staring into the flickering flames, 'and the little lace hankies you sent me. Oh Evie, we have missed you so much.'

Evie's heart swelled when she saw the tears spill on to her little sister's pale cheeks and all the bravado of the night before had disappeared to show a vulnerable child who was scared and helpless.

'Well, I'm here now.' Evie put her arms around Lucy's skinny little body and hugged her, vowing never to let her go again. Her family needed her, and while she had breath in her body, she would not let them down.

'It's good to be home now you're here, Evie.' Jack's strong voice, thick with the Irish intonation surprised Evie for a moment. He hadn't said much last night. Shock, she supposed. And why wouldn't he have a different accent, she thought. He had spent just as much time in another country as he had in his own.

'Help me put this lot away, Lucy.' Evie took the remaining contents of her store cupboard from the bag and put it on the table. So much had happened last night, she had forgotten all about them. But there were rations here that they could make good use of this morning.

A packet of loose-leaf tea, an uncut loaf, a packet of margarine, a pint of milk, a twist of sugar, four potatoes, a tin of dried egg and a few other bits and pieces that would come in handy seeing as her mother's cupboard was completely bare.

'We've got all the time in the world to catch up,' Evie said. 'I'm going nowhere.'

'I'm glad to hear it.' Jack gave her a lopsided grin, looking more relaxed as the heat of the crackling fire took the chill off the room.

'We'll soon warm up,' she said as there was a knock at the front door. When she answered it, Connie was heaving Jack's cart up onto the step and pulling a heavy-looking sack into the lobby. 'It's only nutty slack, but it'll keep you going for a while,' Connie said. 'Luckily, I found some of the wood Jack collected last night – he dropped it on the way home.'

'Do you know who helped you home, Jack?' Connie asked, knowing Jack would never have been able to get back to Reckoner's Row from the dockyard on his own.

'I couldn't say,' Jack answered cagily. He would talk to Evie before he told anybody else. 'I kept drifting in and out, you know...' Everybody nodded, thinking they knew what he meant, but knowing nothing of the sort.

'I've brought fresh dressings,' Connie said putting clean bandages onto the table.

'Oh Connie, what would we do without you?' Evie's heart nearly burst with gratitude. Unaccustomed to being helped by neighbours, she found Connie's kindness overwhelming and only just stopping herself from bursting into tears. Connie wasn't like the rest of them in Reckoner's Row. On the chance occasion Mam talked about her employer, she said Connie was one of those rare women you could tell your deepest secrets to, knowing it would go no further.

'Come and have a cup of tea.' Evie pulled out the straight-backed chair, eyeing the tray her mother had pinched from the tavern. 'I'm sure she intended to take it back, eventually,' Evie said, her face glowing with embarrassment.

'Don't mind me,' Connie said. 'I think you've got enough on your plate without worrying about a tin tray.' She gave a compassionate smile knowing Evie had never had it easy. It didn't look as if things were about to improve any time soon.

* * *

After finishing her cup of tea, Connie stood up to leave. The family would not discuss anything of importance while she was here. And she was sure they had a lot of catching-up to do.

'I'll call in later,' she said, heading to the door.

'Thanks, Connie. I'll keep an eye on these two. They're safe now.'

'I know, love.' Connie patted her arm. 'Back later to change those dressings, hey Jack?' Connie smiled when Jack grimaced, knowing full well that being a typical lad he would have left well alone until his leg dropped off. 'No jitterbugging now, d'you hear me?'

'I couldn't jitterbug before.' Jack managed to laugh, and Evie knew that he would bounce back, come what may. He was going to be her mainstay. 'Thanks for everything, Connie,' Evie said walking Connie to the front door.

'Think nothing of it,' Connie answered. 'If the truth be told, I'm glad to get away from Mim's wittering for a while – now, don't forget if there's anything that you, Lucy or Jack need, you know where I am.'

'We'll be fine.' Evie said, hugging her cardigan around her slim frame and hurried inside to close the front door on the cold weather. She let out a long stream of pent-up panic. What the hell was she going to do now?

* * *

From the shadows of the bridge, he watched the landlady scurry into the tavern on the other side of the jigger. Evie was back, he thought, just like he knew she would be. Opening the palm of his right hand he looked down at the single brass key. Not yet, he thought. Give them time...

12

'You should have seen them, Mim,' Connie said the next morning, 'God only knows when they last ate, and the house was so cold, you could have stored dead bodies in there.'

'And only next door, too,' Mim said, shaking her head. 'What is that mother of theirs thinking of?' It was common knowledge that the widow Kilgaren liked her drink and men in equal measures. 'I'm not surprised they were on their own, she was always gallivanting on her nights off, but I thought she'd turned over a new leaf when she gave the spiv his marching orders.'

'And especially when those two kiddies came home.' Connie nodded, knowing nobody called Leo Darnel by his proper name if they could help it. 'We don't know what goes on behind closed doors.'

'I've a good idea,' Mim said. 'I know everybody said Frank Kilgaren was a hero, but he was an outside angel and an inside devil, if you get my meaning.'

'I know exactly what you mean, Mim,' Connie agreed, 'but we

shouldn't speak ill of the dead – although I do remember he had a temper on him, and even watched her when she was only going down the yard to the lavatory. She's well shot of both of them.'

'She can't half pick her men. I know that much,' Mim said with a sharp disapproving sniff, knowing her longest-serving barmaid liked a good old time, especially when the American ships were in port. Mim took another sip of her morning cup of tea, shaking her head in wonder. She didn't have sympathy for women who neglected their children

'She had a good heart, though, Mim, and that's why I want to help them.' Connie said.

* * *

'How long have you both been home?' Evie asked, watching her brother and sister tucking into their food.

'We came home two weeks into the New Year,' Jack said.

'My good shepherd brought us on a ship,' Lucy said excitedly, not wanting to be excluded from this very important family conversation. She was glad Evie was back.

'You've been home for a month? And nobody thought to tell me.' How could her mother be so heartless? 'I was saving every penny for the boat fair to bring you both home.'

'I did ask Mam why you weren't here,' Jack explained, 'and she said you didn't get on with the lodger.'

'That's an understatement, if ever I heard one,' Evie said, watching the fire splutter into life, but she didn't go into detail. Nor did she tell her brother that bringing him and Lucy home had been a bone of contention between her mam and Leo Darnel.

'So, who is this Darnel?' Jack asked, resting his leg on the sofa.

Evie wasn't sure what to tell him. Although, she was sure he would find out soon enough when he was fit enough to go back into the streets.

'You don't want to hear about him,' Evie said, trying to change the subject. 'Tell me all about Aunt Martha, is she still as demented as she ever was?' Evie laughed, knowing their father's older sister was a bit eccentric, but she had a heart bigger than herself.

'She gave me a box of charcoals so I could keep up with my drawings,' Jack answered, 'I'll have plenty of time to use them now I'm laid up with this thing.' He nodded to his leg. 'And Darnel?' It was obvious he wasn't going to give up asking questions until he got a satisfactory answer.

Evie told him everything. There was no sense in keeping Jack in the dark over their mother's antics. If he was expecting to come home to a paragon of motherhood, he had another think coming.

'We never saw him,' Jack said, 'by the time we got home he'd gone.' Evie was relieved. Her brother was at an age where he would be a handy runner for the spiv's illegal gambling racket. And, skinny as a whippet, Jack could nip in and out of places others could not.

'I never thought she'd throw him out,' Evie said, knowing her mam couldn't manage without a man.

'I bet that was a slap in the gob for her,' Evie said, 'watching him take back all that he'd provided. Well, serve her right. She should have thought about that when she gave the spiv a roof over his head. It's obvious he would take back everything he'd supplied if he wasn't living here.' Evie cut more slices of bread for toasting now the fire had livened up. 'He wasn't in the habit of giving stuff away if he wasn't getting anything out of it. There's no goodness in that cold black heart of his. Did Mam say where she was going or when she'd be back?' Jack and Lucy shook their heads in unison and as the fire thawed the icy room, the two youngsters began to relax.

'How did you get home last night, Jack? It couldn't have been easy.' The dockyards were only a couple of streets away, but she knew it would have been almost impossible to get home under his own steam with an injury like that.

'A man was passing along the dock road, he helped me.' Jack shrugged, unintentionally pushing his lolling sister off his shoulder.

'Did he tell you his name?' Evie dragged a chair from the table nearer to the fire.

'I can't say for sure,' he answered, giving the adorable lop-sided grin she remembered so well. 'It was dark. I was too busy trying to stay alive...' He shifted a little to make Lucy more comfortable.

'Not to worry,' Evie said, suspecting Darnel was at the centre of the warehouse robberies and capable of violence. He didn't make idle threats. 'Would you recognise him as part of the gang on the dock, do you think?' Evie worried Darnel might come here, but Jack shook his head, causing his dark fringe to fall into his eyes. Flicking it from his face, he said, 'I'm not sure what Darnel looks like, but I'd know the ugly fucker who shot me if I saw him again.' Jack winced as he tried to move his leg into a more comfortable position.

'Less of the cursing, Jack,' Evie said giving him two aspirins, which Connie had left last night. 'I understand you're angry and you have every right to be. But you don't have to let yourself down in front of Lucy.'

'Sorry, Luce,' Jack said, nodding his head, 'I don't indulge, but the pain got the better of me.'

'You'll feel better when you've had a bite to eat and the tablets take effect,' Evie said. 'I'll make enquiries. Try to find out who he was. To say thank you, for getting you back home safe and sound.'

'He'll be your good shepherd, Jack,' Lucy said knowingly, wanting to add her thoughts to the conversation. 'Aunt Martha said we all have a good shepherd watching over us, I saw mine on the ship when we were coming home.'

'I think mine was looking the other way when that fella let rip with the bullets,' Jack said.

'Good shepherd?' Evie asked. Her young sister had grown into a character. One minute she was babbling on like a fast-running brook and the next, when she had everybody's attention she was as quiet as a timid little mouse. Evie realised she would have to be patient, give her time.

Lucy was only a baby when she was evacuated. Reckoner's Row was a different place to the one she had left behind nearly eight years ago. A busy port, with a rookery of streets leading up from the docks, was a world away from the tranquillity of the Irish farm she'd been accustomed to.

'Lucy believes in good shepherds.' Jack counted on each finger. 'Angels. Sprites. Leprechauns. Fairies and Furies – you name it, she's seen one, been one or spoke to one.' He gave a tired smile. It had been one hell of a restless night. 'She'll try to convince you they're everywhere.'

'Well, if you see this good shepherd again, Lucy, ignore him.' She was worried Darnel might be up to no good. 'You mustn't talk to strangers,' Evie warned.

'But good shepherds are not strangers,' Lucy said, certain she was teaching her older sister something new. 'They know everybody.'

Evie rolled her eyes. Her sister was obviously the trusting

kind. 'I can see I will have to keep a careful eye on you, Miss Adventure.' Especially until their mother came back. 'Don't you worry about anything,' Evie said. 'I'm here now. And if Mam thinks she can waltz back in here with another man in tow, she'll have another think coming!

13

Connie didn't relish the thought of trying to persuade Mim to accept a stranger into the house. She would have her work cut out, for sure. She had to convince her mother that getting a lodger in was the best solution.

What choice did they have? With trade down because of the bad weather, and men being laid off? Some extra income would not go amiss. And truth be told, it would be nice to have a man about the place. She couldn't magic the money for the jobs that needed doing on the pub out of thin air. Mim had been telling her to use her own initiative since she came back from overseas war work. So that was what she did.

'You are the licensee,' she said to herself, trying to drum up the courage to broach the subject with her mother. Nursing on the battlefields was much easier than this. 'Dad left you the pub in his will.' Albeit with a caveat that Mim would live here for the rest of her days and if the mood took her, she could even help run the pub. Not that the mood took her mother often. Connie only just managed to stop herself from groaning out loud. She knew stealth and cunning were both needed if she was going to persuade her mother that a lodger could be the answer to their prayers.

'A lodger?' Mim's agitation was obvious in the twitch of the muscle in her cheeks and the quiver of her double chins. She was on her second cup of tea when Connie eventually told her.

Turned out in a woollen dressing gown, thick knitted bed socks and devoid of her usual lipstick and rouge, Mim was a million miles away from the corseted, nipped-in black dress and favourite pearls she'd worn behind the bar since her husband died. Mim would brush her pin-curled hair, which had been hennaed and wrapped in a silk scarf, into glossy finger waves when she had a mind. But for now, she was playing the martyr.

'If you expect me to welcome any man, apart from your sainted father, into this house you've got another think coming!'

'Mim, could you do me this one good turn?' Connie asked, resisting the urge to remind her mother it was her name above the door, and she had the final say. But she knew her mother, as stubborn as a determined mule, would not want to be reminded that she had failed the licensing board examination.

'A lodger!' Mim was aghast. 'And I have got no say in the matter?'

'You have,' Connie persisted, hugging a scatter cushion to stop herself from dragging her hair out, while Mim yada-yada-yaddaed about the injustice of Da's bias. 'We both decide.'

'But you made this one all by yourself!' *You cheeky madam* were the three words missing from that statement, thought Connie.

'You didn't give me a second thought.' Mim was determined to get her point across. 'What if he's a mass murderer? What then?' Connie ignored her mother's hysterical ideas.

'He's a lodger, Mim. A paying guest. Whatever you want to call him. But he is not a mass murderer. He's got references.'

'Oh, well that's fine,' Mim said sarcastically. 'He's got references. So we will sleep soundly in our beds. Because nobody with references ever murdered two innocent women while they slumbered.'

'I'm sure we will be safe,' Connie's fingers ached to rake the pins out of her hair and drag every single hair out by its roots, rather than listen to this madness.

'Will we?' Mim wailed, and Connie's eyes rolled heavenwards. *Here we go!* 'As safe as I was when you were gallivanting off all over the world.'

'I wasn't having a holiday, Mim! I had to go where I was ordered. There was a war on. Remember?'

'Oh. I remember all right.' Mim's nostrils flared. 'I went through it – on me own, if you please.' She took a large gulp of tea. Then, holding the cup out to Connie she motioned for another spoonful of sugar. 'For the shock.'

'You were not on your own, Mim, you were down in the cellar with a street full of pissed people.'

'Aye,' Mim said, 'and isn't it a good thing I can depend on strangers in me hour of need, because my only living daughter was off saving every other bugger.'

Connie sighed. Next it would be, *those bloody Germans could have murdered me in me bed.*

'Those bloody Germans could have murdered me, as well!' Mim's dark eyes were wide.

'Mim, you've a scream that could scare the life out of a banshee. Look...' Connie's voice softened. 'I know it was terrifying for you when the bombs dropped.' The two houses at the end of the row, next door to Ada Harris, had been blown to smithereens.

'Terrifying, is it?' Mim asked. 'Well, that's one way of putting it.' Agitated, she had no intention of letting Connie off the hook.

'I'm sorry you had to face the war alone – but you survived. Thank goodness.'

'Goodness had nothing to do with it,' Mim said, 'and talking of being murdered in me bed...' Her eyelids narrowed, and Connie, shrewd enough to know what she was getting at, beat her mother to the finish line.

'Mr McCrea won't be here long. I think it is a perfect solution.'

'I've got money put by.' Mim's voice was hesitant. 'We could use that... if we got desperate.'

'I don't expect you to keep me.' Connie put a gentle hand on her mother's arm, knowing she would never hear the last of it if Mim had to break into her treasured savings.

'It's better than having a stranger under our roof.' Mim screwed her handkerchief into a knot. A sure sign she was hoping to win this argument with emotional intimidation. *Well not this time,* Connie thought. Her mother would not get all her own way.

It was hard enough trying to keep the business going in the dark, some nights working by candlelight, with only half a dozen customers. Much less than they had in the bar before the *big freeze*, as it was now being called. She needed help. 'I'm sure he'll have no intentions of ravishing us in our beds.'

'Don't be vulgar.' Mim stuffed her hanky down the side of the chair, leaning towards the blazing fire and Connie smiled. Her mother had been landlady of this dockside pub for over thirty years and could handle the burliest docker, but she would never allow discourteous or uncouth language in her presence. 'There's been too much of that smutty talk, since the war.'

'Yes, Mim' Connie said, knowing she blamed everything from bad manners to the worst weather in three hundred years on the war. 'Mr McClean was a sergeant major in the Dragoon Guards, you know.'

'A sergeant major.' Mim looked thoughtful, and Connie pressed her lips together to contain a smile. Her mother imagined herself to be of a higher class, because her father owned a grocer's shop, and she had been an only child who hadn't had to scramble for attention – or anything else. 'What's he doing around here, then?'

'He's in marine insurance. Shipping, or some such.' Connie decided, without knowing for sure, that Mr McCrea was in that line of business, because they were the most popular office jobs around here.

'I'll think on it,' Mim said.

'Well, you'll have to think quick, Mim.' Connie said under her breath, feeling victorious as she went out to the kitchen to make another pot of tea.

* * *

Dithering in the arctic kitchen, Connie pulled her cardigan around her shapely figure. She lit every jet on the ancient gas cooker, hoping the slight rise in temperature would thaw the frozen water pipes, knowing it was a good thing she had filled the kettle the night before.

'Don't you know gas costs money?' Mim said, dragging herself from the fire, repeating Connie's rebuke from the night before.

'I'm trying to get heat in the place,' Connie answered. 'Any lodger worth his salt will not pay good money for hypothermia.'

'It's not like you to be extravagant.' Mim's words were laced with curiosity. 'Am I missing something here?'

'No, you're not missing anything,' Connie said. 'Can't we be warm for once!'

'I was only saying...' Mim was still in her cosy plaid dressing gown and tartan bootee slippers zipped up to her shapely ankles, her clothes warming on the fireguard. She sounded most put-out.

'No, Mim, I'm sorry, it's just the worry of the dwindling trade getting me down.' Connie sighed. Mim must understand her need to bring in money to keep the business going. 'Jobs, food and fuel are more scarce now than during the war because of this bloody weather.' She knew, even though it was possible to buy rationed goods – on *the* QT – they did not come cheap.

'And we need a new back door,' Mim said on a shiver and Connie wondered at her mother's expectations. Everybody knew things like back doors and window frames were in short supply and difficult to come by because wood, along with most other household materials, was needed for the export drive.

'A new door is not a priority, I'll put a curtain up to stop the draft,' Connie told her mother. 'We have to make do, like everybody else.'

'The country's going to the dogs,' Mim complained as they went into the front room to eat their breakfast. Connie had a thought.

'What happened to your old lisle stockings?' Connie asked her mother as she poured tea into china cups.

'They're in the dresser drawer. Why?' Mim, insatiably curious, always answered a question with a question if she could.

'I'll stuff them with newspaper and plug the gaps under the doors to stop the cold wind coming in, I heard it on *Household Tips* on the wireless.' Connie had a quick sip of hot tea before resting a double sheet of newspaper against the poker wedged into the fender. 'Let's hope this lazy fire livens up soon, but I think the wood's damp.' Connie waved her hand to clear the billowing smoke from the fireplace.

'Everything is damp,' Mim said, 'and I'm not having my

undergarments on display for strangers to see.' She swiped her day clothes from the fireguard and, taking her seat at the table she ladled two large spoonfuls of sugar into her tea. 'And we're nearly out of sugar.'

'There's no more left in the shops,' Connie sighed, 'but there are other things to worry about. The roof, for a start.' If the snow got much heavier, Connie believed, she would sleep under the stars – certain the roof tiles were not strong enough to hold much more weight.

'You should take it up with the landlady,' Mim said. 'She might put a plaster on it.' Connie sighed, knowing the whole place needed doing up, but so did the country. What hope did they have? 'Since your father died there's been nobody to do all the handy jobs.'

'I'll get someone to look at it when the snow clears,' Connie said, putting a scrape of butter onto a piece of toast.

'If the snow clears,' Mim said. 'The man on the wireless said this could last for weeks.' Spending money on anything – even essential repairs – was anathema to Mim.

'I can't do all the repairs, myself.' Nor would her dwindling takings stretch to the exorbitant cost of replacing the roof.

'Maybe your nice Mr McCrea will do the honours,' Mim said, cutting her buttered toast into delicate-looking triangles.

'His money would bring in extra cash, that's for sure.' Connie ignored her mother's insinuations and continued to eat her breakfast. Mim sniffed as she offered Connie some of her precious jam, brought by a cook off a visiting ship.

'Talking about being murdered in our beds!' she looked at Connie who was shaking her head in disbelief.

'I thought we'd finished that conversation?' Connie said, making sure everything was neat and tidy.

'Ada Harris heard it on the wireless!' Mim said. Connie counted to three.

'If there was no news, I'm sure that woman would make it up,' Connie said, looking at the clock on the mantelpiece. Mim loved the titbits of local gossip, gleaned from the ever-present meat and grocery queues.

'I can't see any other solution than a lodger,' Connie said. 'There's not enough work.' Her retort hid the worry of not being able to pay her way. The die-hard regulars spent nowhere near enough to keep the tavern going.

'It's the same all over,' Mim answered over the rim of her teacup.

Connie knew this cold weather might be good for the kids to throw snowballs, but the frozen streets were now way beyond pretty. 'Snow-capped houses are not so attractive when the gas is on low pressure and the cold weather freezes the water pipes solid.'

'It's the streetlights going out that bother me,' Mim added, shaking her head. 'It's the blackout all over again. The snow's twenty feet high in some places,' Mim said, reading the details from reduced pages of *The Daily Express*. Connie knew her mother enjoyed nothing better than a morsel of misery to wallow in. 'Transport's ground to a halt, and the whole country's come to a standstill.'

'We'll have no money if there's no custom,' Connie said, driving her point home. If only she could get her mother to see how dire the situation was.

'I suppose it'll put the kybosh on my nightcap.'

'That's the thing, Mim: how can we replenish the stock if the drayman don't get paid?'

'How will I sleep without me nightcap? There's nothing worse.' Mim looked thoughtful, blowing into her cup then taking a cautious sip of the hot tea. The conversation was going in a more positive direction, and Connie suspected her mother was about to talk herself into a lodger.

'How much did you say he will pay...?'

'Three pounds ten shillings, with an evening meal thrown in – it's a good price.'

'It's more than most, I'll grant you.' Mim nodded, mulling over the situation, then she said, not without an air of smug satisfaction, 'Cissie Brown gets twelve and six off her lodger *and* she does his laundry. Three pounds ten shillings, you say...?' Connie nodded, no longer daring to breathe. Mim hadn't said a definite 'no', but she hadn't said a definite 'yes' either.

'Three pounds ten is not to be sniffed at, considering the average docker gets a pound for a forty-eight-hour week – this Mr McCrea must have a well-paid job.'

Connie lifted her cup from the matching saucer, gazing into the fire while Mim plotted, weighing up the pros and cons – then she played her ace.

'Mr McCrea said he doesn't mind doing his own washing and ironing...' She heard Mim's horrified gasp, but she didn't look in Mim's direction. It wouldn't do to look eager.

'A man doing his own laundry?' Mim was obviously outraged if her irate tone of voice was anything to go by. 'I've never heard the like in all my days!'

'He was in the army.' Connie watched the dancing fire gain momentum. Nearly there.

'Well, I'll be having no man washing and ironing in my kitchen!' Mim said. 'I'm sure we can come to an arrangement...' Connie sipped her second cup of tea.

'Three pounds and fifteen shillings, with meals *and* laundry thrown in?' Mim conceded. 'And that's me last offer.' She gave a deal-affirming nod of her head.

'You drive a hard bargain.' Connie smiled. 'He only works for the Mersey Dock Board, he doesn't own it.'

'He won't get better, not around here.' Mim knew her own home was a cut above the average. 'What does he do? I'm having no docker in dirty overalls mucking up my antimacassars!'

'I told you. He's suit and tie, works in the office. And here's the supplied references.' Connie took out the brown official-looking envelope, and could have jumped for joy when she gave the envelope to her mother. Three pounds fifteen shillings would go a long way when trade was down.

'They decorated him for his war work, did you know?' Mim asked, peering over her new spectacles, bought from Woolworths. Connie nodded. She knew.

'Thirty-seven, and already a widower...' Mim said, folding the reference and sliding it back into the envelope. By the raised eyebrow and agreeable expression on her mother's mature, attractive face, Connie deduced everything was in order. 'He's got implacable credenzas.'

Impeccable credentials, Connie thought, knowing her mother often got her words mixed up. 'You can congratulate him when he gets here – at half past eight.' She nodded to the clock on the mantelpiece.

'Half past eight! Today? This morning?' Mim's eyes widened as she shot up from the table. 'It's that now, and here's me in me night-shift... It would have been a kindness to tell me!'

Connie had never seen Mim move so fast.

14

When she heard the knock on the front door, Connie felt her insides tighten. There hadn't been a man in the place since her father died six years ago.

'You'll hardly know I'm here,' Mr McCrea had said when he caught her undecided expression, his vibrant blue eyes coaxing. 'I'll be out all day. All I need is a bed and a bite to eat, and I'll be satisfied.'

Be that as it may, thought Connie, heading down the stairs, but would Mim feel the same way? Since she'd decided to take in the lodger, Mim had a face on her like a wet week in Weatherby, and nothing was more miserable than that. Before opening the side door downstairs, Connie took a quick peek in the mirror. Pinching her cheeks to give them a dash of colour, having already removed the pin-curls under her turbaned scarf. But when she got to the door, she was surprised to see Evie, huddling in the doorway, hopping from one foot to the other.

'I hope you don't mind me knocking this early,' Evie said, her arms folded across her slim body trying and keep some body heat. But Connie knew nobody could keep warm in this arctic weather. 'I've come to—'

'Come in,' Connie said standing to one side. 'We don't want to let all the heat out.'

'That's what I've come about,' Evie said. 'I don't want you to think I'm on the scrounge and I didn't sleep a wink for worrying.' Evie didn't want Connie Sharp thinking she was brazen like her mother, who wouldn't think twice about accepting a hand-out. 'I forgot to pay you for the coal last night.'

'You had a lot on your plate,' Connie said, ushering Evie up the stairs. Then, lowering her voice, she said in a confidential hush. 'The brewery make sure we don't go short. They don't want their regular customers going somewhere warmer.' Connie led the way up to the front living room and Evie made a determined effort not to let her jaw drop.

She'd only been in the Tram Tavern once on that terrible Sunday last Summer and had never seen the upstairs living quarters. But even before she got to the top of the stairs, she knew this was no ordinary accommodation. It was like how she imagined a high-class hotel. Even before she followed Connie into the furnished front room, Evie could see this place was a million miles away from the Kilgaren house next door.

This lot must have cost a queer penny, Evie thought, taking in the velvet plumb coloured curtains keeping out the cold draught from eight bay windows and fitting the rounded corner bay, which allowed an all-round view of the area – right down to the docks. Evie couldn't take her eyes off this rare view of the borough and she could even see her lodgings on the other side of the canal, next to Old Man Skinner's haulage yard.

'Come and sit down,' Connie said patting the brown leather Chesterfield sofa so like the one that had graced her mother's kitchen, except this one looked as if it belonged. Evie complied, her feet sinking into the deep-pile carpet that covered the whole floor. No lino here, she noticed, eyeing the kind of luxury she wanted one day. Nobody would ever dream this was a backstreet pub in the heart of the Mersey dockland.

'I can't stay long.' Evie felt the extravagant heat seeping into her frozen limbs, and she knew the kids would thrive in a place as warm and luxurious, and then some. 'I've got to get back to Jack and Lucy.' She felt guilty, knowing their fire was nowhere near as inviting as this one.

'I'm not going to take your money,' Connie said pushing away Evie's outstretched hand. 'We get it off the brewery, like I said, so it's no skin off my nose.' By the looks of it, poor Evie needed all the help she could get.

'I won't take charity.' Evie sounded determined and Connie surmised the girl had something about her that was a million miles away from her parents. She was not going to be the cause of a good jangle, like her mother. And as for her father – well, Connie thought, the least said about Frank Kilgaren the better.

'I pay my way, then I know what's what.' She didn't elaborate but Connie had a good idea what she was getting at. Her family had filled the mouths of Reckoner's Row inhabitants for many a long year, and it looked like Evie thought the time had come for the gossip to stop.

'Suit yourself,' Connie said good-naturedly taking the proffered money, knowing Evie was still as independent as she remembered and knowing there were some around here who would take the eyes from your head and live in the holes. She smiled as she tucked the money inside her blouse, Evie wasn't like that.

'I must get back,' Evie said. 'I didn't want you thinking I diddled you out of the coal money, not like some.'

'I know you didn't, you soft mare,' Connie laughed. 'But say what you like about Rene, she was a bloody good worker until now. No stinting. Always gave me notice if she was going to miss a shift behind the bar...' Connie paused as if remembering, then said, 'Oh, before I forget, I've got some candles here – for when the gas goes off, later.'

'I'm sure we've got candles.' Evie was sure they didn't have any candles, Connie had done enough already. They would manage with the light of the coal fire.

Realising the girl looked a bit shame-faced, Connie nudged Evie's arm and said, 'don't worry about the money. I mean it!'

'Are you sure you can spare them?' Evie asked, knowing she needed every penny. 'I don't mind paying for them.' She knew they possessed only one nub of candle for the whole house next door, so a couple more would come in very handy.

'They cost me nothing,' Connie said. 'The brewery makes sure we're well-stocked – they know the customers won't drink in the dark during the blackout.'

When she disappeared to fetch the candles, Evie allowed her taut body to relax a little. The dark wooden framed pictures on the pale cream walls looked ever so posh and her eyes were drawn to a sepia coloured photograph above the marble fireplace, it showed a young woman in white lace. The style looked straight out of the 1920s. The drop-waist dress showed off her white silk stockings at her slim ankles, her dainty Mary-Jane shoes and flowing veil completed the stylish outfit.

The newly-married girl was smiling up to her new husband dressed in the uniform of a soldier in the First World War, who had his arm around her small waist outside the doors of the tavern, and Evie guessed the adoring couple were Connie's mam and dad on their wedding day.

As she stood admiring the photograph, something struck her. Her own mother had taken all the pictures down when her father's ship went down. She couldn't bear to be reminded of the happiness they shared, Evie supposed. Mam never talked about her wedding day. Never said where she was married. Nor how she met Dad. But he had made sure they knew how much he loved her mother. Adored her. Worshipped the ground...

'Here we are,' Connie said, holding out three long white alter candles. 'But say nothing to anybody – if someone in the street gets wind of spare candles, they'll all want some.'

Evie shook her head. Who could she tell? Connie was the only person in Reckoner's Row who had ever given her the time of day. Except for Danny Harris. Her heart gave a little flutter and she ignored it. Being in the army, he didn't count. He was nice to everybody.

'Thanks ever so much, Connie,' Evie said, bundling the candles under her coat. She'd always been a bit scared of Connie, thought she was a bit... sergeant major-ish, but really she was very kind and not a bit like Evie imagined.

As she headed towards the door to leave, Connie's mother came into the room. Now Mim really was a character and as far removed from the girl in the photograph as it was possible to imagine. Her bleached blonde hair was wrapped in tin curlers and covered with a brown hairnet. But that wasn't the thing that disconcerted Evie as she gave Mim a quick nod of greeting and tried not to look puzzled at the sight of the middle-aged, but still handsome woman, dressed in her nightclothes while sparkling like the crown jewels.

'Any news from your mother?' Mim asked, ignoring her daughter's wide-eyed glare, as Evie shook her head. 'Knowing Rene, she'll be back in a day or two with her tail between her legs.'

'Mim!' Connie's unblinking retort made no difference; her

mother was noted for speaking her mind. 'Evie doesn't want to hear you talking about her mother like that.'

'How could any good mother in their right mind leave their kids? In this weather!'

'She'll be getting the length of my tongue when she does get home.' Evie forced the words through clenched teeth.

'It takes all kinds, I know,' Mim had no intentions of keeping her opinions to herself, 'but this country's gone to the dogs since the war...'

'Don't forget, Evie,' Connie said interrupting her mother before she caused the poor girl any more embarrassment, 'if you need anything, you know where I am.'

'Thanks, Connie,' Evie said, her smile tight. Opening the side-door and stepping out to the yard, where beer crates stacked as high as her head lined white-washed walls, Evie felt privileged to see behind-the-scenes.

'I must go back to my lodgings,' Evie said, 'though, I begrudge paying rent for a room I'm not using.'

'Why don't you move back home? And if it doesn't work out when your mam gets back, you can have a room here,' Connie offered. 'I'm sure it's much better than where you're staying now.'

'Not half!' Evie said, delighted. 'I swore I'd never come back, but I didn't realise I was going to miss the old place.'

'I felt exactly the same when I came back from Italy, after the war,' Connie said, not allowing herself to dwell. 'It's funny how you get used to the noise and the dirt and the smoke from belching chimneys.' Suddenly she started laughing. 'Oh I really missed the belching chimneys and the stink off the dock.'

'All seven bloody miles of it,' Evie joined in and for the first time in who knew how long, she heard the sound of her own laughter. It felt good. Connie wasn't the harridan she had imagined. In fact, she was lovely. Even if she did have to put up with a strange mother.

'It's good of you to offer me a room, Connie...' Evie hesitated, unsure of her next words. 'Don't think I'm being nosey, but does your mam always sleep in her jewellery?'

Connie threw her head back and laughed, something she did often.

'Take no notice of Mim.' Connie lowered her voice. 'We're getting a new lodger today, and she thinks the first thing he'll do is ransack her jewellery. It's only paste, not worth a balloon off the ragman.'

'Oh, Connie you are so funny,' Evie laughed, realising this feisty woman was not as formidable as she first thought. Connie could still hear her laughing when Evie reached number two next door. The sound raised her spirits, knowing Evie Kilgaren had been desperately short of a bloody good laugh.

Closing the high wooden side-gate, Connie heard the rumble of a hackney cab trundling over the icy cobbles at the bottom of the street and the sound spurred her on. Hurrying upstairs she pulled the turban from her head and slid the grips from her pin-curled hair. Leaning forward she gathered the little Catherine wheels into Betty-Grable-style curls and secured them on top of her head with the pins she had removed.

A quick squirt of sugared water held the glamorous coils in place, and her look was finished with a hunter's bow of red lipstick and a dot of rouge on each cheek. She could not greet her new lodger in a turban without her *face* on, not at this hour of the morning.

Connie had finished getting ready when she heard the throb of the taxi's engine outside. Like a young gazelle, she crossed the room and pulled back the lace curtain, sensing Mim close behind her. Craning their necks, they peered down into the frozen street opposite the canal to where a man in a dark Crombie overcoat and black trilby hat was taking two large suitcases from the boot of the black cab, bringing attention from every kid in Reckoner's Row.

'Come and have a look at this, Mim,' Connie called. 'Trust Bobby Harris to stop and say something,' she added when she saw Mr McCrea smile at Bobby's unsuccessful attempted to pick up one suitcase. But she could not explain why her heart did a little flip when the new lodger ruffled Bobby's hair.

'No doubt he's getting all the information he can for his mother, save her the bother of asking when she comes in to clean afterwards,' Mim said with a sniff.

'Looks like he's offered to carry the suitcases the whole three feet to the tavern door,' Connie said, smiling.

'For a small consideration, no doubt,' Mim answered when she saw Mr McCrea reach into his trouser pocket and hold up a threepenny bit. 'Those new threepenny bits are worthless,' Mim said. 'All the silver's needed to pay back the bullion lent by the Yanks during the war.'

'Really?' Connie answered, not taking much notice, more interested in watching what Bobby was up to. Mr McCrea said something, which she couldn't hear, and Bobby nodded. Then, the Scotsman slapped the twelve-sided coin onto the back of his hand. Bobby must have got the answer right, she thought, as the boy raised his hand in salute when Mr McCrae gave him the money.

'He's no spring chicken,' Mim said, raising her chin, taking all in.

'We're not asking him to lay an egg.' Connie's sudden anxiety was making her tetchy.

'By the look of those leather suitcases, I'd say he wasn't short of a few bob, though.' Mim knew if most people even owned a suitcase it would be made of stiff cardboard.

'As long as he can pay his rent, that's all that need concern us.' Connie knew what would happen. Her mother, a wily inter-rogator any secret service would be glad of, would cross-examine every ounce of information out of their new lodger.

'He might be useful after all.' Mim's shrewd expression soft-ened, and Connie watched the fine web-like lines that etched her face disappear.

'No, Mother,' Connie warned when she saw her mother's familiar expression, which told her the quest had begun. Under the hospitable exterior of an ex-landlady, beat the heart of a predator. Whilst removing her dinky curlers with apparent haste, Mim watched Connie hurry down the carpeted stairs to answer Mr McCrea's ran-tan on the side door.

Taking a deep breath and wiping her hands on her skirt, Connie opened the door, her eyes bright. 'Well, you got here then?' She gave him an accomplished smile, ushering him inside.

'Aye,' Angus answered in that deep Scottish brogue as he removed his hat. 'I got here.'

'Here, let me bring these inside.' She bent to pick up a suit-case and Mr McCrea put his hand on her arm.

'You will never lift it,' he said, irritating Connie with his condescending smile. She had been through more than enough to know her limitations.

'I am stronger than I look,' she answered, trying to pick up the heavy suitcase, without success. Taking a deep breath, she smiled. 'I'll leave you to it.'

'I am sure you're capable,' he remarked picking up the two cases as if they were empty, 'but I do not travel light.'

'Come and meet my mother.' Connie tried to sound casual, while calming the fluttering butterfly wings beating inside her stomach. Just then, Mim came downstairs. Her hair was set in perfect finger waves. Connie noticed Mim had even had time to apply a vivid coat of pillar-box red lipstick. Never one to be under-dressed, her mother came over all regal when she had a mind.

'Mrs Sharp.' Mim, holding out her hand, introduced herself as she approached the new occupant of the spare room. 'And you are?' Connie felt her insides shrivel and wondered if she had made the biggest mistake of her life.

'Angus McCrea.' He smiled, shaking her mother's hand. 'But please, call me Angus.'

'I'm sure you would like a cup of tea, Mr McCrea,' Mim said, ignoring his request. Connie knew her mother was deciding whether she liked him. When she was sure she did, then she would she call him by his first name.

15

'Why don't you show Mr McCrea the room?' Mim said. 'My leg's banjaxed this morning.'

'If you're sure.' Connie was sure her mother would have wanted to show the rooms. 'This way,' Connie said in an efficient business-like manner. 'You can have either one, whichever suits.' The first room was the back bedroom adjoining her own, one step up to the right, on the landing.

'Very nice,' Angus said, taking in the polished wardrobe, dressing table and single bed draped in a dark blue candlewick bedspread. The room was adequate for his needs and well-cared-for. 'And the other room?' He asked, requesting to see the room at the front, his mind already wandering. Why was a good-looking woman with a well-turned ankle and shapely figure wasting her time in a backstreet pub?

After showing him the other room, Connie saw him hesitate. His reticence was not the reaction she expected, given both rooms were comfortably furnished. 'You won't find better around here,' she said, thinking he was having second thoughts.

'The rooms are fine, excellent in fact.' His expression changed to one of cheerful approval.

'We have spare furniture if you want to make this front into a sitting room?' Connie ventured.

'That won't be necessary.' Angus preferred being with the families, if they didn't object. He learned a whole lot more that way.

'There won't be any extra charge if that's what you're worried about?' Connie said. 'Although we have the wireless in the living room...'

'I'm not worried about money.' His smile was tight. Something about this woman unsettled him.

'Mr McCrae can sit with us, I suppose,' Mim said, bustling into the room. 'If you want to listen to the wireless, we don't mind, do we Connie?'

'Mr McCrea might have other things to do, Mam, he won't want to sit with us every night.'

'That's kind of you. If it's nae bother, just let me know if I'm getting under your feet and I'll make himself scarce.'

'I'm sure it won't come to that, Mr McCrae,' Mim said. And then the penny dropped. Connie knew what she was up to. Her mother was trying to find out if he would make good husband material and if so, she would do her best to put a spanner in the works – she had seen that look before. *Well, not this time, Mim*, Connie thought. He'd only been here five minutes and she could pick her own men-friends, thanks very much!

'You have a lovely house,' Angus said, charming Mim with a warm smile. 'This front room will certainly suit my needs.' Edging the burnt-orange curtain and starched white net to one side, he could see right up the street and down to the docks. 'This is perfect.'

'I moved to the back on account of the Blitz,' Mim explained, patting her combed-out hair and enjoying the compliment. 'I never moved back in here again, did I Connie?'

'No Mim,' Connie said, amused at how easily Mr McCrea had managed to flatter her mother. 'There's no point in letting good rooms go to waste.'

'I agree,' Angus said, taking in the polished walnut wardrobe, good quality dressing table and expensive looking carpet that covered the whole floor. This was not what he had been expecting in a house round here. 'I'm impressed.'

'We have high standards, Mr McCrea,' Connie said when she noticed him eyeing the deep-pile carpet, which had been an over-estimation for a luxury liner under construction at Birkenhead. She knew if he was of the observant kind, he would see the same carpet graced a few houses around here, not just the tavern.

'None higher, I imagine...' Angus answered with a quiet smile. Her tone was as he expected, was sure that underneath the reserved exterior there beat a passionate heart.

'Breakfast will be at seven sharp, except at weekends,' Connie covered her neck with her palm as an unusual heat rose to her throat under his scrutinising gaze. 'There is an alarm clock supplied, and you will get yourself out of bed.'

'Oh, I'm sure I will.' Angus smiled. 'I have been doing that same thing for a long while.' Connie was too nervous to laugh. She wasn't sure if he was being serious.

'If you or I – we – don't suit, we'll end the agreement, forthwith.' *Oh dear, she was making a right pig's ear of this.*

'Forthwith...' he said, his eyes twinkling. 'Shall I pay you now?'

'Mim deals with the money side of things,' Connie said, refusing to take money from a man in her mother's front bedroom. It didn't seem decent.

'Shall we have tea?' For some unknown reason, Connie Sharp,

who took no lip from any man, and could clear a bar full of sailors in ten minutes flat, couldn't get out of that bedroom quick enough. 'I have a lot to do this morning.'

* * *

'So, you're starting work nearby, Mr McCrea?' Mim found small talk came easy because of the nature of her trade, but there was something about Angus McCrae that left Connie tongue-tied – and she wasn't sure she liked it. 'You haven't picked the best of weather.'

'Nae matter,' Angus replied as he glanced around. This was a damn sight better than most he had seen. The place was comfortable after his long trip from Scotland. Even if her mother was an odd-bod, sparkling like the crown jewels, Angus decided this place would suit him fine.

'It's a nice place you have, Mrs Sharp,' he said, noticing the old dear staring at him like he was the last chicken in the butcher's window.

'We do our best, Mr McCrea,' Mim added, unable to let go of the reigns completely. 'If you would like to come into the drawing room, we can have tea.'

Connie looked to Mim, who sounded like she had her mouth full of some dark fruit they hadn't seen in a long time. When had they acquired a *drawing room*?

'Do you take sugar?' Mim asked, lifting the cut-glass sugar bowl.

'Two please.' Angus smiled when he saw her scoop just one spoonful into his cup.

'Stir that, it will be sweet enough,' Mim said. *Two indeed*! 'I hope you found your room comfortable?' she said, sipping her own sugarless tea. 'We wouldn't want you to feel we were lacking in amenities – the bathroom is just down the passageway, although, because of the fuel shortages, I must ask that you stick to the usual five inches of water when bathing. How long will you be requiring the room?'

'I'm not sure how long I will be here. Is that a problem?'

'Not at all,' Connie blurted before her mother could pin down as many rules as she could think of in the shortest amount of time. 'You come and go as you please.' She handed him his keys. 'This is the side-gate key, and this is the side-door key, which we use most of all. It will save you having to come through the bar every time you need to...' Her voice trailed, and Angus nodded, putting the keys in his pocket.

'What line are you in, Mr McCrae?' Mim asked without preamble. As far as she was concerned, it was best to get as much information as possible. Only then could she decide about a person. 'Insurance,' Angus said, scraping his cup across his saucer, setting Mim's teeth on edge, 'I work all around the country. Only staying long enough to finish the job,' he said, omitting to divulge the true nature of his work.

'I could see that would put a lot of strain on a marriage, Mr McCrea?' Mim said, and Connie glared at her mother who really was the limit. 'Although, I believe you are a widower?'

'Mim. That's none of our business!' Connie worried her straight-talking mother would put him off taking the room before he had spent the night here. Turning to Angus, she said, 'Mim asks the questions that politer people wouldn't dream of.' She gave her mother a warning look. Although she noticed Angus didn't refer to Mim's question.

'Have you worked for the dock board long, Mr McCrae?' Mim ignored her daughter's direct gaze. '... I need to know if the rent will be on time.'

'I'll pay two weeks in advance if that suits?' Angus said

amiably. 'I won't be here until Sunday night and only then until Friday. I will be away every weekend. However, I will pay for the full seven days.'

'That's very generous of you, Angus,' Mim said, brightening at the mention of money. Connie smiled. Her mother had obviously decided she liked him enough to call him by his first name.

'There's no need to pay for days when the room will be unoccupied,' Connie cut in, watching her mother's face gather in an irritated scowl.

'Not at all,' Angus said good-naturedly, 'it will hold my room in reserve, will it not?'

'Yes,' Mim answered quickly. A businesswoman, she wasn't one to look a gift horse in the mouth.

16

'I won't be long!' Evie called upstairs to Jack, who poked his nose out of the warm confines of an army blanket she had bought in the Army and Navy Stores.

Pulling the rough grey blanket to his chin, Jack felt the cold air damp on his skin. When he breathed out, he saw a cloudy miasma billowing into the early morning air and quickly dipped his face back under the covers, reluctant to start another day just yet.

'Lucy's down here on her own, in the back-kitchen,' Evie called, her words sounding like a warning and Jack shivered. It had been two weeks since their Evie had come back home and there was still no sign of their mother. With Connie's expert care, his leg was healing nicely, and he could get up and down stairs now. As soon as it was wise to do so, he was going to find himself a job, and pay his way. He didn't like the idea of their Evie spending all her savings on him.

'I'll be there and back as quick as I can,' Evie called from the front door, and moments later he heard it slam.

'I'm making you a nice cup of tea, Jack,' Lucy called from the scullery and, stretching his good leg, Jack winced as the gnawing pain in his thigh turned to a shooting pain, detonating an explosion of panic inside him. Lord knew what Lucy would get up to, left to her own devices.

'Don't touch nothing, Lucy!' he called, swinging his good leg off the bed and searching for his ice-cold shoes. 'I'm coming down there, now.' Balancing on the edge, he shrugged his feet inside the leg of devastated trousers. Fuel was in short supply, but lit gas was still strong enough to do some damage in the wrong hands. If Lucy burned herself on the gas stove, Evie would make sure he never walked again...

He hopped downstairs on one leg then over to the kitchen door, each excruciating thud screamed through his injured leg. The pain got bad during the night, knocking the bajazus out of him. He had had to come downstairs on his behind to get a couple of aspirins Connie had left.

'Here's a nice cup of tea,' Lucy said, mimicking her older sister who had been waiting on Jack hand and foot. Concentrating on the cup, Lucy slopped hot tea all over the floor before Jack managed to take it from her.

'Evie will go loopy if she knows you've been near the gas cooker,' he gently scolded his younger sister, yet was grateful for the hot, sugarless drink.

'I couldn't let you make it yourself,' Lucy said with an air of importance, 'and I am capable of making a cup of tea, you know. I am ten years old – hardly a child.'

'Thanks, you did a great job.' Jack grinned. 'Even if you did lose half of it on the floor.' He took a huge gulp and the heat revived him.

'Evie said she'll get a good blaze going when she gets back, she heard there was a job going at the coal yard,' Lucy assured him, her nose red-tipped with the cold. Jack felt a wave of regret and shame wash over him because he couldn't be the one to go out looking for a job to help them get through one of the worst winters in living memory. He vowed that as soon as possible – if not sooner – he was going to get back on his feet and do his share.

'My good shepherd said I'm about ready to start fending for myself.'

'Did he now?' Jack said, knowing all about Lucy's 'good shepherd'. At first, he thought the rigid religious practices of their aunt's Catholic beliefs affected Lucy, because Ma wasn't a great fan of religion. But he soon got used to the little nuggets of information purportedly from her good shepherd.

He had never seen this shepherd, obviously, because he was a figment of his young sister's overactive imagination. An imaginary friend who, up until they moved back to Liverpool had been Lucy's constant companion. But now she had become friends with that young snapper, Bobby Harris, whom she met in Saint Patrick's junior school. Evie made sure she and Jack were enrolled as soon as she came back to Reckoner's Row, so Lucy didn't talk about her good shepherd as much.

'I asked him why he didn't stop you having your accident,' Lucy said, huddling close to the diminishing fire as she finished getting ready for school.

'And what did he say?' Jack asked, lowering himself onto the couch, knowing she wouldn't have a clue.

'He said he did help you,' Lucy answered. 'He brought you home on the cart.'

A shiver ran down Jack's spine. He had told only Evie and Connie the details about the stranger bringing him home. As far as Lucy was concerned, they kept the details from her delicate ears.

'He said you were bleeding like a gushing oil well when he

found you by the docks – why were you so far down by the docks, Jack?'

'To get the wood,' he answered, trying to recall what he had said that night. Maybe she had overheard him talking to Evie. 'We needed the wood. For the fire.' Jack had suspected she would forget all about her imaginary friend when they left Ireland. But it looked like he was back. And this time he was a saviour too, issuing golden nuggets of advice.

Jack never doubted his young sister believed the things she said she saw. Nor did he ridicule, as some would. She was going through a phase – an adjustment, Evie had said when he told her. So he accepted the fact. Lucy had an eccentric way of showing the things that went through her mind. However, their conversation was cut short by a knock at the front door.

'Don't forget to ask who it is before you open the door, Luce,' Jack said, knowing his sister would be no match for their mother if she wanted to push her way back in. Evie had left precise instructions not to let Rene back into the house until she was here. No matter how much she ranted.

'It's Aunty Connie!' Lucy called from the lobby, and Jack told her to open the front door. In minutes the kitchen was filled with laughter and chatter and bustling noise that always accompanied Aunty Connie's visits. She never came empty-handed, and Lucy never failed to get excited.

'I thought you might make use of these, Jack,' Connie said, opening a brown paper parcel and taking out a pair of pin-striped trousers. 'They look like they'd fit you,' she said putting her head to one side to gauge his size. 'I know they're a bit Sunday best, but they'll do you a turn.'

'I'll look a proper toff in these.' Jack beamed, unperturbed that the trousers were big on the waist. 'Just the ticket, Aunty Connie. Ta very much!' He made a circle with his forefinger, wanting the two females to turn their back while he shuffled into the trousers. 'Too right, these'll do for me,' he said in that good-natured way he had about him. Always ready to look on the bright side.

'I'd give you a catwalk demonstration,' he said, 'but I'll have to wait for my gammy leg to get better, first.'

'Oh, you'll have all the girls after you,' Connie said with a wink of one of her caring blue eyes. She was glad the dock incident hadn't changed Jack's exuberant personality. He was the one who kept Evie's spirits up, stopping her worrying too much.

'Shall I pour you a cup of tea?' Lucy asked, dramatically throwing herself onto the sofa in surprise when both, in unison, cried 'No!'

'Let me do it,' Connie said, bustling out to the kitchen, just as Evie came through the front door and called a greeting after Connie.

'I'll just get on with building up this fire,' Evie said unbuttoning her coat, but keeping the woollen headscarf around her neck to keep in what little warmth there was to be had, before joining Connie in the kitchen. 'I managed to buy some coal briquettes and a few bundles of wood, but only enough to get a fire going for today. I had to lie about going for a job.' Because of the low pressure due to lack of fuel, the kettle took an age to boil.

'Jack and Lucy are glad to have you back in their lives,' Connie said, knowing the Kilgaren kids were settling back into Reckoner's Row with Evie's complete and willing support.

'I've been to the police station to see if they've heard anything about Mam,' she told Connie in a lowered tone so her voice wouldn't carry to the other room.

'Any joy?' Connie asked and Evie shook her head.

'I have to admit, I am getting worried,' Her brow was

furrowed, alarm bells ringing in her head. 'Mam's always been a roamer, but she's never been gone this long.'

Connie put the tea things on the tray, patted her arm and said, 'Don't upset yourself, she'll be back soon enough.' Not believing her own words, Connie took the tray through to the kitchen, where Jack and Lucy were hogging the fire.

'Come and get a hot drink you two and let some of that heat out.'

As she waited for the knocking pipes to deliver more water for the kettle, a small noise alerted Evie to the window overlooking the back yard. She leaned over the sink and pulled the net curtain across the steamed-up window. Wiping it to get a better view, she looked down the yard and noticed the back-gate slowly closing. Her mouth dropped open, but she didn't say a word. Not because she thought there must be a simple explanation but because she recognised the tattooed hand that shut the back gate.

'I take it you didn't get the job?' Jack asked when he went into the kitchen, and for a moment Evie couldn't think straight. She had made the excuse of going to see about the non-existent job, so she could go to the police station without worrying Jack or Lucy.

However, she had thought no more of the excuse when she was told there was still no news of her mother. Nevertheless, she would have to start thinking seriously about looking for work. Her savings had all but disappeared, and she had no intentions of going cap-in-hand and living off the parish.

* * *

'Hello Evie, long time no see.' Leo Darnel's voice came from behind her as she walked back from the shop on the top road later that day, stopping Evie dead in her tracks. Every nerve in her body froze, and the cold that had seeped into her bones after queuing at the grocers for so long, turned to fear. But she dared not show it even though she was experiencing that dreadful, sickening sensation that turned her insides to jelly. That feeling, which had been an everyday part of her life just two years ago.

Hunched inside a camel coat, Leo Darnel peered at her from under a grey fedora hat. His beady eyes undressed her, making her skin crawl, as he snaked his tongue around the ever-present matchstick, rolling it around his mouth. His hands were dug deep into his pockets while one foot lay flat against the sooty jigger wall at the side of the bridge, out of sight of passers-by. It looked like he was holding up the whole bloody tavern.

Evie imagined him losing his footing on the ice, and landing in a heap on the cold alley slab. The image cheered her somewhat, halting her sign of distress. She had to stay calm. Show no fear. He would expect his sudden appearance to terrify her and it did. But she wasn't going to give him the satisfaction of knowing. He was the kind of man who would revel in his ability to scare the living daylights out of defenceless women. Well, not today, Buster, she thought defiantly.

'Do you have to jump out on people?' She squeezed the words through her teeth, not knowing where she found the courage to rebuke him, although glad she did, as her fear turned to anger. Taking in a deep breath, she studied him for a moment, taking in the sharp features any fox would be proud of. The slim moustache that defined so many spivs. And those piggy little eyes that followed every woman. What did her mother ever see in him?

'The blackjacks 'ad me in the Bridewell all bleeding night because of your mother,' he said, his tone terse, and Evie suspected it wasn't blood that ran through his veins, it was molten anger.

'Why would the police lock *you* in the cells because of my

mother?' Evie asked as a niggling worry grew into full-blown alarm. Darnel didn't like lippy women. 'You'd better not have hurt her,' she warned, knowing her mother could be infuriating, but she was *her* mother.

'Why would I wanna do that?' he said, lifting his shoulder in a half-shrug. 'I loved the bones of that woman.'

'You've got a funny way of showing it,' Evie scoffed, 'stripping the house of *your* furniture.' And because Evie knew he could change his nature on a whim, she was wary. Her mother was not a weak-willed woman, nevertheless he had manipulated her from the moment he stepped foot in Reckoner's Row. But he was not going to do the same thing to her.

'Can't we go inside and have a nice hot cup of tea? I'm bloody freezing out here.' Darnel moved from one foot to the other, blowing warm air into his hands

'I'd rather pull my eyelashes out. One. At. A. Time,' she said emphasising each of the last four words as she hurried passed the alleyway. Buoyed by the number of people on the busy top road, she said, 'our Jack is at home, he'll be waiting for his dinner.' Her brother was taller and, now his leg was on the mend, much faster than the spiv. However, Evie didn't want Jack getting involved with Darnel, and she would do her utmost to make sure he didn't.

'The coppers said I must know something about your mother's disappearance.' The words stopped Evie in her tracks, and she spun around glaring at him, careful not to slip.

'And do you?' Darnel's expression reminded Evie of a wronged kid, blamed for smashing a window when he wasn't even in the street. But she knew better than to be taken in by his feigned innocence. She had witnessed his deceit first-hand.

'I told 'em straight,' he continued, 'I 'aven't seen her since she threw me out last Christmas.'

Evie shot him a venomous look, knowing corruption and lies

came as easy as breathing to Darnel and she didn't believe a word he said.

'I've got to get on.' Evie's head was tilted against the keen north-westerly wind as his hand shot out and grabbed the sleeve of her coat.

'Don't think you can put one over on me,' Darnel spat through gritted teeth, and Evie knew she had to be careful. 'If I wanted to get inside *your* house I would. Like that.' He snapped his fingers.

'There's nothing in that house for you.' Evie jerked her arm from his grip, and even though her heart was hammering, she managed to keep her voice level.

'See... I think I might've left something behind.'

'You'll get in over my dead body!' Evie said, thankful her voice held no evidence of the chilling fear invading her body. 'There's nothing there for you.' Every grain of pluck she seized, helped her lift her chin as she headed next door, towards number two.

'Make sure you bolt all your doors at night, won't ya, Evie?'

She didn't answer. She couldn't. Fear had rendered her speechless.

* * *

'Evie can I go skating on the Cut with Bobby Harris?' Lucy asked as she came hurtling through the back door. Red-faced and breathless, she had been sliding on the ice all morning and bickering with Bobby about who could slide the furthest.

'Ahh, go on, please Evie, let her. Go on, please...' Bobby pleaded. Lucy was his new companion who played a mean game of footie. But she had challenged him to a skating race on the icy canal. He couldn't wait... but his hopes were soon dashed.

'No, it's too dangerous,' Evie answered, peeling potatoes for tea and wondering if the minced meat was too fatty. She wouldn't go so far as to identify what kind of meat it was exactly, and the contents didn't bear thinking about, but she was lucky enough to get it after such a long wait. That particular butcher was what her mother used to call, 'a queer 'eel of an old boot,' which she took to mean he needed watching – otherwise he would charge fillet steak prices for scrag-ends.

It had been a month since her mother had walked out. The police had searched the area and all that could be done had been. But given her history of doing a flit whenever the mood took her, the authorities said she would be back when she got fed up galli-vanting. But Evie's concern was growing.

'But the ice is dead thick,' Lucy wailed, breaking into her thoughts. 'Everybody is skating. I'm the only one who can't do anything that's fun.' She liked being home and she loved their Evie, but she could be a right old misery-guts sometimes.

'Don't you go skating on that canal, Lucy. D'you hear me?' Evie called to her sister who was making her way down the yard.

* * *

'So, still no sign of Rene, then?' Mim asked her daughter over the tea table and Connie shook her head, still not prepared to share the contents of her life in front of Mr call-me-Angus McCrae. He had been here three weeks and his rent money came in very handy, but she refused to divulge every minute detail of Rene's life in front of him. She had been talked about enough in this street. Nevertheless, Mim spoke freely.

'That husband of hers was no saint when he was alive,' Mim said. 'He bashed her about a few times – I saw the bruises.'

'Mim, that's not our concern.' Connie's words disguised a plea to desist from discussing their neighbour's private business. 'He's not in a position to knock her about anymore... and you shouldn't speak ill of the dead – they might come back and haunt you!' Connie wanted to stop the conversation in its tracks and judging by her mother's pursed lips and stony silence, she seemed to have got her way, at last.

'Evie's doing her best,' Connie said, when she could stand her mother's hard-done-by silence no longer. 'She asks nobody for help or support. I admire her fortitude.' But surely, she wanted to say, they have a right to some privacy and not be every teatime conversation, as they had in the past. However, she kept those thoughts to herself.

'It's not normal walking out and leaving two kids to fend for themselves though, is it, Angus?' Mim asked their lodger, who seemed at a loss as to how he should answer.

'This pie is delicious, did you make it, Mrs Sharp?' Angus said, trying to lighten the heavy atmosphere. He liked lodging here. Mim, and her cleaner friend, Ada Harris, were a mine of information when they got together.

'Connie made it,' Mim said curtly. She felt he asked too many questions for her liking.

There was a lull in the conversation and Angus wondered if he had put his great size tens in it again. Noticing a lovely scarlet flush colour Connie's creamy complexion, Angus gave her a warm smile and, not for the first time, wondered why such a handsome woman was still not spoken for.

Trying to ignore his direct gaze, Connie concentrated on cutting up her pie. 'Mim bought the steak and kidney, she has a good eye for meat,' Connie answered, sure the compliment would give Mim cause to bristle with pride. And she did, when Angus addressed her.

'You chose well, Mrs Sharp, and the pastry is the best I've

tasted in a long time.' Angus relaxed when he saw the older woman give a satisfied smile, and harmony resumed.

However, there was something else he noticed about the delicious homemade steak and kidney pie. It did not contain the usual boot-leather cheap-cuts that were the usual fare in these austere times. Some meat being sold these days could be braised in a slow oven for a week, and still not be as tender and succulent as this. Kidney, being offal, was not on ration. But beef of this quality was rare in a backstreet butchers and if it was available, he knew, it would be prohibitively expensive to the wives of dockworkers.

'More pie, Angus?' Mim said, cutting another huge slice.

'You're spoiling me, Mrs Sharp,' Angus said, nudging creamy mashed potato onto the back of his fork knowing the black market thrived around the dockyards – but he wasn't after the men who pinched a bit of beef to supplement their meagre wages. He was after the ones who gave the orders.

'Connie, you are a cook of the highest calibre.' It surprised him to realise that Connie-behind-the-bar was a different woman to Connie-in-the-kitchen, and he raised a quiet smile when Mim, obviously feeling left out, revisited her earlier conversation...

'Rene Kilgaren always picked the wrong man,' Mim said, distracting Angus from his obvious approval of her daughter's cooking. Warming to her theme, she ignored a warning look from Connie. 'Rene became the femme fatale of Reckoner's Row when her beloved husband lost his life fighting for his country.'

'*Beloved*, Mim?' Connie said, her fork stalled between plate and lips. 'She was like a bird in a cage. The poor woman couldn't go to the shops without being interrogated when she got back.'

'She made her bed, so she had to lie in it,' Mim answered tucking into her meal with relish, 'but there's one thing I will say in Rene's favour, she always knew where she could get a decent piece of meat, or a nice bit of fruit – not to mention—'

'Yes, Mim!' Connie said leaning towards her mother. 'Not to mention! You know what they say about loose lips – it still applies. Even though the war's over – rationing isn't!' Connie's voice held a warning note and her mother seemed peeved that she couldn't finish her story about Rene Kilgaren.

Angus, tucking into his tea, appeared not to notice. He was glad of the older woman's indiscretion. Mim was a mine of useful information he would never be privy to under normal circumstances, but as yet she hadn't mentioned where the black-market merchandise was being sold to the hard-working women of Reckoner's Row. But he would bide his time. He was a patient man and would get to the heart of the warehouse robberies soon enough. In the meantime, he was enjoying the hospitality of the tavern's generous landlady.

* * *

After tea, Angus went out to buy an evening paper, as usual. The evening sojourn gave him the opportunity to relay any information he had garnered. His conversation inside the red telephone box outside the tavern was brief. He would have more information tomorrow.

Replacing the black Bakelite receiver, he had a good view of the street and the frozen canal. Connie was shovelling snow from the path leading to the door of the tavern. A truly beautiful woman, both inside and out, he mused.

Friendly. Successful. She could hold an intelligent conversation on many subjects. But she liked to keep private things to herself. Although not here to admire the locals, he couldn't help but be drawn to Connie's womanly charms... It had been a long time since he had enjoyed the love of a good woman. There were two reasons he needed lodgings close to the docks. One was so he did not arouse suspicion, and two – Liza was just a few miles down the coast.

'Here, let me do that for you,' Angus said, taking the spade from Connie's freezing hands. For a moment their eyes locked, and he caught the glimpse of a storm in her blue-eyed gaze that caused a pleasant hum to warm his blood.

'Go on in,' he said while every hair on his scalp stood to attention, every skin cell tingled, every neuron fired. 'I'll do that.' His penetrating gaze lingered, and she lowered her eyes.

'Thank you, Angus,' Connie answered, 'it's good to have a man about the place.'

'I have my uses, Ma'am,' he said cheerfully, raising his hat and Connie raised her eyes to the sky.

'Where do you stand on leaking roofs?' she asked with a cheeky grin that made his heart flip.

'In this weather, I'd position myself very carefully.'

'I'll leave you to it, then,' Connie said, making her way back to the tavern, aware his eyes were still on her – and liking it.

17

Evie dropped the rope that steered the cart holding bundles of kindling and precious coke, which she had queued for all morning. The bag of coke would have to be enough to tide them over until the coalman came on Friday morning, and she was eager to get indoors.

Holding on to her precious purchase was not easy when her fingers were frozen to the bone but somehow, she struggled to drag the cart across the frozen bombsite towards the back of Reckoner's Row, eager to get a good blaze going before Lucy got in from school at half past three. Jack would be half an hour later, having started at Saint Patrick's senior school the previous Monday.

'Hold your horses, lassie,' Angus said, closing the back gate of the tavern and sure-footedly sprinting across the frozen wasteland. 'That looks heavy.' He took the frayed rope from her frozen hands.

'That's good of you.' Evie recognised him. Mr McCrea had been a regular face around the row for the last month and was friendly with everybody. He pulled that heavy cart like it weighed nothing, but she was glad of his help.

'I could have sworn I locked the back gate.' Evie said when she saw the gate swinging open. Her heart hammered against her ribs. Leo Darnel had put a double lock on when he lived here. For security, he had said, but Evie suspected it was his own security he was thinking of.

'Wait here,' Angus said, dropping the rope, but Evie stopped him. She was making a fuss over nothing, she said. Perhaps her mother had returned! Either way, she did not want to involve outsiders.

'That lock's always been dodgy,' Evie said with a skilful nonchalance that had hidden many a family secret. 'You have to make sure the catch sits just right. The lock needs coaxing... Knowing me, I haven't caught it, in my rush to get to the chandlers.'

Angus did not want to frighten the wee girl, but those large footprints leading to the back door belonged to a man. He had seen her brother many times, up and down the street, and Jack did not own a pair of boots, let alone ones that would leave a deep imprint.

Evie was glad when Connie's lodger accepted her explanation, even though she knew the gate was secure before she set off. It was a ritual she had set for herself, to stop her mother sneaking back and upsetting the apple cart with her boozy ways and her iffy men-friends.

Her mother would have a key too. So on her first night back, Evie made it quite clear they must lock the back gate at all times. She made Jack and Lucy promise they must never, ever leave it open, giving their mother easy access. She was so deep in thought she did not even notice the footprints.

'Ta, Mr McCrea,' Evie said taking the rope when they reached the back door. 'I'll be fine from here.' Ashamed of the meagre contents of her family home after seeing the lavish accommodation above the tavern, Evie was reluctant to let the Scotsman into number two.

'Aye, if you're sure,' Angus said, his brow creasing. The girl was hiding something, but he would have to give her the benefit of the doubt. He could not arouse her suspicions at this point in the enquiries.

'Yes... Yes, I appreciate your help, but I must get on,' Evie said, knowing this wasn't the first time someone had opened the gate. Yesterday morning, when Jack put the dustbin out in the entry ready for emptying, the gate was closed but not locked.

'Do you want me to wait while you check the house is empty?' Angus asked, knowing Darnel had threatened the girl because he'd overheard Connie telling her mother two weeks back.

'I'm fine.' Evie's calm tones belied her accelerated heartbeat. 'We're made of tough stuff around the dockside.' Lucy had said she'd heard noises in the night, but Evie put it down to her sister's imagination. Now she wasn't so sure. The worry of her mother – or worse, Leo Darnel – getting inside the house kept her awake at night.

'Do you want me to check if everything is alright?' Angus asked, but Evie shook her head and gave a false laugh. 'Just my overactive imagination,' she assured him and, taking her word for it, he bade her good day.

Once inside, Evie lit the gas mantle. The weak glow did nothing to enhance the bareness of the austere room and picking up the poker from the hearth, she checked there was nobody else in the house. She could see no evidence of a break-in, or that anybody had been in the house while she was at the shops. So, relieved, she busied herself lighting the fire before Lucy got in from school, although it seemed the thought of her sister made her suddenly appear, red-cheeked and breathless.

'Where did you go?' Lucy asked accusingly. 'The one day we got sent home early, because the school pipes were leaking, you're out and every door's locked.'

Evie breathed a huge sigh of relief and almost laughed out loud. Thank God for Lucy, she thought. It must have been she who opened the back gate!

'So, where did you go?' Evie asked, suddenly afraid Lucy had been tempted to go skating on the canal with Bobby Harris.

'We played football on the debris. We used Mrs Harris' gable end as the Liverpool goal post and the bridge wall as the Everton goal post.' Lucy beamed.

'And who won?' Evie asked putting the poker on the fender in readiness for the centre pages of last night's *Evening Echo,* only to see her sister's face descend into a scowl.

'I was up three–nil and Missus Harris called Bobby in for causing too much noise.'

'I hope you didn't give her any lip,' Evie said, knowing her young sister would have a misplaced sense of injustice for her friend, considering the debris an unofficial play area.

'I would never do that, Evie,' Lucy said, feigning shock at such a thought, 'even if she is a moaning auld windbag.'

'Lucy...' Evie's tone held a warning. Nevertheless, she kept her back towards Lucy so she could not see the uncontrolled smile that forced its way to her lips. What could she say? Ada was a moaning auld windbag. 'Don't let Bobby hear you saying that about his mother.'

'He knows what she is, right enough,' said Lucy taking off her coat and hanging it on a nail behind the cellar door. Evie shook her head, contented. What was that child going to be up to next?

* * *

There was a heavy knocking on the front door as Evie, Jack and Lucy sat down to eat the meatless stew known locally as *blind scouse*. Meat, even fatty scrag ends and offal, was in short supply, but there were no complaints from her brother and sister who tucked into the hot meal knowing they were lucky to get it.

Evie knew her savings would not stretch to paying another week's rent *and* buying food. It was either one or the other. But she couldn't let the kids go hungry. Jack's leg was better, and she was glad of the wood he brought home each night, reluctant to ask where it came from as they needed all the help they could get, to eke out the meagre ration of inferior coal. Although Jack was out for much of the day, Evie didn't have the guts to ask what he did with himself, worrying she might not like the answer.

'I'll go,' Jack said, scraping back his chair. But Evie put her hand on his arm. Something akin to excitement ran through her veins. If this was her mother, turning up drunk and clinging to another fella for emotional and financial support, she would give her more than a piece of her mind. She would give Rene her marching orders.

When Evie dragged the door open, she was surprised to see Connie huddled on the step.

'I hope you don't mind me knocking, Evie,' Connie said, pulling her coat more closely around her shoulders.

'Come in,' Evie said stepping to one side allowing her neighbour into the lobby, which was lit only by the weak beam of the gas lamp outside.

'I won't take long, I know you'll be having your tea,' Connie said apologetically. 'But I've got something to ask you, I hope you don't mind?' Through the partially opened door of the kitchen, she could see the place was a damn sight cleaner than it had been the last time she was here.

The conspicuous fragrance of floor polish lingering on the shiny linoleum, skirting boards and spotless paintwork, vied with a tantalising aroma of something tasty wafting through the house.

'Come into the kitchen where it's warmer,' Evie said, about to lead the way when Connie put her hand on her arm to stop her.

'I'm not stopping,' Connie said, giving Evie's heart cause to quicken. She hoped Connie hadn't come to complain about Lucy and young Bobby Harris throwing snowballs earlier. Evie had warned them to keep away from the tavern, knowing she couldn't afford to replace a broken window.

'I was wondering if you could do a few hours in the pub each day?' Connie asked.

A job? Evie had never given a thought to serving behind the bar. That was her mother's job. But a job was a job and she was in no position to turn her nose up at money coming in. No matter how it was come by.

Evie let out a sigh of relief. Connie hadn't come to complain about Lucy throwing snowballs after all.

Evie explained, 'I have to tell you, Connie, I've never even drank inside a pub, let alone served in one. But I'm willing to give it a go if you don't mind showing me what's what.'

She had hoped to secure an office job, now the arctic weather was beginning to lose its bite. An office job would have been lovely and show Jack and Lucy she was someone they could look up to. She wanted to better herself. Not step into her mother's shoes. But beggars can't be choosers.

'You won't have to serve behind the bar,' Connie said, putting her hand on Evie's arm as if to reassure her. 'Mrs Harris slipped on the ice and sprained her ankle – it's a cleaner I'm looking for.'

'A cleaner...?' Evie pulled her cardigan around her in the draughty passageway as her spirits plummeted. She wanted to work in an office. Be someone. Make Jack and Lucy proud...

'Just mornings, say eight 'til ten?' Connie, noticing Evie's hesitation, hoped she hadn't said the wrong thing. 'I've heard wonderful reports of your work and you've worked wonders with this place, if you don't mind me saying.' It was true, the little house at the top of Reckoner's Row sparkled.

'We don't have much, but we're clean,' Evie said with a hint of irony.

'You were the first person I thought of,' Connie said intending no offence. But that wasn't the way Evie saw the compliment. It was obvious Connie saw her as no more than the skivvy she was. Evie put everything into her work, scrubbing, dusting and polishing from morning 'til night. 'Susie Blackthorn said you did a thorough job at Beamers.'

'Did she now?' Evie's forced smile did nothing to reduce the bile that rose in her throat. She still had some savings. And one thing she was sure of, she didn't intend to clean other people's mess for the rest of her life.

She was nineteen years of age and when her mother returned to Reckoner's Row, she would resume her night-school studies and get the diploma in advanced bookkeeping and accountancy that she had worked so hard for up to now. She had ambitions. She was going to be someone. But she would need her savings to pay for her tuition. Evie took a deep breath.

'Eight 'til ten,' she said. Her mind was like a number puzzle, mentally reshuffling her morning chores. 'Would it be all right if I nip back to check on Lucy? She's a bugger for getting up these mornings, and if I'm not here she'll turn over and go back to sleep.'

'Couldn't Jack help?' Connie urged, knowing Evie must be

short of money by now. She knew she had savings because Evie told her, but they wouldn't last forever.

'Jack leaves earlier than Lucy,' Evie answered quickly, plucking at the skin on the back of her hand, thinking she had blown her chance of a bit of work and felt she had to explain.

'I'm worried about Jack,' she whispered, 'I don't think he's been going to school since he got back from Ireland. He's out of here before we get up and sometimes, we don't see him again until last thing at night.'

'I'm sure you are worrying over nothing, he's a good lad, got his head screwed on the right way.'

'What if he's got in with a bad crowd?' Evie's voice cracked to a squeak, 'I've got every angel and saint harassed with prayers, begging them to make sure he's not up to mischief.'

'I understand your worries,' Connie said, 'but the best thing you can do is ask him outright.'

'I suppose I'll have to if I want to sleep at night,' Evie said knowing Connie was the only person who could allay her fear that the kids would be taken away again. But there was still a bit of *us-and-them* she could not shake free.

'It can't be easy for you...' Connie said in her straightforward way. 'With three mouths to feed, I thought you'd jump at the chance of a bit of extra cash.'

Evie didn't know if she should be insulted or humiliated at Connie's thoughtless remark and realised she felt both. Connie obviously thought she would jump at the chance to get down on her hands and knees and scrub her floors for a pittance, and only because the charlady left her in the lurch!

'Thanks for the offer, but I can't have Lucy sagging school, as well as Jack.' Evie opened the front door, letting Connie know their conversation was over.

'Well, if you change your mind, you know where I am,'

Connie called over her shoulder, as she headed down the tiled path. Closing the door, Evie fought back tears of disappointment. A cleaner? A bloody cleaner? The money she had spent, and the effort she had put into her studies would not be wasted by mopping floors and cleaning ashtrays! She would find a reputable office and work her way to the top. If only it were that easy.

'Is everything all right, Evie?' Lucy asked when she resumed her seat at the table. 'Your eyes are all glassy, like you want to cry.'

'I'm fine, Lucy.' Evie put on a bright smile. 'Let's eat our tea.' *While we still can.*

'I thought it might be *the missus*,' Lucy never addressed her mother as such, like other children would, Evie noticed. And who could blame her? Rene was hardly the maternal kind. Letter writing was not a strong point either, she was too busy worrying about herself to keep in touch with her offspring.

'I thought we'd be looking forward to a bit of fisticuffs,' Lucy laughed, her angelic Irish lilt, deceptive to the unwary, hid a sense of humour far beyond her years. She had a way about her that made you want to smile, Evie thought, watching her young sister mop up the vegetable gravy with a slice of bread, but beneath that angelic exterior beat the heart of a maverick. She would have to keep a close eye on this one.

'Have no fear, Lucy,' Evie said looking at the cooled, unappetising mish-mash of food on her plate. 'I'm here. Everything is fine.'

'When do you think Ma will come back?' Jack asked when Lucy took the empty plates out to the kitchen. Evie shrugged.

'All I do know is, she'll have a lot of explaining to do when she gets back,' Evie said in a low voice. 'I went to the police station again, but they still haven't heard anything.'

'It's a wonder they haven't reported her to the cruelty people,'

Jack said, unperturbed by his mother's absence. Evie supposed that having lived away from home for seven years, the link between her mam and her siblings had weakened. After all, she thought, Mam hardly ever put herself out to go over to Ireland to visit them.

It was left up to her to go and make sure they were well and being cared for. Not that she minded. Not one bit. Evie wished she could have stayed with them or brought them home. But it was far too dangerous. The docks and surrounding areas had taken a nightly pounding and she had to console herself with the fact she was doing the best thing for them.

'Did that woman call around?' Jack asked.

'The woman from the church?' Evie asked and he nodded. 'She called earlier in the week, to check everything was as it should be, make sure everything was clean and that we had enough to eat.'

'Did she give you the advice you were looking for?' Jack knew Evie was worried about keeping a roof over their heads and wanted to know if the landlord could throw them all out with Mam not being here.

'Yes, she said that because I am over sixteen, I am legally responsible to look after you and Lucy and as long as the rent gets paid the landlord can't evict us without good reason, so there's no need to worry Lucy with details.'

'Her imagination doesn't need much encouragement, right enough,' Jack said, 'but Ma's been gone weeks. Somebody must have seen her.'

18

'Rene did this kind of thing during the war,' Mim told Connie and Angus. 'Left me high and dry behind that bar many a time. If she found a generous Yank who liked to treat her, you wouldn't see her arse for dust.' The longer Rene was away, the blacker Mim painted her, Connie noticed.

'She's never usually gone this long.' Connie's forehead pleated in a frown, she knew Evie had a lot to contend with, it was a heavy load on those young shoulders of hers.

'And still no sign?' Angus asked, having finished the delicious oxtail soup, which his landlady had made earlier. He was amused to see Mim noisily sucking meaty jelly from the bony tail of the ox.

'None,' Evie looked to her mother, grimaced and gave a little shake of her head.

'You never knew what that one was up to.' Mim paused in her endeavour to extract every morsel, holding the thick bone between her fingers and thumbs while resting her elbows on the table. 'Kept her cards very close, she did.'

'It's unusual for women to walk away from their family, don't you think?' Angus enjoyed their nightly chinwag around the tea table, not to mention the priceless information he was able to glean, and the fact that Rene was involved with one of Liverpool's most notorious, albeit slippery, villains was cause enough to be interested in her whereabouts. 'It's not unheard of, though.'

'And how would a shipping insurance clerk know such a thing?' Mim's eyes narrowed. Like the rest of the borough she was naturally suspicious of strangers; around these parts it could take years to be accepted. 'Men don't usually bother themselves with things like that.'

'She must have run away for a reason.' Angus remained unflustered; his information gathering during the war had stood him in good stead for his latest line of work. 'A woman won't leave her family for no reason.'

'Who said she's run away?' Connie asked, stirring her cup of tea. 'What reason would she have?'

'Did she need a reason?' Mim asked with a touch of sarcasm, wondering why Angus was so interested in Rene Kilgaren. 'What would it be?'

'The usual,' Angus answered, casually putting his cup back on the matching bone-china saucer, addressing Connie directly. 'An unhappy marriage, debt. That kind of thing.'

'If that were the case,' Connie replied, 'most women would have scarpered years ago. Women are a tough breed around here. They stick it out through thick and thin.' Most didn't have the luxury of flitting when the fancy took them.

'What do *you* think made her run off into the night?' Mim asked later when Connie gathered her night clothes from the fire-guard, where they had been warming, wanting nothing more than to relax in five inches of bathwater.

'I couldn't say,' Connie answered, clearing away the dishes. She didn't want to discuss Rene in front of Angus. She knew he was more than a little interested in the locals, but Rene's kids were not mixed-up in anything sinister. She was sure of it.

'Here, let me help you with that, Connie,' Angus said taking the tray of crockery, while Mim could not help but notice the way his eyes lit up when he spoke to her daughter.

'Will you be staying in Liverpool?' Mim asked, her imagination running away with itself. She would have to tread carefully. She wanted to see her daughter settled. Even though Connie was cracking on a bit, she was still young enough to give her grandchildren.

But what if Angus was the one to set her daughter's heart on fire? And what if he wanted to take her back to Scotland? Mim hadn't reckoned on that. The thought filled her with dread. This fella could whisk Connie away, and it would be the war all over again, with her being left alone to manage the tavern.

'Rene's a widow, so it's not husband trouble,' Connie said breaking into her thoughts, 'but Evie told me that Leo Darnel is sniffing around again.'

'What about debt?' Angus knew he was sailing close to the wind, asking so many questions. He knew that no men around here troubled themselves with what they called 'women's jangle'. They kept their own counsel and expected to be informed only on a need-to-know basis. That way, they remained blissfully ignorant of their wives' womanly woes.

'The whole country's in debt because of the war,' Mim answered, 'we can't all bugger off.'

'Aye, it cost, true enough,' Angus replied, 'in money and in loved ones...' He picked up the clean tea towel and awaited the first plate. Connie experienced a rare frisson of pleasure towards Angus who offered to dry the dishes she was washing while Mim put her feet up in front of a blazing fire in the front room, listening to the wireless.

'So, is this your night off?' Angus asked, and Connie nodded. She didn't want to speak of loss, financial or otherwise. 'Do you fancy going to the pictures?' he asked, and Connie stiffened. Up until that moment she had not thought of Angus in any way other than him being their lodger. She liked Angus, he was a decent man, who was good company. But he was the lodger. Look what happened when Rene's lodger got too settled. No, Connie thought, she didn't want to complicate matters by going on a date.

'Another time would be lovely, Angus,' she said, wishing he hadn't asked.

* * *

Mim looked at the clock. It was well past her bedtime and Connie was reading. Angus had just retired to his own bedroom, so she felt it was safe for her to the same.

'I'm off to the land of nod, Connie. Don't stay up too late.' Connie bit back the reminder that she was thirty years of age and would go to bed when she bloody-well felt like! Instead she said a cheery, 'goodnight, Mim,' and carried on reading her book. She would just read to the end of the chapter, then she would turn in. The tavern had been quiet all night and she had locked up early. Connie could relax. If only she could get that damned invitation out of her head...

'Want to join me in a little nightcap?'

Connie didn't hear the door open and her head shot up from her book, her tired eyes now wide awake.

'Oh you did give me a fright!' Connie laughed self-consciously, her heart thudding against her ribs.

'I didnae mean to startle you,' Angus said and the mischievous look in his eyes told Connie he might already have had a nightcap before he came into the sitting room. 'I saw the light on, I thought you might like a bit of company?'

'I was just finishing this chapter,' Connie answered, closing the book and resting it on her lap. She watched as he ambled over to the sofa and, with the grace of a panther, he poured them both a drink. Maybe she would like a nightcap after all.

* * *

His confident nature made Connie feel safe, yet vulnerable at the same time.

'I waited for Mim to settle down.' His voice was redolent with good breeding: deep, measured, and with perfect enunciation, causing ripples of pleasure that caught her breath. She could listen to Angus all night. 'She's late tonight,' Angus said, rolling the glass in his hands.

'I think she suspects something is going on between us.' Connie gave him an incredulous look, but just saying the words gave her palpitations. 'If only she knew we were just putting the world to rights.' Connie's words sounded composed, but inside she felt anything but... She had grown to look forward to their nightly chat when Mim retired for the night and the fact that he'd asked her out made her feel he liked her – a lot. But for the last few nights, her mother had taken to staying up later and Connie knew Mim suspected any red-blooded male in their right mind could not resist jumping her bones as soon as her back was turned. The thought caused a small gurgle of laughter to erupt in her throat.

'Care to share?' Angus asked as he handed Connie her drink. The nightcap relaxed her, and they chatted about this and that as the time just slipped away.

'I thought the war years were exhilarating,' Connie said,

looking down at the drink in her hands, feeling her face suffuse with a heat that was not triggered by the alcohol. 'I know that's not how we're supposed to remember those awful, angry days,' she said, sipping her drink, savouring the warmth seeping through her whole body. 'But, with so much devastation, there was also the exciting anticipation of not knowing when your number would be up.'

'Daring death to find you, and so very thankful when it didn't,' Angus said in that melodic tenor, urging her to continue, enjoying the radiant beauty in her eyes.

'I've never discussed my wartime experiences with anybody,' Connie said. 'Yet, it seems the most natural thing in the world to share them with you, Angus.'

'I'm flattered,' Angus said quietly, emptying his glass and silently offering Connie a refill. She shook her head, refusing another drink. She wanted to tell him about her time in Italy, and she wanted to be clear-headed when she did so.

'Mim wouldn't understand,' she whispered. And after a moment's silence she said, 'do you want to know a secret?' Angus nodded, and Connie took a deep breath. She was going to tell him something she had never told another living soul. She didn't understand why, but she suddenly found it important he should know.

Maybe she just needed to speak about it. Or, perhaps it was because he was passing through. She would not see him again once he left here. Or, maybe it just felt right.

'I was married in Italy...' Connie watched his reaction carefully, and knew that if he ever played poker, he would give no clue as to the hand he had been dealt. '... In a beautiful little white chapel with no roof – blown off in a raid the day before...' Her words, like cinders under a door, were scratchy, and she paused for a moment, her throat tightening at the painful memory.

... Sam had just placed the ring on her finger. His smiling eyes gazing into hers.

The planes seemed to come from nowhere. Strafing the holy ground with bullets. His hand was still clutching hers as he fell. Sam was dead before he even hit the floor.

Her own injury led fellow medics to believe she would never have children of her own. The damage caused her to lose the unborn child she was carrying. Sam's child. When Matron told her she might never carry another child it was of no consequence.

Sent home when she was strong enough to travel, Connie worked behind the bar of the family pub, and vowed never to nurse again.

'When Mim started asking questions, I told her I couldn't talk about it...' Angus reached out and took her hand, sensing how hard it was for Connie to open up like this. 'My wedding day was far too traumatic to discuss with anybody.' Connie's eyes glistened. 'Married and widowed within moments.' Silent tears rippled down her cheeks. 'That's got to be a record, right?' She gave a teary half-smile.

Angus listened in companionable silence, sensing this was the first time Connie had spoken about this immensely important episode in her life. As she talked, he stroked the back of her hand with his thumb.

'It should have been your new beginning,' Angus whispered and for the first time since that awful day, Connie felt she could finally talk about the horror of it all.

'As the sun broke through the clouds the following morning, they buried him.'

'I am so sorry you had to go through all that,' Angus said. Connie nodded, relieved she was able to unburden herself like this. Angus understood completely, letting her talk without interruption. Holding her hand, he showed how much he cared, and Connie was so very glad she had found somebody she could tell it all to, but most of all she was glad that somebody was Angus.

'I didn't have time to grieve,' she said, shivering when the grey, dead ashes shifted in the grate. Angus put his arm around her, and it seemed the most natural thing in the world to nestle into the warmth of his body and relive her experiences. Now the floodgate of secrets was open, it was almost impossible to close them again. She felt that if she didn't speak of it now, she never would, and it would eat her up from the inside, and reduce her to a cold, bitter old woman.

'A storm of bullets shattered every stained-glass window of that beautiful church on the hillside,' she said, re-living the moments. 'There was an enormous explosion. Everything went black. I was pinned to the floor of the nave by a statue of Saint Jude,' she gave an ironic laugh. 'The patron saint of lost causes.'

With hindsight, and the slow progress of time, Connie felt able to accept the emotional wounds of her past. She had grown a tough layer in a way she never thought possible. 'I grew strong enough to accept that when my unborn child was taken from me, it was not a punishment from God, as I had always believed.'

'It's war. Plain and simple,' Angus said, understanding completely. 'Man's inhumane ruthlessness to man has nothing to do with a divine deity.'

'I returned home when I was able and kept the whole tragic event to myself.'

'Mim still doesn't know?' Angus asked, gently stroking her cheek.

'Certainly not,' Connie answered sleepily. 'It was far too personal to share. The one good thing about serving abroad was that nobody needed to know. Talking about it would have made it real. I wasn't strong enough.'

'And you are strong enough now?' His concerned words weaved through her hair and Connie sighed.

'I felt able to tell only you, Angus'

'Then, let's keep it between ourselves,' Angus said when Connie looked up into his handsome face, her eyes red-rimmed, 'I trust you, Angus,' she said as he gently pulled her close, and Connie knew without a doubt her secret was safe.

'Knowing all this would be the undoing of Mim, she couldn't keep something so important to herself – she would tell Ada Harris, and before you know it, the whole town would be in on it.' Connie was surprised at how much she was enjoying this new intimacy between them. She shifted a little and looked at him, really looked. His pale eyes, so full of compassion, held a myriad of comforting words he didn't need to say. Without speaking she lay her head back down and could hear the rapid beat of his tender heart, confused by the new feelings she was now experiencing.

'Mim raised me to have standards...' she said as if to herself. 'And they are high!'

'I bet you never had trouble reaching them.' Connie could hear the smile in his voice, and it warmed her.

'There's no rush to be off, is there?' she said, feeling bolder, and he shook his head, holding her like he was offering her a lifeline – and she gladly took it.

The blazing coals had long since cooled by the time he finished telling her of the wife he too had lost during the war. They had more in common than Connie thought. He told her about his life as an only child on a small island off the coast of Scotland where his family were crofters. He was silent for a short while, as if mulling over their revelations, and Connie was content to be cocooned in his arms, listening to the soothing beat of his heart.

'I wanted a son,' Angus said eventually, as if talking to himself, 'but it was not to be.'

'My arms ached with longing for a child,' Connie said, 'but I knew I could never fill them.'

Feeling the devastating, familiar tug of maternal longing, Connie knew it was getting very late. She reluctantly must go to bed, even though she didn't want to break their intimate new bond. Understanding. Loving. Angus had captured her heart. And she feared he would hold on for dear life.

'Just a short walk tonight, I think.' Angus said as Connie unfurled herself. He would have liked nothing better than to stay here, just the two of them. Heaving a great sigh Angus knew he had a duty to take a nightly stroll and telephone to give updates. Then he must ring Liza. Poor, bewildered Liza... The war had not been kind to her.

'Thanks for listening, Angus,' Connie said, 'everything is much clearer now.'

'I'm glad,' he answered, watching her walk barefoot towards her bedroom. She was the most beautiful, enchanting woman he had known for a long, long time. 'Goodnight, Connie.'

'Goodnight, Angus...' she said, closing the door.

* * *

Evie gave Lucy a cup of hot cocoa and they settled down, lost in thought, reluctant to leave the fire for the cold rooms upstairs. Jack was still not in from his nightly jaunts to who-knew-where and Evie prayed he was not getting into trouble. Since his leg healed, he was never still.

'Somebody's ready for her bed,' Evie said when Lucy yawned, her eyelids growing heavy. Moments later the front door closed with a bang and Lucy's eyes were wide again. Evie breathed a sigh of relief.

Red-faced with the cold, he headed straight for the fireplace and steam rose from his damp clothing. Although Evie was wracked with worry, imagining he was up to no-good, she couldn't bring herself to ask. She might not like the answer.

'I'm done in, so I am,' Jack said, stretching his back, 'my bed's calling me, for sure.'

'I put in two hot bricks wrapped in a pillowcase, to take the chill off the sheets, so be careful where you put your feet.' Evie said. They couldn't afford hot water bottles, even if there were any to be had in the shops. So the next best thing was a couple of house bricks, heated on the fire. At one time they would have used the oven shelf, but since gas was so scarce it would take a fortnight to warm up!

When Jack finished his cocoa, Evie lit the stub of a candle, and Jack took it down the yard to the lavatory, leaving it there overnight, a ritual to stop the pipes freezing. Rinsing the cups under the freezing water, Evie watching Jack from the kitchen window, his second-hand trousers flapping around his ankles. She sighed, wishing she could buy him some that fitted. But her saving were being eaten up.

How was she going to cope when the money disappeared altogether? She thought her mother would have been home long before now. And there was no sign of any office work. With experienced clerks and office-workers being laid off because of the bad weather, it was impossible to compete.

Maybe she had been a bit hasty, refusing Connie's offer. She was their only hope of bringing money into the house. Unlike others, she would not take charity, refusing to go cap-in-hand to the parish priest and beg a handout. Not that they had anything of value. Even Uncle Bill, as the locals called the pawnshop man, would turn his nose up at the stuff her mother left behind.

'Do you think that fella Darnel came back?' Jack said after Evie told him later about the back gate.

'He wouldn't dare,' Evie said, dismissing her brother's fears. Jack could be a hothead when his family was threatened, and she didn't want him going in search of trouble. 'There's nothing here for him, now Mam's not here.'

'You let me know if he shows up and he'll get a puck in the gob he won't forget in a hurry.' Jack balled his fists and stood like one of those fairground boxers of the olden days, and even though she laughed, Evie was under no illusions that her brother didn't mean every word.

'Oh, I forgot!' Jack said, his eyes bright. 'I got this for our Lucy.' He took a small pad of unlined paper and a tin of pencils from under his jerkin. 'She likes to draw – and she's good at it, too.' Lucy, wide awake, jumped off the couch and threw her arms around her brother's neck, delighted with her rare gift.

'That's good of you, Jack.' Evie sounded cautious and alarm bells rang inside her head. Jack didn't mention where he got them from, she noted. *Please, Lord, don't let him turn into one of those warehouse robbers.* That kind of gift didn't come cheap.

'Don't worry, Evie.' Jack could see the worry clouding her eyes. 'It's not what you think.'

He was bound to say that, she thought, holding her head high. 'How do you know what I think?' she asked, her words clipped. Jack tapped the side of his nose, his blue eyes twinkling.

'Because, like a Mother Hen, you care too much about us little chicks.'

* * *

The residents of Reckoner's Row were tucked up indoors and the deserted street was silent, save for the low buzz of one-sided conversation in the red telephone box on the corner.

'There's still no sign of Rene Kilgaren and I've just seen the lad, Jack going into the house.' Angus McCrae's words were low, reticent. He kept his back to the small windows of the telephone box. Pulling the brim of his trilby low onto his forehead, his words disappeared into the black mouthpiece of the Bakelite receiver.

'No sign of Darnel, either,' he said. 'Although, he's in the vicinity, there was another dockside robbery last night that had his sticky hallmark all over it. And there's evidence of a disturbance at the family home, nothing taken – quite the opposite in fact.'

'Does the girl know anything?' a voice on the end of the line enquired.

'I'm positive she has nothing to do with the transportation or storing of stolen merchandise.'

'Can you be sure?'

'Not as yet,' Angus said, 'but they have very little from what I've witnessed. They seem trustworthy, not so sophisticated they could lie their way out of something as big as this.'

He omitted to give any information regarding Jack's shooting for the time being. Connie told him in confidence. The kids could do without investigators crawling all over their home in search of evidence. Angus was more than capable of handling that side of things himself. 'Evie and her siblings loathe Darnel, not least because he lured their mother away when she was needed most.'

'In what way?' asked the tinny voice on the other end of the receiver.

'The girl, Lucy, has been unwell, and Mim – Miriam Sharp, my landlady – has her ear to the ground as far as the neighbours are concerned. She told me the older girl has no work, so not much money.'

'And they haven't seen their mother since the elder girl, Evie, came back?'

'Apparently not,' Angus answered. 'By all accounts Rene often took a midnight flit...' He looked around, making sure there was nobody around. Everybody knew the tavern had a telephone. It was the only property in the street that did. Angus knew the residents of the row would find it strange to see him using a public telephone box in this weather. 'Although, Rene Kilgaren hadn't left home since she threw Darnel out and brought the children home.'

'Do you think she knows about Darnel's involvement in the warehouse robberies?'

'Almost certain,' Angus answered.

'Goodwill to all men, what.' The voice on the other end sounded amused.

'Something like that.' Angus knew about Rene's frugal living conditions. She could be enticed to Darnel's racketeering ways on the promise of a good time, or money. It wasn't beyond the realms of possibility.

'Do you think the older girl has any information about Darnel's activities?'

'I doubt that very much,' said Angus, looking out towards the deserted street. 'She has too much on her plate keeping her family together to get involved in anything shady. But Connie – Miss Sharp, said Jack Kilgaren told her the robbers had broken into a bonded warehouse. He saw the weapons on their flat-back lorry when he was collecting wood.'

'Good work, Angus.' The voice held a satisfied note. 'He would be a star witness. Someone is bound to slip up, let me know.'

'Will do.' Angus heard the ping when he placed the receiver onto the cradle and pushing open the stiff, red telephone box door, he made his way back to the tavern.

Connie's sweet perfume lingered on the landing, elevating his tired spirits. He was enjoying this assignment and was in no hurry for it to end. A man of habit, he closed his bedroom door and, sitting on the edge of the comfortable single bed, he unfastened his tie and his mind wandered.

Connie... Dependable Connie. Everybody's friend.

Angus' eyes were drawn to the flower-papered wall that divided them. She was feet away. Yet it could be a thousand miles. He was glad she had married, even if only for a short time. It was proof, if any were needed, that she was a warm and loving, red-blooded female, and not the spinster he had first took her for. That would be a terrible waste of a good woman, he thought.

Smiling, he noticed the outline of two hot-water bottles under the covers. Connie must have put them in when he went to the telephone box.

Tossing his socks into the laundry bin provided, he lay on top of the bed. His hands behind his head in the dark, and he stared up at the cracked ceiling watching the occasional arc of a vehicle's headlights as it crawled over the icy bridge.

A relationship with Connie could never progress, he thought with more than a hint of regret. Although, admittedly, he was growing fond of her... too fond. He didn't want to hurt her, and he wouldn't be here long enough to sustain a permanent relationship.

He had been here longer than usual, but as he told the powers-that-be, Darnel had raised his game from stealing booze and cigarettes to cracking bonded warehouses. Stealing war weapons to sell abroad was a hanging offence.

Jack's information about the weapons stored for overseas

shipping was a breakthrough. He would make a star witness. Darnel would know that, too.

A small creak of the floorboards jolted him from his thoughts. Connie was still awake, and he imagined her moving around the large square room next door. She was edging a sticky drawer back into place, trying to be quiet so as not to disturb anybody. Her mother especially.

'Connie! Is that you?' Mim's strident call showed she was not as considerate.

Who else would it be? Angus thought, deferring a mirthless chuckle. Mim likely suspected he was in Connie's room. Ravishing her daughter to within an inch of her life. But nothing could be further from the truth... Seven long empty years.

He never expected to find another woman who could set his pulse racing. But that night, when he was looking for lodgings, he knew he had to get to know Connie Sharp.

19

Angus decided he would have a pint in the tavern after work, instead of going straight upstairs to his room overlooking the docks. Mim would be cooking the evening meal and it was safe to say this would be the only time he could have a private word with Connie.

The tavern, ever popular with dock workers, was busier than of late given that the ice was beginning to thaw, and the country appeared to be on the move again. It was also one of the best places to watch the comings and goings of the locals.

'Busy tonight,' Angus said to Connie who had started pulling him a pint. She nodded as she slipped the glass of dark beer across the bar and shook her head when he offered her the money to pay for it.

'There's a couple of American ships in, and the dockers are having a whip-round for Sid Harris – he hasn't been able to work since he was coshed during a warehouse robbery.'

Angus knew all about it, because Connie told him. He also knew that she helped Jack that night, and he worried that Darnel might put Connie in danger

'Poor Sid is an old soldier, who lost half a foot in Flanders, working out on the dockside in all weathers,' Connie was saying. Her dander was up, Angus could tell. 'If he doesn't get some kind of reward for the bravery he showed that night, I'll eat my hat.'

'That would be a sight to see,' Angus said giving her a smile that would charm the birds from the trees. Connie flicked a bar towel in his direction and, smiling, went to serve another customer.

'… An American ship came in that night an' all.' Sid Harris' words were slurred as he leaned against the bar. It was obvious he had had a skinful.

'What night was that, Sid?' Angus asked. It was amazing what information he had gleaned once the customers got to know him – or at least, once they thought they had got to know him. It seemed any friend of Connie's was a friend of theirs.

'That night… you know.' Sid waved his forefinger at something Angus could not see. In his inebriated mind he knew what he meant, but the trouble was, nobody else did.

'Do I?' Angus asked, and Sid looked at him through bleary eyes, swaying on the spot.

'The night before I got whacked over the head, and took a fractured skull fer me trouble,' Sid mumbled, scratching his grey-stubbled chin and narrowing his eyes to a narrow slit in concentration. 'Anyway, as I was saying…' Angus didn't know what he was talking about but thought it wise to listen. '… The drinking led to good-humoured banter, you know what the locals say about the Yanks – over-paid over-sexed and…'

Angus was taking mental notes. It appeared there was something Sid needed to get off his chest.

'Sometimes you get the odd skirmish, but nothing serious.' He shook his head. 'Nothing I can't handle. I've helped Connie eject many a leery customer who thinks she's an easy target. I fought in the trenches you know...'

'So I've heard, Sid... another?' Angus nodded to Sid's pint glass.

'Aye, go on, then. Seeing as you're offering,' Sid moved from the bar and headed to a table. 'I'll just be over here, rest me poor feet.' Angus watched him zigzag across the chequered floor of the bar and plonk himself down at a table opposite.

'Has he got on to his war days, yet?' Connie asked with a smile. It was good to see Angus coming into the bar after work.

'Aye,' said Angus, returning Connie's beautiful smile. 'I think he's in the mood for talking. I must sit down for this one.'

'Well, don't let him keep you gabbing all night,' she said, pulling the second pint and putting it on the bar. 'Mim will have the tea on the table at six o'clock sharp.' Angus gave a low chuckle and saluted from the brim of his trilby.

'Yes, Ma'am,' he said, and Connie flicked her hands, urging him away from the bar. They both laughed. Angus had brightened her life so much, it would be a bleaker place when he left. But she didn't want to think of that now.

'Hey?' Sid looked puzzled, and he thought for a moment, his forehead pleated in a concentrating frown. 'Oh aye,' he said, 'I was telling you, wasn't I?

'Better start from the beginning, Pop,' said Angus, 'I came in halfway through the conversation.' Angus knew the locals were notorious for keeping information to themselves. But Sid seemed willing to sing like a canary tonight.

'So you did. Well...' Sid took a sip of his beer and wiped his mouth with the back of his hand. 'It were like this. Wednesday nights the Shipwrights have a meeting in the snug at seven o'clock.'

'The Shipwrights?' Angus asked thinking the conversation had taken a strange turn.

'Aye,' said Sid reaching for his pint. 'They used to build wooden ships, now they repair them. Some people call them artisans, highly skilled, like... Anyway, every Wednesday they have a get-together in the snug over there.' He nodded to a small private room separate from the bar. 'Don't suppose they like mixing with us riff-raff.' He gave a low chuckle and wiped his mouth while Angus waited patiently for him to get to the point.

'So, that night, a few Yankee sailors came into the tavern. They'd had a skinful, singing dancing, eyeing up the ladies.' Sid took another sip of his pint, to dramatically heighten the tension, thought Angus. He waited.

'Well, that's the Yanks for ye,' Angus said in his low Scottish brogue, drinking his pint of bitter while taking all in. His interest piqued, he was thrilled he had followed his instincts and come into the bar after work.

'Well, Rene...' Sid wagged his finger, pointing drunkenly to an empty chair and meandering through his memories. 'Lovely Rene... you know Rene... everybody knows Rene... you know, the barmaid.' He shook his head as if to clear it. 'Well, she seemed to know the Americans well, because they supplied Darnel with ill... illic... knocked-off booze, and Darnel supplied the sailors with the female attractions, so to speak.' Sid took a well-worn tin out of his back pocket and slowly filled a cigarette paper, careful not to spill the precious tobacco – all the while airing his vital observations.

'The Yanks have a never-ending wallet of notes, and the ladies like to be treated.'

'How come you were in here that night?' Angus knew the night-watchman would usually be on the dock making sure the warehouses were secure, any time from seven at night.

'I usually call in before my night shift, have a quick gill, give Connie a hand, collecting glasses if she was busy. That was two nights before I was bundled into that warehouse – to keep me quiet while they made off.' Sid lowered his voice, looking all around the bar, 'they told me to keep shtum, but...' He shrugged his shoulders again. 'I'm passed taking orders. Sid Harris will do what he likes from now on.'

'Good for you, Sid' Angus could have jumped up and punched the air, knowing that Rene Kilgaren was in here two nights before Jack got shot. But he must remain calm. This was his lucky day.

'Aye. Guns and everything! There must have been ten... no twelve of the buggers. One pulled a gun out and pushed me into the warehouse. Told me to keep my mouth shut or else. Then he cracked me over the head.'

'Who did? Darnel?'

The older man nodded, obviously running out of steam.

'Bastards!' Angus cursed, disgusted they could treat a war hero like Sid in such a way.

'Aye, they're the scum of the earth, who neither work nor want for anything.'

'Did you get a good look at them?' Angus asked, suspecting he was asking too many questions but unable to stop himself. Nevertheless, in his inebriated state, Sid didn't notice.

'They all had balaclavas over their faces, except for the hot-head and Leo Darnel.'

Angus felt his adrenaline soar. Sid could even describe the goons who assaulted him. 'Darnel was there right enough, trying to calm the hot-head down. But I'd recognise the eejit with the gun. Irish he was.'

Angus gave a silent groan of disappointment. Every other person in Liverpool seemed to have an Irish accent. It would be like looking for a needle in a haystack. Then a thought struck him, and he reached into his pocket.

'Did he look anything like this man?' Angus showed Sid the picture.

'That's him! That's the bugger. Thought he was John Wayne, he did!'

'I'll tell you what, Sid, you don't half have some exciting escapades,' Angus said, keeping his cool. It wouldn't do for the locals to know what he did to earn a crust. They would treat him with suspicion for hoodwinking them into thinking he was a regular bloke, one of them, and not a senior undercover detective working on behalf of the port insurers.

'... He was a trigger-happy bastard – heard a rat over by the coal hills and bang! Not a second's hesitation.' Angus said nothing but gave a low whistle. Evie and Connie had both managed to contain the information about Jack being shot and he suspected that was only because Mim and Sid's missus hadn't found out.

Lucy didn't know the true details either. They had all been told Jack fell over and Connie was cleaning it each day. 'The place was heaving, everybody was having a fine old time. Singing. Dancing. You name it, the locals were having a ball.'

'Rene Kilgaren was enjoying the American's attention.'

'In what way?' asked Angus, filling his pipe.

'She was just larking about, having a laugh and a dance, the way they do, but she kept looking over the sailor's shoulder, tormenting him, like.' Angus presumed Sid was talking about Darnel. 'He must have been wound up, the way he broke that glass.'

'Broke the glass?' It was like pulling teeth trying to get a straightforward story from Sid now. 'And then what happened?'

Angus' pulse was racing, but he couldn't be sure if it was because of hope or frustration.

'Grabbed her by the wrist and told her she was drunk. She didn't seem sloshed, like,' said the wiry watchman. 'She could drink enough to sink a battleship, that one – I've seen her in a worse state than that, and she's been capable.'

'Of what?' Angus asked with a practised grin. Sid chuckled, he was a man's man.

'She could get herself home.' He paused thinking about the day. 'She stormed out in a huff and he left too.'

'Did you see him again?' Angus asked and Sid nodded his head, seeming to have lost interest in the conversation about Rene.

'What about Rene?' Angus asked. 'Did Darnel say where she had gone?'

'I asked him, like, and he said she went off in a huff. Talking to some fella. He left her to it.'

'That doesn't sound right,' Angus watched Sid's eyebrows pucker. 'He was always possessive from what I heard.'

'He was edgy, like, drank quite a few whiskeys.' Sid laughed and leaned on the table. 'Here, you're not a copper, are you?'

'Me?' Angus knew his luck had just run out, and quipped, 'What do you think? Anyway, I'd best be off for my tea, otherwise Mim will skin me alive.' He laughed, finishing his pint. It was time to go. Sid shook his head at the absurdity of his own question and smacking his lips he said, 'Aye, you're right. Our Mim doesn't like snoops – well, who does?'

Angus considered Sid's last comment at leisure as the old man's eyes grew heavy.

'It's time to go, old fella,' Angus told Sid, who got up from his seat and, wending his way to the door, waved his flat cap drunkenly as he went.

'Mim will have our tea on the table,' said Connie, who had just finished checking the till before the part-time barmaid took over.

'I like your hair,' he said admiring her mahogany curls. 'Have you done something with it?'

'Done something?' Connie said, patting the result of an uncomfortable night's sleep in a head-full of steel curlers. 'Not really.'

20

'Evie!' The rapid thump, thump, thump of small feet racing along the landing kept time with Evie's thumping heartbeat. The frantic calling of her name penetrating a quickly forgotten dream, and at first, she imagined the child's voice was part of her nocturnal slumber until the bedroom door swung open with such force it banged against the wall. Evie's eyes opened wide, trying to adjust between wake and sleep.

'Evie! Save me!' Squinting, Evie focused on her sister's small frame scrambling over the bed.

'What's wrong, Lucy, did you have a bad dream?' The silver glow of a frosty moon shone through thin net curtains, giving no sign it was night or morning and Evie unfolded the bedclothes, hoisted herself up to rest her elbow on the pillow. Jack said their young sister was prone to nightmares since they came back from Ireland. And who could blame her? Your mother running away from home was enough to give anybody the heebie-jeebies.

'There's a man on the landing!' Lucy hissed between her teeth. 'I think he's dead!'

'Behave yourself!' Every nerve in her body screamed and Evie said the first thing that came into her head, being woken so dramatically. She took a deep breath, trying to calm her racing heart. 'You've had a bad dream that's all. Nobody can get in here.'

She listened, pulling on the bedclothes. As the icy air hit her, she grabbed her young sister's hand and dragged her into the bed, putting her by the wall. 'Go back to sleep.' She could brain her mother for putting the child through this much distress. Evie stroked her sister's hair, and Lucy drew her knees up under the faded nightdress that had once belonged to her, and she was shaking.

'I'll have a look, shall I?' Evie wanted to check Lucy hadn't wet her bed, as she had the previous night, when she had a nightmare.

'No! Don't leave me!' Lucy sounded terrified, and Evie scooped the child into her arms.

'It's all right, Lucy,' Evie whispered. 'Jack's a light sleeper, he would've heard something.' Lucy snuggled into her big sister, too afraid to look up.

'You've had a bad dream, that's all.' She folded the child in her arms, patting her back, whispering soothing words. 'Shh, go back to sleep. You're safe with me.'

'But he's here,' Lucy cried, 'he's here!'

'Who is Luce?' Evie's mouth was paper dry. 'Who did you see?'

'A man! A big man and he's not moving.' Lucy's eyes had a wild look about them. The child believed she had seen someone on the landing. Evie heard night terrors could be as realistic to the victim as real life itself.

'I'll go and check, you stay here,' then, in a light-hearted voice that would be sure to ease Lucy's distress, she said, 'It might be your good shepherd, asleep on our landing. If it is, I'll puck the gob off him – waking me up at this hour.'

Dotting her toes on the freezing lino, Evie located her slippers, certain she would find no strange man asleep on the landing, nobody would get past their Jack's bedroom door at the top of the stairs without him hearing.

The candle had almost burned down, and she cupped the flame as she picked it up. The creak of the rusting hinges sounded much louder in the silence of the night, and Evie steeled herself to look around the bedroom door. But all she could see was a wall of darkness. Nothing stirred. She closed the bedroom door, tiptoeing across the floor to Lucy.

'See? I told you there was nobody there.' As she and Lucy settled down to sleep, the sound of the creaking bedsprings drowned out the click of the closing front door.

* * *

'I'll see Evie after breakfast.' Connie felt heart sorry for the girl who'd had no life to speak of. Nineteen years of age and saddled with two kids, it didn't look as if she would have much of one for the foreseeable.

'They said on the wireless the worst of the bad weather is over. Maybe her ladyship will come back to her kids,' Mim said, causing Connie's eyebrows to pucker in confusion. Her mother said the daftest things sometimes. The weather was warmer, and there was hope the worst was over. But she had no clue why her mother would think the weather would bring Rene home and she had no intentions of asking. 'I asked Evie if she wanted the cleaner's job, when Mrs Harris sprained her ankle,' Connie said, 'but she wasn't interested.'

'Maybe she has funds of her own?' Angus said stirring his bowl of porridge oats, which Mim insisted on giving him each morning. If anybody would know what was going on at the

Kilgaren's, it was Mim – his wonderful mine of valuable information.

'I doubt she's got a penny, otherwise she wouldn't huddle inside a coat that was three sizes too big,' Mim said. 'I'm sure her mother's got a decent coat she could wear?'

Connie got up from the table. She had a busy day ahead and had no intentions of sitting here listening to her mother's narrow-minded view of the Kilgaren's. 'You were glad of Rene, when she worked behind the bar.'

'Aye,' Mim said, 'she brought in the customers, that's for sure. That's why she could afford a coat with a fur collar.'

'If you need me, I'll be sorting out the airing cupboard,' Connie said, suspecting the coat had more to do with Darnel than it did to Rene's tips.

* * *

'Here, let me help you with those,' Angus said when he saw Connie lifting heavy blankets out of the airing cupboard.

'Thanks, Angus. I promised Evie I would pass these to her.' She handed them to Angus. 'We have no need for so many, and poor Evie's desperate.'

'You've a heart bigger than yourself,' Angus said in a voice that could stroke kittens.

'Give over,' Connie laughed, her face growing warm, surprised at how much the compliment lifted her spirits. With each passing day she thought more about Angus, sure he felt the same way, too.

Angus noted the pink tinge illuminate Connie's beautiful face. He had given the matter some thought and decided he had to be honest with her. Hoping she would forgive his deception, he swallowed hard.

'If I tell you something,' Angus said, 'you won't throw me out, will you?'

Connie stiffened. This was the bit where he was going to tell her he had a wife and ten kids. 'It depends what you have to tell me,' she said in a voice that held no warmth.

'You remember when I told you I was working in insurance?' His tone was unusually hesitant as he stood on the landing with an armful of bed linen. Connie nodded, hardly trusting herself to speak. 'And you remember when I asked you if you knew Leo Darnel?'

'Are you testing me for dementia, Angus?' Connie managed to say, and he gave a low, deep chuckle that fanned the flickering flame in her heart.

'No, I'm not. I'm trying to tell you the reason why I had to lie to you.'

Connie felt her heart sink. She had been instantly attracted to Angus from the night he walked into the bar, and she thought he felt the same way. Why else would she have trusted him with her biggest secret?

'I am working for Marine Insurance, but not in the way you might expect.'

'Spit it out, Angus, I haven't got all day.' His hesitation was making Connie unusually impatient. He was in insurance, then he wasn't. The man was a bloody puzzle, she did know that much.

'I'm an undercover detective, working for the Marine Insurance Company. They are the underwriters for many of the dockside warehouses. It is my job to find out who is behind the warehouse robberies.' He saw Connie's pallor blanche, and he worried he had made the biggest mistake of his life, telling her the truth in such detail.

'I suspected as much.' Connie was annoyed, her indignation obvious in her steadfast glare. 'How dare you?'

'Let me explain, Connie,' Angus pleaded, 'I didn't want you to find out from someone else.'

'Do you know what would happen if certain people found out I was harbouring a detective?' Her lips curled in disgust, never having felt so betrayed. 'This community doesn't like a snitch.' Connie's voice was low, one hand leaning on the doorframe and the other on her hip, her tone deepened ominously. 'And that's what they would see me as!'

'I will never put you in any danger of being known as an informer,' Angus said, mesmerised, like any hot-blooded male, by her sensual poise. He had never seen her more provocative. As his feelings for Connie grew stronger, he knew he must tell her the truth.

'You had better hope Mim doesn't get wind of it,' Connie said. 'There are two kinds of people she cannot abide, snoops and snitches. She'll have you up the road as soon as look at you.'

'There's something I have to tell you, Connie.' Angus would never have told Connie who he really was if he didn't feel so strongly about her. 'Can you keep a close eye on the Kilgaren family?'

'You want me to keep *dixie* for you, an' all?' Connie could not believe he had the gall to ask.

'Keep dixie?' Angus asked, confused, then he realised what Connie meant. 'No, I don't want you to be my lookout. I just want you to let me know if you think they might be in danger.' When Connie looked worried, he said, 'We know Darnel is involved in the warehouse robberies, and we also know he used to hide his contraband next door, and when Rene turfed him out, he left a number of valuable items that could put him away for a very long time.'

'What kind of valuable items?' Connie asked, too intrigued to be subtle. She should know better than to ask questions, but this time she couldn't help herself.

'Ration books. Points. Coupons. Cigarettes. Booze... Guns.'

'Guns!?' Connie could hardly get the word out of her mouth. 'Bloody hell!'

'So now you understand why I have to keep this between you and me,' Angus said, his voice low. Connie's head was spinning.

'I've got to tell Evie,' she said, 'the kid's got a right to know.'

'No! Don't do that,' Angus said quickly. 'The less she knows the better it will be for everybody.'

'Except Darnel,' Connie said, realising she had no choice but to keep quiet if she wanted to see that crook behind bars.

* * *

By Monday, there weren't many coppers in Evie's purse, the cupboards were bare and, for the second week in a row, she could not pay the rent. She had spent every penny making sure they wanted for nothing. And while she had the money, she lavished all she could on them.

Now she realised, she should have been a lot more sensible. She could have bought Jack a coat and trousers, she could have got the locks changed.

Sitting at the table, she scraped the last of the margarine on two cut slices of bread for Lucy's breakfast. Her sister didn't notice she had eaten nothing, kept going on just a cup of sugarless tea. But at least it was hot. She must look on the bright side.

Although the bright side was getting more dim with each passing day. She had applied for every office job in Liverpool. But her efforts were fruitless. She would have been better saving the money she paid in postage and put it towards buying food. The rent would have to wait.

'Are you all right, Evie?' Lucy asked when Evie came into the room with a comb that had most of its teeth missing.

'What made you ask that?' She combed her sister's waist-length hair into two perfect plaits. Lucy would be warm in school, at least.

'Your face looks pinched, like those poor women who slope into the pawnshop when they think nobody's looking.'

'Well, aren't you the observant one?' Evie said, making her voice as bright as she could, knowing she could not let Lucy go to school worried. The child could not concentrate on her studies and Evie had no intentions of putting heavy burdens on her sister's shoulders, knowing from personal experience how much misery that caused.

'It's this cold weather, gets everybody down, not just me. Roll on summer, hey Luce!'

'Roll on summer!' Lucy said with a smile, 'as long as you're not worried.'

'That's the spirit, Lucy.' Evie put the final touches to her sister's bows. 'Nothing at all to worry about. Now, finish getting ready before you're late.' Evie would have to go cap in hand to Connie, she had no choice. She prayed the cleaning job was still available. Pride was not an option – she could not let the kids starve. Nor could she afford to lose the roof over their heads. As Lucy scrambled under the table to fetch her shoes, there was a loud knock at the front door.

'If that's Bobby, tell him I'm ready, and not to go without me,' Lucy called from under the table. Bobby Harris had been calling for Lucy since she started at Saint Patrick's junior school. Evie suspected Bobby found her sister's mad-cap attitude a challenge to his own.

'Come in, Bobby, she won't be long,' Evie called down the lobby and Bobby sauntered into the kitchen as Lucy, on hands and knees, backed out from under the table with a pair of scuffed leather T-bar shoes. Moments later, the two children were heading out the door.

'Hiya Bobby! Hiya Lucy,' Connie said with a smile, as the two passed her on the step, 'Ta-ra, Bobby! Ta-ra, Lucy!'

'Ta-ra, Connie' they called in unison and Connie smiled. She never would have thought Bobby Harris' best friend would be a girl and was unsure whether to be glad or disappointed the boy spent less time in the pub. Not because she wanted him to collect the glasses, but because she missed his lively chats and cheeky banter.

'Hello, Connie,' Evie said, coming out to close the front door. Nobody closed their front door in Reckoner's Row from early morning until last thing at night, but since the weather had taken a turn for the worst, everybody closed it trying to keep out the draughts.

'Hiya, Evie, have you got a minute?' In her hand she gripped a pillowcase. She turned to make sure Bobby and Lucy were out of earshot. 'I hope you won't be offended, but I've brought these, Evie.' She lifted the pillowcase, Evie looked puzzled and stepped aside to let Connie into the house. 'What is it?' she asked.

'Just a few blankets and sheets – all spotless!' Connie assured her as Evie popped her head out of the door to give Lucy a final wave. 'If you don't want them, I can always take them to the Red Cross shop.' Connie didn't want Evie to feel as if she was lumbering her with second-hand cast-offs. 'They're in perfect condition, no stains or patches and they've all been laundered.'

'Oh, Connie! Are you sure?' Evie watched Lucy and Bobby head up the steps by the canal before closing the front door. She didn't want the rest of the street to see her business.

'Let's have a cup of tea,' Evie said as brightly as she could manage. She'd had a sleepless night, tossing and turning, worrying about everything from the kids to where the next meal was coming from. And, to put a top hat on it, their Jack didn't come home until nearly midnight, and was gone before she could tackle him about it this morning.

'Problems?' Connie asked, noting Evie's expression. It couldn't be easy for her.

'The usual,' Evie sighed. She didn't want to burden Connie with her woes either.

'A problem shared...' Connie said, taking a seat at the table, glad to see that it was now covered in a clean, bright gingham cloth and not the old newspaper that it once had.

'Lucy's been nagging me to let her go skating on the Cut, and if she thinks I will say yes, she's got another think coming.' Connie was a good friend. The only friend she had. She was an understanding soul she trusted, but there were details of family life she preferred to keep to herself. What if their Jack was up to no good? It was easier for a young lad to get into trouble as not these days.

'Are you sure it's just about Lucy?' Connie asked as Evie poured the boiling hot tea into plain white cups. Evie nodded. She couldn't tell Connie what was worrying her – that she was failing as a guardian and a provider. The two things that she felt should come naturally.

'You're worried about something else, I can tell,' Connie said in that gentle, persuasive tone that was as far away from the tavern as it was possible to be. Evie felt her throat tighten and the sting of tears behind her eyes.

'Don't be nice to me,' she said with a wobbly smile. That would be her undoing. She was proved right when Connie, without a word, lightly touched her arm. The gesture spoke a thousand words. It said she understood. It said she cared. And that's when the floodgates opened, and tears rolled down Evie's pale cheeks.

'I feel terrible,' Evie said, pinching the skin on the back of her hand, a gesture that told Connie the girl was almost at the end of her tether. 'Sometimes I find myself thinking, if the kids go back to Ireland where they were happy, I wouldn't have to sacrifice my hopes and dreams to look after them.' A dry sob shook her body. 'And then I hate myself for thinking those things.'

'No, you shouldn't think that,' Connie said sympathetically. 'You have done everything you can for Jack and Lucy. None of this is your fault.'

'It's my fault if there's no food on the table tonight,' Evie said, 'although, I suppose I could go along to Uncle's and pawn these pristine bedclothes you gave me.'

'I suppose you could,' Connie said, unperturbed by Evie's belligerent tone.

'I'm not ungrateful for your help, Connie, but what chance do we have of getting out of this hand-to-mouth existence?'

'Well, you can stop feeling sorry for yourself for a start,' Connie said in her usual pragmatic way. 'You've done a grand job of looking after Jack and Lucy, and you kept a roof over their head...'

'Not for much longer if I don't find the rent money before Friday,' Evie said. 'Connie...' Her empty stomach growled, and she knew the only thing she might eat today was humble pie. 'Did you manage to find anybody to take Mrs Harris' place?'

'No, not yet.' Connie knew what Evie was getting at, and she wasn't going to humiliate the girl by making her grovel for the job. 'I don't suppose you'd consider changing your mind?'

There was a moment's pause and the almost inaudible sigh that left Evie's body was a palpable sign of relief to the landlady of the Tram Tavern.

'Well,' Evie answered in the most indifferent tone she could manage, 'I suppose if it would help you out...'

'That's fantastic!' Connie cried jumping up from her straight-backed chair and nearly knocking it over. 'Can you start today? Now?' Evie nodded, too full to speak. The cleaning job was not what she wanted, but she was in no position to pass it up. Where else was she going to find a job so close to home, and with hours to suit?

* * *

Jack moved along the road with his head down and his hands as deep into his ragged pockets as they would go. Now his leg was mended he intended to help Evie as much as possible. Take that strained look off her face, if he could. She had sacrificed every-thing to look after him and Lucy. Her savings. Lodgings. Freedom – even the hope of getting her dream job in an office.

This morning she'd tried persuading him she wasn't in the least bit bothered about having no decent shoes. Even if by some small miracle there would be a knock on the front door and the offer of a much-coveted office job was hers for the taking, how could she afford shoes when she had spent all her money on rent and food? It was impossible.

Jack heard the commotion before he saw the woolly mongrel, which was unfortunate because, with hands still in his pockets, the dog ran out in front of him and took him clean off his feet. With no way of saving himself he landed on his chin while the dog slid to a shuddering halt behind him.

Jack saw the old man, Skinner, waving a half-eaten sandwich. 'You robbed my dinner again – you greedy, useless hound!'

The dog was in big trouble, for sure, and he watched it skulk back to its master with its tail between its legs. But, instead of chastising the dog, Jack watched Mr Skinner give Rex the rest of the butty, while scratching his half-chewed ear.

'What am I going to do with you, ay?' Skinner asked the dog, then noticed Jack lying on the cobbled road. 'Did he run you down?' the old man called, and Jack stalled an acerbic answer, getting to his feet.

The old man beckoned him over, and he hobbled across the cobbled street.

'You all right, son?' asked the owner of the haulage yard, his bowed legs encased in brown corduroy trousers while on his head he wore a brown felt hat, the rim of which looked like every moth on the planet had nibbled it.

Although head and shoulders shorter than himself, Jack could see the old man was as strong as the Clydesdales that pulled the canal boats. He had hands like Wimpy shovels.

'He can get a bit boisterous when there's food on the go. Sorry about that.'

'Ah, tis fine,' Jack said, agreeable. 'I'm used to the rough and tumble of farm life.' An excitable dog knocking his feet from under him was nothing at all.

'Well, that's good of you, lad,' Skinner said, when Jack shook his outstretched hand to show there was no hard feelings.

'I was just about to have some dinner, there's plenty if you want some – by way of apology, like.'

'That'd be grand,' Jack said, eager for a bite to eat. 'Having had no breakfast this morning, me belly thinks me throat's been cut.' He grinned and followed the old man into the stable yard. Taking in the familiar smell of horses he had grown up with and so loved.

'I've seen you looking through the gates, many a time,' the old man said. Jack found an oil spot on the floor of the yard and he focused on it. He could have this yard cleaned up in no time at all.

'I wasn't looking to pinch anything!' Jack said quickly. 'I was looking at the horses.'

'I know, lad, I know, that's why I asked you in here.' He opened the door of a brick out-house at the top of the yard, 'this is the cookhouse. It's where we mix the provender to feed the horses.'

'Oh, that brings back memories,' Jack said, inhaling. 'I loved working with the horses when I was evacuated to Ireland,' he said. His world was a happy place when he was around the horses and, when he closed his eyes, he was transported back to Ireland by the delicious smell of boiling beans and oats mixed in treacle, which the horses loved, and he was partial to as well.

Entering the cookhouse, Jack luxuriated in the warmth that seeped into his frozen bones and began to thaw him.

'You like horses?' Mr Skinner asked and Jack nodded.

'It's always been a dream of mine to work with them.'

'Can you start Monday?'

'Beg pardon?' Jack asked, not daring to hope he had heard right.

'That's your job if you want it, lad,' said Skinner, 'I need a lad to fetch fresh bales of straw for the bedding. My old bones are getting very much worse for wear of late and climbing those steps to the hayloft is a job I don't mind sharing I can tell you.'

'You mean, you're offering me a job!'

'Aye, if you're willing,' the old man said. 'You can earn thirteen shillings and sixpence a week, Monday through Saturday noontime, and if you work late Saturday, I'll give you an extra shilling on top. Deal?' He held out his big gnarled hand and Jack took it, shaking it hard. 'Be hopes you're more gentle with these here horses,' said Mr Skinner.

'Does anybody else work here?' Jack asked as they sat in the lovely warm cookhouse eating bacon and egg, which he cooked in a baking tin on the fire. Old Man Skinner, as Jack thought of him, stuffed great rashers of bacon and fried egg between two thick slices of bread – and Jack had tasted nothing so delicious in all his days.

'Aye, there's the blacksmith and a few vans lads who go out with the carters, and the head horse keeper, Brick Macmillan. He'll give you your orders when I'm not around.'

'When you're not around?' Jack asked finishing his lid of hot, sweet tea.

'Aye cooped up in that ruddy office trying to make sense of the paperwork – it were never my strong point.'

He showed Jack where he would work after they'd had their fill of food and huge mugs of tea and introduced him to the horses. Jack could barely contain his excitement.

'Eight o'clock, Monday morning,' Skinner said a short while later, walking Jack to the huge double gates. 'Don't be late. Come on, Rex, you scoundrel.'

When Jack turned to wave goodbye, the auld man and his beloved dog had already disappeared into the office. Evie might not be best pleased if she found out he had no intentions of going back to school ever again. But he would cross that bridge when he came to it. Maybe it would be best to say nothing to her for the time being.

He didn't notice the blast of cold wind as he walked home, head held high, hands in pockets, whistling a jaunty tune. Nor did he notice the figure under the bridge staring into the frozen canal.

* * *

'Stop hiding in your mother's shadow and let people be your friend,' Connie said later when the lavatories had been scrubbed and the floors mopped, and they were having a mid-morning break. 'And I know you think I'm being harsh, Evie, but you need to realise you have the determination and strength your mother never had.' Poor Evie was stronger than she imagined. And she was going to need that strength in the weeks ahead.

'It doesn't feel that way sometimes,' Evie answered, 'I feel as if I'm trudging through treacle and getting nowhere fast.'

'Have the police heard anything?' Connie asked and Evie shook her head.

'She'll come back when she's good and ready, I suppose.' She didn't want to talk about her mother and quickly changed the subject. 'I'm sorry I let you down over the job the other day,' Evie said. 'Pride made me jump the gun.' Evie hadn't intended to tell Connie she was on the lookout for better things, it popped out. 'I was expecting to walk into an office job when I got my certificate... but...'

'Think no more of it.' Connie's face beamed. 'At least you're next door, and you won't have to start before Lucy goes off to school.'

'Are you sure?' Evie could not keep the relief from her voice and Connie nodded.

'There's something else I wanted to ask you,' Connie said. 'How do you fancy going over my accounts?' Evie couldn't believe her ears! She felt privileged, being trusted with something as important as the tavern's accounts which gave her lacking pride a much-needed boost.

Connie smiled. 'You can take the books home and give them a going-over. Mim's getting slapdash, and I haven't got the time.'

Being given such responsibility delighted Evie. 'I'd love to. I won't let you down.'

'I know you won't,' Connie said, 'and there'll be a few bob in it for you now that the weather's getting warmer, fuel shortages are lessening, and people are getting back to normal. I hear Beamers opened up again yesterday.' Connie thumped the table with the pad of her hand. 'I shouldn't have said that, now you will want to go back there.'

'I made a promise to you, Connie,' Evie assured her. 'I won't be going back to Beamers.' She couldn't bear the thought of that snooty Susie Blackthorn looking down her nose again. Anyway, Evie thought, she didn't have a decent pair of shoes for an office.

'And the men are getting more work on the docks so they're coming back into the tavern, boosting the coffers. Happy days!'

'I won't lie, Connie, it will be good to have money coming in again.'

'Aye, things might look up for all of us,' Connie said. She didn't mention Angus suspected the Kilgarens might be in danger. She didn't want to frighten Evie. Nor did she want word getting back to Mim, who was well known for throwing a wobbly when she felt aggrieved! Her mother had a deep distrust of police after they arrested her dad for being drunk in charge of a runaway dray horse that caused havoc on the dock road. No, some things were best kept quiet. See how the land lies.

'What do I owe you for the blankets?' Evie asked, worrying that her purse was almost empty.

'Nothing,' Connie said, shaking her head. 'I need the room. Mim got them from the army and navy surplus. It's no use me having unused spare blankets taking up space, when you and the kids can make use of them.'

'You don't have to feel obliged because Mam used to work with you.' Evie would hate to be a burden on Connie's good nature.

'It's no trouble at all.' Connie said, her eyes bright. 'Your mam was a good worker and as honest as the day was long.' Connie threw her head back and laughed. 'Well, most of the time, but I could always trust her with the contents of the till – and she would never dream of helping herself to the stock. In my book, you can't ask more than that.'

'Thanks ever so much, Connie.' Evie felt an unfamiliar swell of pride. She had heard nobody say good things about her mother. Then again, she had had little to do with the neighbours, so she didn't know what they thought.

'Your mam isn't as awful as she's painted,' Connie said with a knowing smile. 'She picked the wrong men, that's all. Bastards, every one of them.'

'Is that all men?' Evie asked. 'Or just me mam's?'

'Just your mam's' Connie said. 'She could pick a winner with her eyes closed, but she couldn't pick a good man if she fell over one.'

'What about Dad?' Evie didn't know whether to be insulted, but as it was Connie, she knew she was telling the truth.

'Don't ask me about him, for God's sake! You wouldn't be impressed. Remember him as he was.' Evie wasn't sure she wanted to, recalling some screaming matches that went on inside this house when her father came home on leave from sea.

But one thing Connie was right about – her mother never went for the pipe and slippers type of man. Evie found it easy to talk to Connie and had learned that a trouble shared was less of a burden. Connie was wise, as well as knowledgeable. She knew everybody, and they knew her. But she also knew when to speak out and when to keep silent. Evie had never had a friend as good as Connie. A few moments later, Angus came into the bar, instead of using the private side door.

'Hello, Angus.' Connie said. 'I thought you'd have gone to work by now.'

'I had to make a call,' Angus answered, and Evie wondered if the twinkle in his eyes when he looked at Connie was her imagination playing tricks? On closer inspection she was certain. The look he gave Connie could have melted snow.

'I'll get on, shall I?' Evie said, knowing whatever went on between Connie and Angus was none of her concern. There was only the bar left to polish and then she would get off home in time to cook some dinner for Lucy and Jack.

'I need to show you where the polish is. Bye, Angus' Connie answered quickly, pushing Evie towards the cleaning cupboard.

'Bye, sweetheart,' Angus called, sauntering out of the bar. 'I'll see you this evening.'

'Was it my imagination or did he call you...?' Evie asked, wide-eyed.

'It was your imagination!' A deep red honeycombed pattern broke out on Connie's neck showing her obvious disquiet at the Scotsman's endearment. Evie busied herself in the store cupboard and smiled to herself. Well, well, well, she thought. Connie and Angus?

She couldn't think of a nicer couple.

'He's not who he seems, is he?' Evie said putting away her cloths and polish and she saw caution in Connie's eyes, which confirmed her suspicions.

'He's – and you've got to keep this to yourself – he's a...' Connie stammered, which was most unlike her.

'A scuffer?' Evie said, and Connie's look of surprise told her she was right. 'You don't have to live with villains like Leo Darnel to sniff out police. Clean shirt every day, clean fingernails, treats everybody with respect and has that air of authority about him.' Connie managed a wan smile when Evie said, 'he's either police or church and I don't see a dog collar.'

21

'You won't say anything? To Mim, I mean,' Connie was sitting at one of the round tables opposite the bar when Evie came through, after putting her pinny on the back door of the small anteroom laughingly known as the staff room, except two staff couldn't fit in comfortably at the same time. Two china saucers held matching cups of hot tea beside which sat an identical plate of corned beef sandwiches, cut into triangles.

'It's none of my business,' Evie said, her stomach growling at the sight of the sandwiches. She'd had nothing but a couple of spoons of vegetable soup since yesterday teatime. Any more and there wouldn't have been enough for Jack and Lucy to eat. 'You've been good to me and my family, Connie. Now it's payback. If my silence is the one thing I can give you, then you can have it with pleasure.'

'Thank you, Evie,' Connie said giving her friend a hug. 'You don't know how much that means to me.' In that moment, there was a silent assurance between the two women that would last a lifetime.

'I think I do.' Evie raised a knowing smile. Angus could not arouse suspicion in a place where everyone knew someone who was doing something that was a bit off-centre of legal.

'His easy-going manner and friendly banter is a boon in the bar,' Connie said, and Evie could see her friend was obviously captivated. 'But I can't tell Mim he's a detective. Not with the "arrangements" she's got with tradespeople. She'd have a canary.' The two women laughed at the thought.

'Come and have a butty,' Connie said, tucking into her sandwich. 'Mim made them, so the corned beef's as thick as doorsteps, hope you don't mind.'

'Mind?' Evie said dragging a chair out and sitting opposite Connie. 'Why would I?' She picked up a sandwich took a bigger bite than intended, immediately aware that Connie must think her so greedy. Ashamed, she swallowed hard. 'I don't know what I'd do without you.'

'It's a butty, not a five-course feast.' Connie flicked her hand as if swatting a fly, suspecting the food meant much more to Evie than a mere sandwich. She also suspected, rightly, that Evie had not eaten a proper meal since she came back to Reckoner's Row.

'I'm glad you took up my offer,' Connie said, 'the job might not be what you expected but...'

'It's a job,' Evie answered matter-of-factly, 'and I'm glad of it.'

'You won't always be a cleaner,' Connie said, causing the girl's eyebrows to rise. 'You've got ambition and guts – how did you get on with your final examinations, last summer?'

'Passed with flying colours, I can call myself a bookkeeper.' Evie grinned proudly. 'But it hasn't done me much good so far, every time I go for an interview, they want experience. How do I get experience if no bugger will employ me?'

'Something will turn up, I'm sure,' Connie said.

'Aye, probably my toes,' Evie answered with a laugh. This morning's work had put a spring in her step, brought a bit of security she hadn't felt since she left Beamers. It was good to get out of the house, away from her own miserable worry of where the next meal was coming from.

'If I could get me hands on me mother,' Evie said, finishing her sandwich, 'I'd wring her bloody neck for leaving those two poor kids. What kind of mother does that?'

'Don't be too hard on her,' Connie said, 'circumstances made her like that. She didn't have it easy.' *Especially with your domineering father*, she wanted to say. But out of respect for the girl's dignity, Connie decided not to open old wounds.

'I wouldn't know,' Evie said. For some unknown reason, she suddenly felt as if a dark cloud was resting on her shoulders. She didn't want to talk about the old days.

'Have the police heard anything yet?' Connie asked, changing the subject.

'No, they've scoured every haunt she visits, but no one's heard a peep.' Evie sighed; even she was beginning to worry.

'What about the spiv, has he heard anything?' Connie was surprised he still showed his face, but now she understood why. He was keeping an eye on Evie.

'He wouldn't tell me if he had,' Evie said. 'He's not the sharing type where I'm concerned.' She decided not to mention his ominous warning. Probably trying to frighten her if the truth be told. Well, Evie thought, if he came anywhere near number two, she would be ready for him – and so would their Jack.

'Some spivs will help you out, but not him, he's downright bloody evil,' Connie said, suspecting Rene must have been desperate to leave her kids. She'd never been gone this long before. 'Your mam might be a lot of things,' Connie said, 'including foolish where men are concerned, but she was a good wife. Never played away while Frank was at sea.' *Even though he was a swine.* Connie kept that thought to herself. The way he treated Rene was little short of cruelty. But she wouldn't say anything to Evie. Rene told her those things in confidence.

'Last time Darnel was in the tavern he tried selling knocked-off stuff to Mim. But even she won't touch the stuff he sells – and that's saying something.'

Evie didn't ask why, but Connie told her anyway. 'Mim will buy off anyone if the price is right.' Noting the surprised look on Evie's face, she laughed, 'oh don't let that "lovable old lady" act fool you, Mim can make a penny scream. If there's a chance she can make on a deal you can bet your life she'll take it – but, to give her credit, she won't touch anything from Darnel, and if you've got any sense neither will you.'

'You must think I was born yesterday,' Evie said. 'If I never saw him again it would be too soon.'

'Good on you,' Connie knew that even poor people had codes of decency and even though their flexible scruples allowed them to share in a poor docker's booty, they would never fill Darnel's over-stuffed coffers if they could help it. In these harsh times, Connie knew many housewives felt justified in buying off the black market, because of the prolonged austerity caused by the war, they felt they must fill that gap between the amount their men earned, and what they were actually paid.

'I expected better days to come when the war ended,' Connie sighed, 'but rationing has got worse instead of better.'

'People round here don't steal from their own, though,' Evie said, draining her cup. 'But Leo Darnel would steal from his own mother if he had a buyer lined up.'

'I don't know what your mother ever saw in the ugly little runt.' Connie murmured.

'Me neither,' Evie answered. 'He's not a patch on my dad, if he were here today none of this would have happened.'

I could be sure about that. Connie thought, getting up, a signal that break time was over.

Evie put the empty crockery on to a tray and headed to the small kitchen behind the bar.

'Our Lucy's been having nightmares, even wetting the bed,' she said, feeling she could share a confidence with Connie, 'and our Jack's out all hours of the day and night. I'm worried sick.'

'Where does he go?' Connie's dark eyes were full of concern. She could only imagine what Evie must be going through, never having been fortunate enough to have kids of her own.

'I don't know,' Evie answered. 'He says he's just knocking about with a few of the lads – but that seems a bit far-fetched in this weather? He hasn't been back to school even though his leg is better.'

'You must be at your wits' end, love,' Connie said, feeling heart sorry for the girl's predicament. But Evie never complained before, and she wondered if all this upset was a strain on Evie's nerves. Her worries about her siblings would be compounded by the lack of money to buy a loaf of bread.

'Here,' Connie said, 'put that in your purse.' She sloped a ten-bob note into Evie's hand. 'You did a smashing job today.'

'But I've only worked one morning,' Evie said, 'I can't take this for one morning's work.'

'We'll sort it out another time,' Connie said, having no intention of taking the money back. 'You've got enough on your plate as it is. How long has Jack been sagging school?'

'He hasn't been back since the incident.' Evie picked up a clean bar towel and began drying the cups, she still could not bring herself to refer to the shooting as such. 'As soon as his leg was better, he was up and out. He has money, but I don't know where he gets it from, he won't say.'

'Have you asked him where he goes?'

'He said I've not to worry, I'll find out in good time.'

'What did he mean by that, d'you think? Connie needed to know so she could tell Angus, therefore helping Evie.

'I'm worried he might be in with a bad crowd.' Evie felt her throat tighten. She had kept her worries locked inside her for so long that letting them out made them sound so much worse. 'I don't know what to do about it.' There was a catch in her voice. 'To tell the truth, I feel like I'm drowning and can't find a lifebelt.'

Connie took a deep breath, the poor girl must be out of her mind with worry, and yet she still managed to put a smile on her face. Never let others know her burden. 'Tell me to mind my business if you like, Evie, but if Jack was mine, I'd move heaven and earth to find out what he was up to.' Evie nodded. Connie was right, and she talked a lot of sense. She should find out what he was up to. Turning a blind eye was never the answer.

'I'm sure there's a simple explanation. Maybe he's working?'

'Who'd give a kid a job in times like these, when grown men can't get work?' Evie asked.

'Maybe you're right,' Connie said putting beer mats onto tables, 'but not knowing and worrying, is worse than knowing and trying to help.'

'I suppose so.' Evie was placing the newly washed towels along the bar, her last job of the morning when she saw Lucy coming into the tavern. 'You don't mind our Lucy coming in, do you, Connie? I told her I might still be working when she finished school at dinnertime.'

'Of course not, love,' Connie said, handing Lucy a bag of crisps and a small bottle of lemonade. Lucy was thrilled and, taking her spoils and feeling very grown-up frequenting a public bar, she went to sit by the window and wait for Evie.

'Evie, can I go skating on the Cut with Bobby Harris? Pleeease,' Lucy pleaded, her red cheeks mottled with the cold, her coat wide open, 'Can I Evie, please, go on,' she coaxed. 'Can I?'

'I've told you once and I won't tell you again!' Evie had to be strong. Her heart wanted to give her sister all she desired. But that was a foolish way of thinking. She didn't want Lucy turning into a little madam who felt she only had to pout, and she would get her own way.

Lucy's scattering of freckles stretched into a scowl at her older sister, who was more of a mother to her than her own had ever been. 'It's not fair,' Lucy whined, 'we do nothing that's fun!'

'Bobby's been warned to stay away from that canal, too,' Connie told her. 'The ice is a foot thick in some places, but much thinner by the bridge.'

'Don't you dare go down there, Lucy,' Evie warned.

'I won't.' Lucy shrugged her disappointment. 'Even though every kid in the street's been skating on the canal. I'm the only one who hasn't. It's not fair.'

'Neither is a rainy day!' Evie told Lucy, nuzzling her out of the tavern. 'Now, let's get you home to take off those wet socks and hang them on the fireguard to dry.'

'You look tired, Evie,' said Connie, 'and who could wonder...'

'My heart's in my mouth worrying about her and Jack,' Evie said. What little she had saved had gone through her fingers like water, especially when she had to pay top whack for everything.

'Here,' Evie said holding out the ten shilling note, 'let me pay you for the crisps and lemonade'

'You will not!' Connie would not dream of accepting a penny. 'I'd be insulted!'

'I can think of worse ways to insult somebody,' Evie laughed, 'but I won't take them for nothing, I must pay my way.'

Connie sighed and nodded; she knew Evie's independence meant everything to her and hoped one day Evie would gain confidence in her strengths instead of believing she was not good enough. 'You get off home and give Lucy her lunch, and I'll see you again at three this afternoon, if that suits?'

'That's smashing,' Evie beamed. Slipping her arms into the capacious coat that had doubled as an eiderdown, Evie gave a sigh of relief knowing she had money to buy food and coal.

'Thanks for listening, Connie. You're a godsend,' Evie said, heading towards the door.

'You're the godsend, Evie,' Connie said. 'You've done a fine job – the place hasn't looked so clean for ages, but don't tell Mrs Harris I said that,' she said, following Evie, who emptied her bucket of dirty water down the grid and handed the bucket back to Connie, as Jack was coming down the steps leading from the bridge, not a sign of his recent injury.

'What's the matter with her?' Jack nodded to his younger sister who had gone skulking to their own house, next door. 'She looks like she lost a tanner and found a farthing.'

'The little madam wants to go skating on the canal with Bobby Harris!' Evie's eyes opened wide at the absurdity of Lucy's request.

'I'll have a word.' Jack sounded much older than his years as he went on ahead, following Lucy. Evie noticed his flimsy jacket, knowing the first thing she was going to do when she got her week's wages was to go to Cazenue Street market, to see if she could buy Jack a second-hand coat, to protect him from this awful weather.

'I'll be in soon,' Evie said, giving him a tight smile. Jack nodded once more to Connie and whistled a happy tune as he sauntered home.

'I don't know what I'd do without our Jack,' Evie said to Connie, 'I'd go scatty if he was mixed up in anything dodgy.'

'I'm sure he's one of the good guys,' Connie said in a fake

American accent. Then, more thoughtfully, she said, 'I didn't recognise him when he came back from Ireland, he looked older than his fourteen years, so mature and healthy-looking.'

'That'll be the fresh air in the Irish countryside and all that good food – a far cry from living around here.' Evie shivered as a cold wind whipped in from the River Mersey. 'He goes out all hours, looking for wood for the fire... along the canal, around the docks, that worries me.'

'He's got his head screwed on,' Connie said, suspecting Jack was the reason Darnel didn't hound Rene, when the kids returned from evacuation.

'I must be off,' Evie said, giving Connie a little wave as she headed to number two. With her head bent against the biting wind, Evie didn't notice a lurking figure step back into the shadow of the bridge.

* * *

After walking Lucy back to Saint Patrick's junior school, Evie carried on to the top road to get a few necessaries with the money Connie had given her. She was feeling more relaxed, knowing at least they had something to eat tonight. She pushed the key into the Yale lock on the front door.

As she entered the long passage on her return, she detected the faint aroma of tobacco. If their Jack was wasting precious coppers on ciggies, she would have it out with him once and for all. It was hard enough trying to keep body and soul together, food-wise. She was not having money wasted on those disgusting habits.

Opening the kitchen door, Evie got the shock of her life. A huge fire was blazing in the hearth, and the room was toasty warm. She had decided not to use the last of the coal until the kids came in later.

'Jack! Jack! Have you used the last of our coal?' Evie called out thinking he was in the back-kitchen. But there was no sign of him. If he had lit the fire, and had then gone out again, there might be a new face in heaven by nightfall!

But there was still no answer from Jack, and that's when Evie got her second shock. There, sat right in the centre of the table was a box. A wooden box with *Produce of Ireland* stamped in red letters on all four sides. Full to the brim with food. Evie examined the contents.

There was a huge chicken, bigger than any she had seen before and bald as the day it hatched. Potatoes wrapped in newspaper. Carrots. Turnip. A large green cabbage. Tea. Sugar. Cheese. Bread – and more. She had never seen so much food in one box.

'Jack, are you here?' she called. But Jack didn't answer. Evie was confused, running upstairs she soon discovered her brother wasn't up there either. She would have to wait for him to come home to find out, once and for all, what he was up to. Where did he get the money from to buy this lot? Was it even theirs? And if not, who did the hamper belong to? Chicken was like gold around here, and so expensive it was a rare treat even at Christmas, and only then if people had enough readies to buy one.

Drawn to the chair by the fire, Evie had not seen such a blaze in that hearth since she got back. What precious coal they did manage to buy was frugally eked out to save fuel for as long as possible. Mesmerised by the dancing flames, Evie wondered when she was going to wake up. Things like this didn't happen in real life, so she must be dreaming. Her eyes lingered on the food and her mouth watered at the memory of a chicken dinner she once had when Darnel lived here.

Darnel?! What if he had enticed their Jack into doing something dodgy for easy money? Running illegal gambling in dark alleyways or street corners? All the while keeping an eye out for the local bobby on his beat. Collecting coppers from housewives chancing a little flutter with the old man's hard-earned wages. Thoughts of police knocking on the door turned Evie to stone. She could not move with the fear of it. What was Jack getting himself into?

22

We might be honest, Evie thought, but we're also hungry. And it would be a mortal sin to let good food go to waste. Her family were in need?

'Something smells delicious, our Evie,' Jack said coming into the kitchen, red-faced with the cold. His mouth watering as he began to stir the huge pan of scouse Evie had made. 'It's even got meat in it, not the *blind* meatless stew Mam used to make.'

'Just some scrag ends of lamb I managed to buy from the butcher's,' Evie said pointedly. Letting him know that everything in that pan had been bought legally. He threw his cap on the back of the door along with his frayed jacket.

'Do you know anything about this?' Evie, hands on hips, nodded to the box of food and glared at her brother waiting for an explanation. 'Where did all this stuff come from?'

'Why are you looking at me like that?' Jack's deep voice came out in an incredulous squeak, 'I didn't bring it in.' He stared back unflinchingly and with a sinking dread, Evie knew he was telling the truth.

'Then, if you didn't, who did?' Her voice came out as a

whisper and she looked at the clock on the mantelpiece. It said half past four. She had been so busy worrying, and getting their evening meal ready, she had forgotten about Lucy. 'We'll talk about this later,' Evie said, worried about her sister. 'Did you see Lucy when you came out of school at half past three?' Evie's question was loaded with accusation. The emphasis was not lost on Jack; she could tell by the way he lowered his head, not looking in her direction that he was hiding something from her. A true test of his honesty was in that one small action. Their Jack could not look her in the face and tell a lie.

'I haven't seen her,' Jack said, 'and she should have been home ages ago. I'll go and look for her.' Jack headed towards the door and Evie glared at him in his haste to be out of the house.

'You haven't been to school, have you, Jack?' Evie's voice was thick with accusation. Without warning, Darnel's veiled threat sprung to mind, and she knew he could ruin this family one way or another if he so wished.

'I know where she might be. I've just seen something,' Jack said, 'and you won't like it.'

'Oh please, don't tell me she's done something stupid! I don't want to hear it.' Jack pulled on his jacket and shook his head. 'The canal's thawing and I saw kids on the bank on my way home.'

'Not Lucy!?' Evie could hardly say the words and Jack didn't answer as the sound of running feet and anxious voices caused her to gasp in horror, with terrible thoughts racing through her mind. Her spine jerked upright. Lucy had asked time and again if she could go on the canal with Bobby. She wouldn't... would she?

She's but a child, said an ominous voice inside her head. *She will if she thinks she can get away with it. That's half the fun.* Daring kids like Lucy and Bobby did not think of the consequences. A pair of perishers when they got together. Lucy would be curious, knowing the ice would disappear completely in a day or two.

The rise in temperature brought a much-needed thaw. But with it came floods, burst pipes and overflowing guttering, quelling the initial revelries of spring days to come. It also defrosted icy canals, ponds and rivers.

'I hope they haven't...' Evie's words trailed as a dark cloud of dread descended on her shoulders. 'I've got to find Lucy!' Grabbing her coat off the back of the door she headed to the front door, following Jack.

* * *

The thunder of boots on cobbles told Evie that people were running towards the bridge.

'What's happened?' She stopped a scurrying woman who was dragging her coat on in her haste to get to the canal.

'Something in the canal...' the woman, breathless from running, called over her shoulder. 'I haven't seen people move so fast since the Blitz.' Evie felt her heart shoot to her throat, and she slammed the front door shut. Jack was ahead of her as she raced towards the steps leading to the bridge. This was one of her worst nightmares, being played out before her eyes.

* * *

'Has your Bobby been home from school yet, Mrs Harris?' Evie called from the steps, her words whipping away on the fierce March wind. Since the snow had thawed, everything was damp and slippery, so Evie stayed close to the sandstone wall.

'I was just coming to ask you the same question about your Lucy,' Mrs Harris was being pushed along the street in an old-fashioned bath-chair by her soldier son, Danny. 'If that sister of yours has persuaded our Bobby to go on that canal and anything has happened to my lad,' called Mrs Harris, 'I won't be responsible for my actions.'

'Beg pardon, Mrs Harris?' Evie's anger sliced her words. 'I hope you're not insinuating... Our Lucy's from a respectable home.'

'I'm not incinerating nothing, I'm telling you,' Ada Harris answered. 'Our Bobby's got his paper-round. Now they'll be late! He gets his wages docked if they're late.'

'Is that all you're concerned about, his wages!' Evie shot Mrs Harris a venomous look, too worried to give her neighbour the unedited version of her scathing thoughts. She knew the older woman was livid when Evie stepped into her shoes at the Tram Tavern.

'Good Lord!' Evie prayed the two tearaways were not the reason for the commotion and hurried on up the stone steps.

'Try not to worry, Evie,' Danny left his mother at the foot of the steps, struck by Evie's large panic-stricken eyes, stark against the pallor of her freckled complexion. Evie had never had it easy.

'They should have been home from school ages ago and...' Evie could not bring herself to tell Danny about Lucy's good shepherd. She had warned her sister about the dangers of talking to strangers. This 'good shepherd' could be a figment of her over-active imagination. But now she couldn't be so certain.

'I saw kids larking about earlier on the other side of the bridge,' Jack informed Danny, his voice full of regret. 'I wish I'd warned them off there now.'

'You didn't speak to any of them?' There was frustration in Evie's words and Jack remained silent. She knew she had hit a nerve. Jack would put himself in danger before he would let any harm come to Lucy, and she had all but accused him of neglecting his duty to their young sister.

'I hope your sister's not leading my son down the garden path.' Mrs Harris' voice was full of scorn and loud enough for all to hear. 'What's in the cat is in the kitten, so I've heard.'

'I'm sure he doesn't need much leading.' Evie snapped, although she hadn't meant to speak ill of Bobby. He was a good kid. His mother, though, was a bitter pill. 'Let's worry about who led who, later,' Evie mumbled, surmising Mrs Harris must be just as worried as she was. This was not the time for finger pointing. She was civilised enough to be magnanimous.

Struggling against the crowd, Evie tried to calm herself. Maybe their Lucy wasn't even at the canal. She was a good girl. She did as Evie told her... so why wasn't she home? Her mind was a whirlpool of contradictions. Local children came home from school at midday, as Saint Patrick's was only five minutes away. Then again, school finished at three-thirty, but it was now turned four o'clock! Evie was losing the battle with panic.

'It'll be dark, soon,' a voice said, as if they needed any telling.

'Lucy doesn't like the dark.' Evie's voice rose when she saw the crowd leaning over the wall on the other side of the bridge. She was determined not to show the guilt she felt, the irresponsibility. Allowing her sister to wander the cold streets while she had thought only of filling her growling stomach and what she would say to their Jack when he got home from God-knows-where? 'Oh Lord, please let them be safe!'

'We'll find them,' Danny said, and Evie blanched, not realising she had spoken aloud. 'They've grown up around the canal. They know the dangers.'

'Lucy hasn't,' Evie snapped, his reassuring tone doing nothing to comfort her. 'That canal bank will be slimy after the thaw.'

'Someone said there's a body in the water!' a man said running past them.

'Please, God, no!' Evie could not contain the whimper in her voice as the crowd surged forward and she tried to elbow her way through.

'We'll go on ahead.' Jack and Danny were bigger, stronger. They could get through the throng easier than Evie.

Connie, who had caught up with Evie, put a protective hand around her shoulders. She knew Evie must be out of her mind with worry. As she herself was. She liked the Kilgarens. She liked their determination, and the way they never expected hand-outs or something for nothing. And Bobby... the kid was like her own. She imagined her own darling boy would have been every bit as sparky as Bobby Harris.

Connie took a deep breath that snagged in her chest. All this, the fear and the caring brought back that familiar gnaw in the pit of her own stomach. But now was not the time to think of herself. Evie needed her to be strong. Because that was something she had been proficient in when nursing in war-torn Italy.

'Kids don't keep track of the time,' Connie said, curtailing grave thoughts and bringing first-rate training to bear. 'Something catches their eye and they can't help being inquisitive.'

'Lucy's scared of her own shadow,' Evie said. 'Something's happened. I know it.'

'You know what kids are like.' Connie prayed that any minute Bobby and Lucy would show their grubby faces, wondering what all the fuss was about like nothing had happened.

Evie strained her neck, frantic to get a better view of the canal. 'She's done nothing like this before.'

* * *

Mrs Harris saw her eldest son running down the steps towards the water with young Jack Kilgaren. Evie was doing a better job of looking after those kids than her mother, she supposed, although she would never dream of telling her so. And another thing, she thought, mollified when she saw the worry lines etch Evie's pretty face – young Lucy could not persuade a whirlwind like their Bobby to get up to mischief. The little bugger could do that all by himself!

* * *

'They're here!' Danny's commanding military voice carried through the misty evening air as people jostled to get a better look over the soot covered sandstone wall. Evie watched Danny disappear below the bridge, followed by a crowd of onlookers. But before she had time to descend, Danny scrambled back up the muddy embankment. 'I've got to get to the police box!'

'Why? What's happened?' Evie's heart pounded in her chest.

His determined expression told her this was not good news as she ran towards the steps leading down to the water, stumbling in her haste.

'What's the matter? What's happened?' The crowd parted to let her through. Evie's tongue stuck to the back of her throat, her heart hammering against her ribs.

'Lucy!' A voice inside her head screamed as tears filled her eyes. 'Has she fallen in? Oh, dear God! No!' Danny hurtled back to the bridge after finding a policeman, and Mrs Harris watched from the other side, her mouth slack.

'It's our Bobby! It's our Bobby! Isn't it?' Her face was devoid of colour.

'No, Ma, it's not our Bobby.' Danny's voice was low and the

look in his eyes told Evie he did not feel the same way his mother did. In that moment time stood still.

'I didn't mean nothing by it, Evie, love… It's me nerves.' Ada Harris, aware of her oldest son's regard for the girl, knew she had to be cute where this one was concerned. Otherwise their Danny might do something daft, like fall headlong for the likes of Evie Kilgaren.

'A body in the Cut!' a voice cried, as Danny looked back over to where his young brother lying on his stomach, on the canal bank.

'I'd better get down there quick, before our Bobby jumps in and get the body out himself.'

When Evie reached the canal, she saw Lucy outstretched on her stomach beside Bobby. She was trying to roll the huge floating object towards the bank with a plank of wood. Bobby was using his net trying to retrieve the distended torso, but to no avail.

'I bet it's a shop window dummy,' Bobby called, pulling the belt of a herringbone coat open to reveal a black, pencil-slim skirt. Around the throat was a bright red scarf, which Evie recognised immediately. Because she knitted it last summer.

No! Please God… No!

23

A large crowd gathered on the bridge, some hanging over the sandstone wall to get a better view. Danny reached the two kids first, but they weren't paying any attention to him. The bloated grey mass that was once a vibrant human was openly, ghoulishly, fascinating them.

With one hand, Danny hoisted Lucy away from the water's edge by the belt of her black gaberdine mac. Struggling like a caught fish on the end of a line, she kicked out, punching the air, desperate to keep her front row view of the proceedings. Lucy did not intend to go quietly. But, as he held the wriggling child in his iron grip, Danny also caught hold of his young brother, Bobby.

'We nearly got it, didn't we, Luce?' Bobby was breathless with excitement, his face flushed 'but it kept rolling back an' we couldn't get a good hold! Could we, Luce?'

'It was down there, under the bridge, just bobbing along.' Lucy's excited Celtic twang speeded up when Danny placed her on the muddy canal bank. 'So, we got a big stick, huge it was, because Bobby's fishing net broke, you see and—'

'Then a dog jumped in...' Bobby interrupted. 'I didn't know it was a body at that point—'

'Not until the dog pushed it against the bank and I tried to grab it.' Lucy took over the conversation.

'But you couldn't get hold,' Bobby interrupted. 'So, I got the stick—'

'Enough!' Evie put her hand up to stop the animated commentary of events so far. 'What the hell were you doing on the canal bank?' Evie's insides were turning. She felt sick with relief and revulsion. 'I've been going out of my mind with worry.'

'Me an' Bobby thought we'd be 'eroes!' Lucy's eyes were anticipation-bright, while Evie straightened her back, feeling ashamed for her sister's obvious lack of understanding for the enormity of the situation.

'Turn on the waterworks, Luce,' Bobby whispered, arranging his face into a more sympathetic appearance as the bank filled with uniforms. Fire brigade. Ambulance men. Police and even men with cameras. 'We'll get our picture in the paper.'

'We are heroes, even if our Evie doesn't think so,' Lucy added. But Bobby rolled his eyes heavenwards when moments later, absorbed in the excitement by the water, Lucy forgot to cry.

'How much trouble are we in?' Bobby lost all hope of receiving any reward money and would count himself lucky if he got away with only a telling-off.

'Enough,' Danny answered, 'you mark my words.'

'You know about the dangers of the canal, don't you?' Evie shook Lucy's shoulders, her relief turning to annoyance.

'I'm so sorry, Evie,' Lucy said as the waterworks starting for real and relief finally flooded through Evie's body. Her sister was safe, and she wanted to hug the living daylights out of her.

'But that's not the end of the matter.' The child had been warned to stay away from here and had defied her. 'When we get you home, you will feel the weight of my hand across your arse and you won't sit down for a week!' Evie knew she would never lay a hand on her sister, but it wouldn't do her any harm to worry for a little while.

'Will she come for me, too, Danny?' Bobby asked, slipping behind his older brother.

'I doubt it,' Danny said, admiring Evie's pluck, 'but she's fierce when she's got a cob on.' Even though her marine-coloured eyes narrowed in annoyance and Evie fixed her lips in a hard line, she still looked beautiful.

'Stand back!' a police constable ordered, as events had been few since the war, this was causing quite a stir. Two ambulance men brought a wooden stretcher. The firemen hauled the body from the water a while later and everybody including the children surged forward, and Evie shot out a restraining hand, pulling her curious sister close and covering Lucy's eyes with her coat, dreading the nightmares she would have after seeing this. Bobby wrinkled his nose in disgust, while Danny and Jack didn't take their eyes from the gruesome haul.

'What would make a woman throw herself in the canal?' Evie asked, casting only a quick glance at the body, which must have been underwater for weeks, given the length of time the canal had been frozen.

'Who said she threw herself in?' Jack answered, engrossed in the careless conversation between two policemen...

'It looks like her scarf got caught on an old pram wheel at the bottom of the canal, dragged her down, I'd say.' A large crowd had gathered – men going home from the nearby docks, shop workers finished for the day. Even the traffic on the bridge had come to a standstill. Evie looked to Jack, who seemed transfixed. The gruesome incident had drained his complexion of all colour.

'It might not be her, Jack,' Evie said, moving Lucy to one side out of earshot.

'Mam wore a coat like that one, on the night she left,' he said as Evie pressed her fingers to her lips, determined not to cry out in front of the child.

'Lots of women own a coat like that.' Evie said, refusing to accept the inevitable, but she could not stop the dreadful thoughts filling her head. 'If there's anything we should know, Jack, I'm sure they'll tell us soon enough.' She put her arm around his waist and her other arm around Lucy's shoulders. She suddenly felt helpless.

Imagining the task of becoming a mother to her siblings seemed insurmountable. She wanted a career. She wanted to travel. Do things that women from around here didn't do... She didn't feel grown-up enough to look after a ready-made family. She felt like a lost child.

* * *

'I know the way, Mr North,' Angus told the morgue keeper, covering the chequered floor tiles in a few long strides as he approached the mortuary. He could see movement on the other side of the door and rapped on the opaque glass.

'Ahh, Angus!' said Alfred 'Birdy' Finch, the coroner, who, in Angus' estimation, was far too cheerful for this time of night. Dressed in a white post-mortem gown, a rubber apron, gloves, and galoshes, Birdy waved a gigantic knife.

The mortuary was large and in the centre was a gleaming white porcelain examination table upon which the bloated head of the drowned woman was propped up on a small wooden block. Along the far wall a wooden table displayed weighing scales, microscopes and various sized glass jars containing small body parts in clear fluid.

North pulled an overhead light closer to the body, so he could get a better view while the wireless played an energetic swing-band tune, reminding Angus of the night before, when he'd taken Connie to see Snake-Hips Johnson at the Palais.

Birdy suddenly switched off the wireless and Angus concentrated on the matter in hand. 'So, what have you got for me tonight, Birdy?' His voice echoed off the white tiled walls as the mortuary keeper took photographs of the body. 'Time of death, at least?'

'You're always so bloody impatient, Angus,' Birdy said, preparing his tools. 'Did you listen to the football on the wireless last night?'

'Lindy-hopping.' Angus answered, causing Birdy to explode in a rumbling crescendo of laughter.

'You? With those great platters on the end of your legs?'

Angus shrugged. He and Doctor Birdy Finch had served the police force before, during and after the war in their own expert capacities and knew each other like brothers.

North, getting closer to the corpse, took photographs while Angus covered his nose with his hand, convinced Birdy must lack any kind of olfactory awareness. That body was putrid.

'I can only give an estimate of the time of death,' Birdy said after examining the naked body. 'Six weeks, at least, I'd say, given that was when the canal froze over.'

After bagging and tagging samples of blood stains, semen, powder, dirt under the nails, photographed various small scars and a tiny butterfly tattoo on the victim's right shoulder, he could inform Angus of a few things.

'Caucasian. Female. Late thirties, early forties. Brunette.

Green eyes.' Birdy said dissecting the body. 'Has given birth. Death was not caused by drowning.'

'Really?' Angus was sure this was a case of suicide, or even accidental death.

'See this...' Leo beckoned Angus over and lifted the eyelids. 'There is evidence of *petechiae* in the conjunctiva – the mucus membrane.' Angus nodded. He had seen plenty of post-mortems.

'So, you know these dark red specks inside the eyelid and on the forepart of the eyeball are caused by increased pressure in the head caused by...'

'Strangulation?' Angus felt a dip in his stomach when Birdy nodded. 'So someone murdered her.' Do we know who she is?' he asked, and Birdy pointed him to the long table on the far side of the room. 'She had one of those leather bags that cross over the body – like a bus conductor's – the contents are drying out over there.' Angus went over to where each item was laid out.

A stub of pillar-box-red lipstick. A gold-coloured compact, containing traces of damp face powder. A small leather concertina purse. Empty. A ration book, last date stamped 21st February 1947. The soggy identity card stated she was Mrs Rene Kilgaren. Widow. Lived at number two Reckoner's Row. Angus felt a cold shiver run through his body.

Jesus wept.

24

'Who could afford to leave us all this?' Lucy asked the next morning when her curious eyes spied the box that had been left on the step yesterday, and her innocent remark made Evie's stomach lurch. *Yes,* Evie thought, *who could afford to gift something like this?* The man from the school board had been yesterday. He'd told her that Jack hadn't attended school even though he was on the register. *Please, God, keep him away from Leo Darnel.*

'I don't know.' Jack heaved the box from the back kitchen to the next room, plonking it on the table under the sash window. 'Whoever it was must have strength, it weighs a ton.' They all stood looking at the box as if waiting for something to happen.

'Let's see, now,' Jack said. He was trying to keep everything normal for Lucy's sake. 'Bloody hell,' he gasped emptying the box, 'would you look at all this!'

'More potatoes, carrots, a cauliflower...' Lucy's eyes were wide in amazement when she squealed.

'Fruit!' Jack had a Christmas morning expression on his face. 'Apples and bananas!'

'What's a banana?' Lucy asked, peeking over his shoulder,

but Evie didn't respond. She couldn't. Her thoughts were jumbled and her reactions slow. Mechanical. She didn't know what to do. She must get some breakfast ready. Light the fire. Act normal on a day when nothing seemed normal anymore. She hadn't slept a wink all night. What if that... that body was her mother?

No. It couldn't be. Someone would have told them.

'We haven't had grub like this since...' Jack was obviously not having the same concerns as his older sister when faced with food they hadn't seen since before the war. All Evie could think was: why would someone give away all this good food, buckshee?

'*Five on Kirrin Island Again.*' Lucy squealed with excitement when she spied the Enid Blyton novel. 'And an embroidery set – look at the little bobbins of coloured cotton! This must be for you, Evie.' Evie raised an eyebrow but said nothing. Her sister certainly knew her own priorities when she said; 'I haven't read this one, I love *The Famous Five*. Evie, can we have a dog like Timmy?'

Evie was glad the child did not dwell on yesterday's terrible drama, thankful for her resilience. Reaching into the box Jack took out a box of charcoals and a drawing pad. Taking a sharp breath, he gave a low whistle. 'Well, would you look at that. Now aren't they a sight for aching eyes?'

'Do you still draw, Jack?' Evie smiled when he nodded, his eyes glowing. She must act normal, for all their sakes. Because no matter what the future held, she was the one who had to keep this little family together. 'Remember when you changed the pattern of the wallpaper in the parlour with a crayon?'

Jack thought for a moment and grimaced.

'I remember not being able to sit down for a good while.' His voice was taut, and Evie knew it was not the time for reminiscing.

'Here, you have them,' she said. Jack could draw anything he set his mind on. 'I was thinking a while back we should have pictures on the wall.'

'Aye,' Jack replied as Evie left the box and went to set the table for breakfast, 'we should have some pictures. Lucy, would you like me to draw something for you?'

'Timmy!' Lucy replied. 'A dog like Timmy.'

Listening to her siblings chattering in the kitchen, Evie put porridge oats into a pan and added cold water. It wouldn't take long to get breakfast ready. What if the body in the canal was her mother? Evie's heart hammered against her ribs. What if Mam was never coming back? The situation had never occurred to her before now.

Mam always came back. In her heart Evie knew the answer, but her thoughts refused to take in the enormity of her situation.

A dark cloud seemed to hover at her shoulders, and she had a sinking feeling that this time would be very different. However, for Lucy's sake she would keep her fears to herself. She didn't want her sister having any more nightmares.

'This fella is the spitting image of...' Jack stopped talking and put Lucy's novel, which she had just handed him, on the table as Evie brought the breakfast to the table. He realised that if he told his sisters that Timmy reminded him of Mr Skinner's dog, he would also have to explain where he was every day – instead of studying at school.

'Who does he remind you of, Jack?' Evie asked, pausing as she placed the breakfast tray beside the 'gift box'.

'Let's hope these weren't delivered by mistake,' Jack said, quickly, so as not to alert Evie. 'We'll be in a fine mess if somebody knocks claiming the box belonged to them.'

'No,' Evie said examining the box as she put it on the sideboard. 'It says *Kilgaren. 2 Reckoner's Row*.'

'We can't let good food go to waste,' Jack said. And Evie knew, in his world, everything was black or white. Nothing in between. *Please Lord, don't let Leo Darnel come and demand his payment*

* * *

'You've got to eat something, Evie,' Jack said through a thick slice of buttered toast from the loaf of bread that had been part of the 'gift box'. Evie shook her head, knowing nothing put her brother off his food, thank goodness, and who could blame him. Food was more scarce now than it was during the war, and Jack had a lot of filling out to do. But she couldn't stomach food just now.

'Don't worry, Evie, we won't always be poor.' Jack's voice was low, his eyes hooded, staring at his empty bowl so she could not gauge his expression. 'One day we'll be able to buy fresh chicken, plucked and cleaned ready to go straight into the oven whenever we please.'

Evie gave a small cynical laugh. 'I couldn't imagine being that rich, chicken is expensive.' She had eaten it only when Leo Darnel brought it in from who knew where?

'That was deeeelicious!' Lucy sat back in her chair and rubbed her stomach. 'Thank you, Evie.'

'Do you want more toast, or more porridge, Lucy?' Evie asked and smiled when Lucy shook her head and said, 'I'm as full as an egg, I think I'll draw.' Then looking at the box the child asked, 'Can we have chicken for tea tonight?'

'Of course you can, Lucy,' Evie said, glad they had something to look forward to, Tonight they would feast. Tomorrow she would make soup with the carcass.

She had seen Leo Darnel on the bridge, mingling with the crowd. Was the gift box a bribe, perhaps? To keep her mouth shut about all the things she knew. About him and his bent business dealings? Evie focused on the smoke stain above the fireplace.

She would have to keep her wits about her. Lucy would need watching.

The child had another nightmare, last night... And she was sure all this talk of a good shepherd was mere childish imagination. What if Darnel had sent someone to keep an eye on all of them? Questions. So many questions.

'What made you go down to the canal, Luce?' Evie's hands curled around her teacup to stop them from shaking as she watched Lucy shift in her chair.

'Bobby saw something in the water, and we went to have a little nose around.'

'It's not safe down there, you must promise me you will not go there again.' Lucy promised and Evie said, for good measure, to make sure her sister got the message: 'You never know, you might meet the bogeyman.'

'Been listening to Valentine Dyall on the wireless, Evie?' Jack smiled, at one with the world now his belly was full. 'You're as bad as she is. You know our Lucy's overactive imagination springs to attention every time she reads an Enid Blyton, and yours does too, when you listen to *The Man In Black*.'

'I'm trying to keep her safe the only way I know how, Jack.' Evie's lowered voice was determined, as Lucy sat on the sofa drawing. 'If I have to scare the living daylights out of her to save her life then I will.'

'I drew a picture of Timmy, too' Lucy said. 'Shall I show you?' Jack and Evie nodded, and she produced the unlined drawing book Jack had given her. Evie's mouth fell open with surprise when she saw a rumpled mongrel dog whose beautiful dark eyes seemed to twinkle on the page.

'Did you draw this, Lucy?' Evie asked, and Lucy nodded, her eyelids fluttering like butterfly wings in flight.

'I don't know where you two got the talent from, I can't draw breath.' They all laughed as she took the boiling kettle off the fire and went out to the back-kitchen to wash the dishes. Jack stood by her side, and wiped as she washed.

'There's something I have to tell you, Evie.' Jack's tone was sombre. 'I don't want you losing your rag over this, because I've decided.' He put down the faded tea towel, some parts of it so thin you could see through it.

'Here's another picture for you, Evie!' An excited sing-song giggle tucked into the nooks of Lucy's words and Evie wanted to tell her 'not now.' But Jack shook his head.

'I'll tell you later,' his expression told her – he didn't want Lucy to hear what he had to say.

'Righto,' Evie said drying her hands, 'let's have a look at what you've done, Luce.' What was so important that Jack wanted it kept secret? Taking hold of Lucy's drawing, every nerve, every muscle, every sinew in her body jarred as panic screamed through her veins.

'He's my good shepherd,' Lucy said innocently.

* * *

'If Rene drowned, her lungs would be full of water. Her body would have floated to the top, and she would have been discovered before the water froze over.' Angus said. His words were low in the telephone box. 'As it is, there was no water in her lungs. She died elsewhere, and her body placed in the water later.'

* * *

Connie remembered that freezing night when the first snow came. 'One minute, Rene was here, dancing with a Yank and having a good time,' her voice cracked. 'Then, when I looked for her to come and help behind the bar, she'd left.'

'I'm just going to inform them,' Angus said. In his professional capacity, he had given the same news to many people. However, this case was too close to home.

'At this hour?' Connie looked at the clock. It had gone midnight. Angus nodded. 'Then I will come with you.'

'Was that the night she died do you think?' Connie asked Angus as they left the tavern.

'We can pinpoint it to that night because it was the night the canal froze over.'

He had his eye on the target. But couldn't let the Kilgarens know he was lodging in a back-street boozer to gain evidence, until his suspect was hooked. Nor could he risk Mim finding out he was a detective, because, as sure as eggs made omelettes, his main source of information would clam up and ship him out if she knew who he really was.

'Poor Evie,' Connie whispered as tears flowed. 'Orphaned and left to bring up two kids. She's barely a kid herself.'

* * *

Evie felt her pulse quicken when there was a firm ran-tan on the front door. Jack went to answer it and when he came back into the kitchen accompanied by Connie and Angus. Evie noticed Connie's smudged mascara and wondered if she had been crying. And the strangest thing, Angus was holding her hand.

'What's the matter?' Evie asked. 'Come in, come in' She stood aside, holding the door open to allow Connie and Angus into the narrow hallway, outside the rain was drizzling down.

'We've got something to tell you, Evie.' Connie's voice was low and cracked with emotion. Evie knew immediately they weren't here on a social visit. Connie could barely look at her while Angus removed his trilby and seemed to be guiding her towards the kitchen.

'I'm sorry to have to tell you this.' His voice sombre, Angus stood below the gas mantle in the centre of the room, his full six feet two inches casting dark shadows on the wall as Connie reached for his hand once more. 'The body in the water was your mother.'

Tears were running freely down Connie's attractive face, now red and blotchy, and all Evie could think was, did she have enough coppers for the gas meter? She didn't speak for a moment, remembering that grey, distended... thing that was pulled out of the water. It didn't look human. How could it possibly be her mother?

'No, it couldn't be,' Evie sounded very matter-of-fact and spoke to Connie like she was a child. 'You see, Mam always comes back.' Evie saw Connie grip Angus' hand, and that one small gesture sent a hammer blow to her stomach – her legs weren't strong enough to hold her. Someone had sucked the air out of her lungs, and she was gasping.

Her life had changed in the short time since she opened the front door! She lost track of what was being said to her. Bewildered by the shocking finality of her mother's death.

'I'm fine,' Evie said eventually, heading to the scullery, and Connie followed her automatically filling the kettle at the copper tap.

She must keep going. Act normal. For the kids' sake. She could hear Angus talking to Lucy in the next room. Connie was talking too, but Evie couldn't make sense of the words. She felt ice seize the core of her body and she began to shake. Jack put his arm around her. She was not fine. Nothing would ever be the same again.

'You're strong enough for everybody, Evie.' Connie's words were meant to soothe her. Evie knew that. But they didn't. Instead, in that moment, she knew all her hopes and dreams of bettering herself and getting out of the backstreets had suddenly exploded into smithereens. She had other, more permanent responsibilities now.

'Lucy needs you to be strong,' Jack said gently.

'I know,' Evie whispered, 'and I'll never let her down. You can depend on me.' But who did she have to depend on?

'The authorities are carrying out a full investigation,' Connie said, taking over making the tea. 'But between me and you, going by the marks around her neck, your mam's death was no accident.'

'I would never have expected Mam to fall in the water, drunk,' Evie felt stunned, hearing the words said out loud. 'She could take her drink – she used to say she had hollow legs.'

Connie, the feisty landlady who could clear the bar as good as any man, was dabbing her tear-filled eyes. Jack went back into the other room and Evie suddenly felt the need to know everything. Every little detail.

'Please Connie, I need to know. Tell me.' Evie asked the woman who had become a good friend. Connie nodded her head.

'But please don't say a word about Angus,' Connie said, 'especially not to Mim.'

'I won't. I know how important he is to you.' Evie took a deep breath. 'What a bloody mess.'

* * *

Mim, stirring her morning cup of tea and still in her tartan housecoat, heard a heavy ran-tan on the side door. She hadn't had time to take her curlers out before Ada Harris ran in with the news.

'Have you heard the latest!' Ada was breathless, as if she had run all the way. Mim nodded to the straight-backed chair as she poured her friend a cup of tea, noting there was no sign of an injured ankle.

'Angus told us all about it,' Mim said, aloof. 'He knows about these things, on account of being in insurance. He'd seen the body and everything.' *So stick that in your pipe and smoke it, Ada Harris.* 'Those poor Kilgaren kids are orphans now,' Mim said before she passed on all the gory details, adding a few more for good measure.

'Strangulated only yards from her own front door,' Ada had a faraway look in her eyes, imagining the scene. *Trust bloody Mim to get the news first.*

'The body was quite emancipated,' Mim said, thrilled she had surpassed the local gossip.

'Well, it would be, wouldn't it?' Ada said, the edges of her thin lips puckering in disgust knowing Mim would milk this latest news for all it was worth.

* * *

Don't faint, Evie thought, resting a freshly cut slice of bread on the fire fender with a toasting fork. She had never fainted in her life, but when her skin prickled with clammy heat, and her vision darkened she feared losing control.

'Aren't you having any?' Jack asked when she gave him and Lucy their supper.

'I'm not hungry,' Evie said. Connie had dipped in and out all day, making sure they were all coping.

'You must eat, Evie. It doesn't matter how upset you are, you must try to get something down. An empty sack won't stand.'

'I'm fine,' Evie said, 'don't you worry about me.'

Evie watched Lucy finish her supper of buttered toast and hot malted milk, her young eyes growing heavy as they gazed into the flickering flames of the coal fire, and Evie knew she could never, would never desert her family. These two youngsters were the most important people in her world. Ambition came a poor second to the wellbeing of her family.

In no time at all Lucy was asleep. Connie had suggested sending Lucy next door, to her mother. Mim loved company and would squeeze every last drop of information out of the child by way of innocent conversation. But she wanted Lucy here, by her side, tonight.

'Murdered? Holy mother of God!' Jack's handsome face drained to ashen when they discussed the news.

'They think so' Evie said, still hardly able to believe it herself. 'I know, she might not have been the best mother in the world, but she didn't deserve to die the way she did.' Evie said, her throat tightening, and the tears that stung the back of her eyes finally rolled down her cheeks. Swallowing hard, Evie knew she had to be strong for the kids. They had been through so much.

25

The only thing Danny Harris longed to do when he lined the street with other members of the local community, was take the awful pain from Evie's heart. He watched as she and her younger siblings followed their mother's hearse the short distance to Saint Patrick's church.

Everybody in the surrounding area of the dock road had turned out to say their final goodbye, but one thing still troubled Danny, and it had done so since he heard the news of this woman's tragic death. He could not be certain, but he was as near as damn it sure he had recognised the man who was with Rene on the night she died.

Evie didn't know what she would have done without Connie these last few weeks. Her friend had taken on a new vitality, making copious cups of tea for neighbours who popped in to make sure her and the kids were managing after the terrible news, and the ensuing funeral, which Evie could only cope with by concentrating on Lucy and Jack.

The whole of Reckoner's Row turned out, and every house paid their respects by keeping their curtains closed until after the funeral at Saint Patrick's Catholic Church on a gloriously sunny April morning. Evie was relieved when the church roof did not collapse on her mother's coffin, as Rene had always said it would. The church was packed. Some had come to support Evie, Jack and Lucy. Some – like Ada Harris – had come in case they missed something. And one in particular, whom Evie was totally unaware of, stood at the back of the church and watched...

* * *

The news of Rene's demise was the sole topic of local conversation in the Tram Tavern. And Mim, who had taken over the tavern in her daughter's temporary absence, shared a running commentary of events that proved so popular, the takings over the bar escalated at a rate of knots.

* * *

Evie managed a weak smile. Connie was the tonic she didn't know she needed.

'Don't worry about your tea and sugar ration,' Connie said filling another plate with ham sandwiches. 'Everybody has brought something to add to the table, and a little extra to help out.'

'I don't know what I'd do without you over these past few weeks, Connie.' Evie gave a tight smile. She hadn't cried today.

'That's what us women do, love,' Connie answered in her no-nonsense way. 'We roll up our sleeves and we get stuck in.'

It was another couple of hours before everybody had either drifted off to their own home or had carried on to the tavern.

'This is the first time the house has been empty,' Evie sighed, glad of a bit of peace to gather her thoughts. She was glad Mam had a good turn-out. There had been no funeral for her father, just a mention in Sunday Mass.

'Lucy is going back to school tomorrow,' Evie told Connie as they sipped a cup of freshly made tea. 'I want to keep things as normal as possible.' Her sister needed something to concentrate on. Not that Lucy would see it that way. 'She's certainly enjoying the attention, and the kindness of neighbours,' Evie said. 'She hasn't been affected by Mam's death the way...' Evie's chin wobbled and tears stung her eyes. It didn't seem right that the girl didn't grieve her own mother.

'I'm not one to speak ill of those who can't answer back,' said Connie, 'but she didn't know Rene that well. You have been more of a mam to her.'

'Everybody has been so kind,' Evie said. She had discovered the people of Reckoner's Row were not the accusing, unfriendly gossipmongers who had nothing better to do than show their contempt for the Kilgarens, as her mother had led her to believe. They showed their concern in lots of different ways. Even in their own time of need. Each morning, she would find a loaf on the step, or a pint of milk, a pan of soup – and never a hint of who had left them. Helping out like she was one of their own.

'Well, I'll let you get on,' Connie said, finishing her tea, 'you must want a bit of privacy. I'll get back to the tavern and see what Mim's up to.'

'Thanks for everything, Connie.' Evie gave Connie a hug and said again, 'I don't know what I would have done without you.'

'Same as always, I expect,' Connie said, heading towards the front door with Evie following behind. 'You'd have coped.'

'I'm not so sure about that,' Evie said. 'I still have to find out who left the gift box.' She waved to Mrs Evans from number six who called up the street.

'There're rabbits in the butchers, Evie, do you want me to pick you one up?'

'No thanks, Mrs Evans, we're having corned-beef hash tonight.' Evie smiled when her neighbour nodded and continued on her way. She saw Angus rounding the corner and Connie went to meet him.

Evie was glad she had some time to mull things over. Everything had been so hectic of late, she felt things were beginning to slip. And she still hadn't found out what their Jack was up to.

'Come here,' Angus looped his arm for Connie to link him. 'Any news?' he asked, and Connie shook her head, saying nothing as they sauntered the short distance to the tavern.

'Do you fancy a little walk?' Angus looked straight ahead, not wanting to break their tenuous link only to see Connie consumed by a hoard of prying drinkers in the tavern. He saw her nod out of the corner of his eye and they continued on passed the tavern and up the road toward the bridge.

'Tell you what,' he said a short while later, squeezing her arm closer to his body, 'what do you say we get some fish and chips for supper?'

'If the chippy's still open,' Connie said realising she hadn't eaten since midday, 'I'd love some.' A cosy supper with Angus, and her mother downstairs in the bar sounded just the ticket.

She and Angus had not spent time alone since that wonderful night they went dancing. Angus held her in his arms as they danced closely together, and for all Connie knew, there might not have been another person in the ballroom.

Over the last few weeks she had grown fond of the Scotsman

and she would be sorry when he had to leave, which was one reason she did not want to get too close. However, what she wanted and what she longed for were two different things.

When they entered the warm, steamed-up interior of the chip shop, the delicious aroma of cooked chips made Connie's stomach growl. She hadn't realised she was so hungry, and she couldn't wait to get back home with Angus.

As they walked arm-in-arm, turning back into Reckoner's Row, Connie felt her good humour take a dive when she saw Ada Harris hobbling towards them. That was all Connie needed. When Ada saw her on the arm of the good-looking Scotsman, it wouldn't take her long to blab to Mim.

'Hiya, Connie,' Mrs Harris called from the other side of the road, her smug tone letting Connie know it was too late to worry now, 'and hello, Mr McCrea. Just out for your nightly stroll?'

Connie and Angus answered in unison. 'Hello, Mrs Harris!'

'No phone calls tonight, Mr McCrea?'

'Not tonight, Mrs Harris,' Angus called back.

'Nosey cow,' Connie muttered. 'If you ever need information and Mim's disappeared off the face of the earth, Ada's your woman, she will fill in the details. The two of them would put you lot to shame.' Connie laughed, and her steady pace was a sign that, for the first time since Rene had been found, she could relax a little. Life in Reckoner's Row had returned to its usual hubbub of activity. It didn't take long for people to get back to normal. The war years had given them a determination to get on with life, tomorrow could take care of itself.

Angus hugged her linked arm close to his body again and a piercing thrill caused Connie's chin to raise higher, her backbone straighter. That one small gesture changed everything. The air seemed charged with his presence, fizzing with life and laughter.

His involvement in her life was the start of something. She

would even go so far as to admit she had fallen head over heels in love with this man. And though she didn't want to think of it now, she would miss him when he went away. Nothing would ever be the same.

'No doubt she will break her skin to get to tell Mim what she saw tonight.'

'Is that such a bad thing?' It wasn't what Angus said, but the way he said it that caused an unsettling quiver to take over her body.

'Shall we let Mim know we're back?' Angus asked, heading towards the door of the tavern.

'I'll put her supper by the fire to keep warm.' Connie felt reckless. 'Just the two of us tonight, hey, Angus?' Her eyes lingered on his for a moment longer than was necessary. And she could tell, he knew what she meant. As secrets purred like ghosts looking down on the living, Angus quietly closed the side door. Tonight was theirs alone.

* * *

'What did I tell you?' Connie said later, after checking on Mim who went to bed with a headache immediately after locking up the tavern. 'I've left two aspirin and a glass of water on her bedside table. They're still there and she's fast asleep.' She felt so happy. She and Angus had spent a lovely night together. 'Is there anything I can get you before I turn in?' Connie asked, and he looked up at her from the sofa, his eyes tender.

'Just you,' he said patting the space beside him on the sofa, and maybe a brandy to finish off the night.'

'Why did you come to live here in Liverpool?' Connie asked after settling down beside him. There was just enough light from the fire to see the faraway look in his eyes.

'For the excitement,' he said rolling the brandy glass between the palm of his hands. 'And my wife.' This latest piece of information brought Connie up sharp. She hadn't expected him to discuss his wife tonight.

'You must have loved her very much,' Connie said, covering up a covetous stab of something that had hovered in her heart since the first time she met him.

'I still do,' Angus said. 'She was everything.'

'She was a lucky woman.' The words were out of her mouth before Connie could stop them. Angus said nothing as his tender gaze turned into something deeper and held her captive.

He put his arm around her and gathered her close. The intimate gesture was the most natural thing in their world of late, and Connie burrowed into his arms, her yielding lips waking a hungry passion that had for so long lay dormant...

'I'm the luckiest man alive to have found you,' Angus murmured through his kisses. His deep voice low and husky as his fingertips lightly following the outline of her face, her neck, her arm...

Connie's sensual response flooded her body at his touch. And her breathing quickened, surrendering to delicious shivers. Longing to feel his skin on hers. Connie drew him towards her bedroom, knowing tonight would be special for both of them...

27

'It's not easy settling back into civvy street, but you'll get used to it,' Angus said amiably to Danny Harris, keeping his eyes and ears open for any clues that might help in the capture of the warehouse robbers or Rene Kilgaren's murderer.

'I don't fancy working in Uncle's yard forever, I want to buy my own wagon,' Danny said after taking his first sip. 'But since Da's been laid off the dock, Ma depends on me to bring some money in.' Owning his own business had always been a dream of Danny's, but it looked like he would have to put it on a back burner for the foreseeable.

'Civvy street not the place you remembered?' Angus grinned, standing at the end of the bar where he could observe unfettered.

'You've hit the nail on the bonce, old son!' Danny said. He loved his mam, he really did. He also loved treacle tart, but he was sure he would get fed up with it if he ate it every single day. 'I want to be king of the open road in my long-distance lorry. See the countryside. Get the soot out of my lungs. Be my own man. No ties. No restrictions... But Ma has other ideas.' There was a lull in the conversation while the two men cogitated, lost in their own private thoughts. Angus enjoying the new closeness he and Connie shared and...

'Have you seen Evie?' Danny said, breaking into his thoughts and Angus told him she was in earlier mopping floors and emptying ashtrays. Danny looked troubled and it wasn't long before Angus found out why.

'Evie's really good with people, you know. Friendly, without being forward. There's always sparkle when she's around. She listens, you see.' A slow smile spread across his handsome, weathered features. 'She has many attractions, don't you think, Angus. A beautiful face, a cracking figure and a fine pair of legs.'

'Not that you've taken much notice?' Angus gave a low rumbling laugh. Danny lifted his glass as if he would drink from it, and then put it back on the bar.

'A fine girl is Evie,' Angus said. Danny looked as if he had something else on his mind, and then Angus realised what it was.

'D'you think she'll let me take her to the pictures, Angus?' To hell with what his mother said about her mother's carry-on.

'I'm sure a night out would do her good after what she's been through. But what about Susie?'

'Susie's just a friend of my sister's,' Danny said. The drink was giving free reign to his tongue. 'Not being there for Evie, when she had to go through the horror of identifying her own mother. I can think of nothing more tragic.' He lowered his head and was quiet for a while. 'I should have asked her if she wanted support. I know that. We're friends and that's what friends do isn't it?' Angus nodded but doubted Danny noticed. 'She'll think I don't care. But I do.'

Angus had never seen Danny like this; he didn't seem the kind to wear his heart on his sleeve, though he suspected he felt things deeply. Danny was one of those men who didn't think it was appropriate to bear their soul to an all and sundry.

'Since the canal incident,' Angus said referring to the discovery of Rene Kilgaren's body, 'Evie's had more friends than she knows what to do with.'

'I only spoke to her for a short while after the funeral,' Danny said. 'I should have asked if she needed anything.'

'With hindsight we are all wise, and she would probably have said no, you know how independent she is.'

'Evie was the first to offer her condolences and her help when Ma's brother, uncle Bill, died. So why couldn't I do the same for her?' Danny looked at Angus like he had the answer, but all Angus could do was let him talk. Then, Danny said something that really caught Angus' attention.

'It struck me,' Danny said, 'I might have been one of the last people to see Evie's mother alive. I feel guilty for not telling anybody... but, you see...'

'What's that?' Angus was all ears. They say men speak the truth when they are in their cups, and Danny had certainly had a few tonight. So now was the time to pay attention. 'What do you mean?'

'I heard Rene arguing with a man,' Danny said. 'Fierce it was, too. I'd just said a stiff goodbye to Pa, who was awkward, as usual and you know what Ma's like.' Angus nodded. It was common knowledge that Ada Harris worshipped the ground her soldier son walked on. 'Pa's more reserved. Like me.'

'You heard Rene arguing?' Angus urged Danny to continue, growing impatient for information, he couldn't believe his luck. He didn't want Danny meandering down the scenic route.

'I was returning to barracks after a forty-eight-hour leave, halfway up the stone steps... I heard raised voices under the bridge.' He swilled his drink around the bottom of the glass, but he drank none of it. 'I remember slowing down, in case she needed help, but didn't want to butt in, it sounded like a lover's tiff.

But...' he shrugged, 'I didn't think much of it, I was concentrating on getting to Lime Street to catch the last train. Memories of that night have niggled inside my head like burrowing woodworm since they fished Rene out of the canal,' Danny said. 'Something I can't put my finger on... I hadn't given the canal incident any more thought once I caught the bus into town... You don't mind me telling you all this, do you Angus?' Danny asked, wiping his mouth with the back of his hand. He liked the genial Scotsman – well, everybody did, he was a good man who got along with everyone. Angus always had time for folk. 'I had to tell someone. I couldn't go to the law with a suspicion. And when I saw you in here tonight, I knew you were just the man who'd understand.'

'I'm always here to listen, Danny.' Especially when it was in the public interest.

'I didn't know the voices at first, the hailstones battering the cobbles muffled them,' he said, 'but then, as the hail slowed, I recognised Rene's voice echoing under the bridge.'

Hardly able to believe his luck, Angus quietly sipped his pint, standing at the bar, nodding in all the right places.

'Rene's words were slurred, after a drinking session in here,' he said. 'I remember her words.' Danny imitated the woman's high-pitched voice. '"*You stay well away from my kids, they don't need nothing from you, and I don't want no police sniffing 'round my 'ouse!*"' But this is the baffling bit. The man who was with her said, "*If the police turned up, they wouldn't be looking for me.*" He sounded like he was trying to keep his temper in check, you know?'

Angus nodded even though he wasn't too sure what Danny was alluding to.

'Or that might be my imagination, considering what's happened, I'm not too sure... But it's what he said next that baffled me even more. He said, "*I squared that when I got back. I went to the police and they told me I had nothing to answer for, nothing to fear..."'*

'Nothing to fear?' Angus asked, adrenaline pumping through his body. 'What do you suppose he meant by that?' He didn't want to sound too eager, but this was getting interesting.

'Rene sounded angry, called him a coward,' said Danny. *"Believe me, Rene"* he said, *"I'm not a coward! And if you call yourself any kind of a mother you would be with them now – not making a fool of yourself – not throwing your legs up to any passing serviceman who'd look twice."'*

'What happened then?' Angus asked. He was taking nothing for granted at this stage of the investigation, but this latest turn sounded very promising.

'I heard a slap. And then everything sort of went quiet except for shuffling.'

'Shuffling?' Angus asked. He didn't want to lead Danny to say something he might not have heard, but he had to be sure he understood what he meant.

'Yeah, you know like... I dunno, feet scuffling the canal bank... well, groaning, I suppose.'

'Groaning?' The young man looked nervous and he shifted, looking around the bar, making sure he was not being overheard, his neck turning as red as a cock's comb. 'You know... groaning. Like they were... making up... You know.'

'Ahh,' Angus said when the penny dropped. Danny might seem like a man of the world with his cheeky banter after two pints, but he was as inadequate about discussing *that kind of thing* as any other man. 'Get a good earful, did you?'

'Here! None o' that.' Danny's colour crept further up his throat. 'The traffic was busy, so it took ages to get across the bridge. I heard a loud splash in the water. Then the man stormed off. He was halfway down the towpath before I could cross over the road, I could see him.'

'Did you recognise him?' Angus asked, his heart beating faster. Danny Harris could be a key witness to Rene Kilgaren's demise.

'It was dark, there was a power-cut, and though there was a full moon it kept going behind the clouds,' Danny said, 'I was on the top of the bridge, looking over, but couldn't make out if she followed him because there was a lull in the traffic by then.'

'Did you hear a scream, or a cry for help?' Angus lifted his empty pint glass, offering to buy Danny another, not interrupting.

'When I got over the other side, there was no sign of anybody. The water was calm... there was nobody in sight... I thought I imagined the splash.'

'If you could hear it over sound of traffic...' It must have been a big splash, thought Angus.

'I had to run for bus into town. Otherwise I'd have missed my train and been put on a charge for getting back to barracks late... And, if truth be told,' Danny said, 'that's the reason I haven't been to see Evie. I felt ashamed for not doing more to help.'

'It's not your fault. You weren't to know,' Angus said, eager to get more information. 'Could the man under the bridge have been Darnel?' Danny shrugged. Sitting at the end of the bar, he looked like he had lost a shilling and found a tanner.

'Nah.' He shook his head, 'Don't think so. He was down the dock road, helping himself to merchandise, waiting to be off-loaded from a warehouse onto a waiting ship, according to local sources.'

'Local sources?' Angus looked puzzled and Danny tapped his nose.

'Like the three wise monkeys... I see all, hear all, say nothing. Know what I mean?' Angus nodded, realising the shutters were coming down. Danny had said his piece and there was no use asking for more information.

'Terrible business,' Angus said. 'I feel so sorry for Evie and those poor kids.' He had been in the game long enough to know when he had outstayed his welcome. He had gathered a lot of information tonight and mustn't be greedy. 'Aye. Well, that's me done,' Danny said, downing what remained of his Dutch courage, and deciding to go and see Evie. 'I'll bid you good night.'

'Mind how you go,' Angus called as Danny, hands in pocket, wended his way out of the bar. Now it was time to see Connie. Mend fences. Make love.

* * *

Alerted by the knock at the front door, Evie seized the poker.

'Who's that at this hour, Jack?' She didn't like opening the door once she had locked up for the night.

'Put that down, you'll do someone a mischief.' Jack took the poker from her hand. 'I'll go.'

'Be careful,' Evie whispered, feeling her heart swell with pride.

'Like you said, things will change around here, and one of them is me taking more responsibility, not putting everything on your shoulders.' Evie was genuinely relieved, realising that since they had found their mother's body, Jack had gained a maturity that wasn't there before. She listened, assuring Lucy that everything would be fine when she heard voices at the door. One voice belonged to Jack, but the other one was not so clear.

'Come in, come in,' she heard Jack say. Lucy, curled up on the couch, was reading an American comic that Bobby Harris had lent her earlier.

'Go right in, she won't mind,' Evie heard Jack say and when

the kitchen door opened, she could have knocked their Jack's head off, for letting Danny Harris see her looking like this! Her hands, red raw from scrubbing the tavern and keeping this place spotless, went to her hair. Coiled into Catherine wheels and secured with hair grips, a turbaned scarf covered her hair.

Her face was pale, devoid of lipstick or rouge, and her old frock was hidden by a full-length wraparound pinny. *Making do* wasn't a national duty in this house, it was a way of life!

'Hiya, Evie, I hope you don't mind me barging in like this,' Danny said, wringing his cap. feeling as if he had a pond of frogs jumping about inside him. A feeling he had never experienced before.

'It's a bit late,' Evie said, feeling irritated, 'couldn't it wait until morning?' A knock on the front door at this hour was rarely good news. Look at the state of him, she thought. Drunk as a Lord.

Danny perched on the edge of the sofa, aware that he was the centre of their unwavering attention. 'I thought I'd better pop in to see if... to say how... to just...'

Evie sighed. Some men just couldn't show their sensitivity when they're sober, she thought, some had to get a few pints down them to loosen their tongue.

'I know.' She gave him a tight-lipped smile. 'We've had that many people knocking to offer their sympathy, haven't we Jack?' Jack nodded, amused at his sister's fluttering hands, and inability to keep still.

'I didn't mean to intrude,' Danny said, making to get up from the sofa. 'It was a mistake coming so late.' He had nothing to offer in the way of sympathetic words and he wanted so to hold her, comfort her, tell her everything would be all right.

'Don't mind us,' Evie said, 'take us as you find us. Isn't that right, Jack?' Jack nodded. He had never seen their Evie's face go so red before.

'Would you like a cup of tea? We have nothing stronger.' Not that she would give it to him if she had any alcohol in the house, he looked as if he'd had enough already.

'Tea's fine,' Danny said. 'No milk, two sugars, please.'

'You'll have one and like it! We're not made of sugar!' Evie's eyes widened.

'One's plenty,' Danny answered, chastised. He loved her feistiness, it reminded him of a lioness protecting her young. Moments later, she offered him a cup of tea from the brown muggen pot on the side of the range, waiting to hear what he had to say.

Danny could not blurt out what he knew. Not now. Not in front of the young ones.

'I was wondering if it is too soon to ask if you fancied going to the pictures one night?'

'The pictures?' Evie felt as if someone had hit her with a door! They had found her mother floating in the local canal – almost outside their own house – and he wanted to know if she would go to the pictures! The cheek of him.

'No thank you,' she said curtly. She had never been on a date in her life, and now was certainly not the time to be thinking of such things.

'Someone in the tavern said *It Always Rains On Sundays* is on at The Commodore.'

Evie could not believe Danny asked her out, especially at a time like this. And who wanted to see a film about the weather anyway!

'I'll think about it,' she said. And for the first time in a long while, Evie had something to smile about.

28

'Over my dead body!' declared Ada Harris, the following day, when her son announced that he intended to take Evie to the pictures.

'I'll make sure you get a good send-off,' Danny said over the top of the evening newspaper. Blimey! Anyone would think he'd just told his mother he would join the foreign legion, instead of asking a girl out.

'Isn't it bad enough she's stolen my job?' Ada's voice was high-pitched as she cleared the table. 'Now she's stealing my son, as well! You must need your head read.'

'Ma don't say things like that, it's not nice.' Danny's calm tone was determined. Evie had agreed to go to the pictures with him and he had howled with laughter when she said she wasn't struck on watching a religious film about the weather. Her face had gone a lovely shade of pink when he explained it was about an escaped convict who hid in his old flame's corrugated air-raid shelter in the back yard, but she is a married woman now, and....'

Evie had a good long think, and Danny recalled gazing at her. Enjoying the moment. Although, she hadn't looked too sure when he first asked her out, she seemed glad when her brother Jack said a night out would do her the world of good. Danny was relieved when she agreed to think about it.

Getting up from the chair, Danny looked out of the window at the dark sky, lit by thousands of tiny stars, all signs of snow had disappeared, and everywhere was shiny. He'd show Evie a good time, he thought as his mother came back into the room.

'I'm not keen on that picture.' Ada said. 'It's pictures like that that give people funny ideas.'

Danny rolled his eyes heavenward, knowing his mam had some funny ideas. But he was flummoxed as to knowing what they were. 'It's a good thing I didn't ask you, isn't it?'

'I only said she could have my job until I'm better, as a favour to Connie,' Ada said, knowing it was Connie who had suggested taking the girl on. 'What's in the cat is in the kittens, that's what I say. That mother of hers was a trollop of the lowest order.'

'Well, I wouldn't know about that because she won't go to the pictures with me.' Danny decided to keep his mother in the dark with regard to Evie. He would bide his time, wait until Evie was ready to socialise.

'Susie Blackthorn's a nice girl, she'll go with you,' his mother said.

* * *

'You do me a favour, and I will do favours back.'

Evie, on her way home from queuing for an hour outside the butchers on the top road, heard voices coming from the haulage yard. Not one to pry, she thought she recognised Leo Darnel's voice, but she couldn't be sure. If it was him, he was up to no good. She had heard his smarmy tone many a time when he was trying to persuade her mother to hide loot in the cellar.

'I'll not be asking for any favours!' There was no doubting the second voice. Evie recognised her brother's Celtic lilt. However, she stopped herself from bouldering through the closed wooden gates, knowing if their Jack was up to no good, she wanted to get her facts straight before she tackled him about it.

'Easy boy. Watch who you're talking to.' Evie knew she was right when Leo Darnel's words took on a steely tone. Peering through a gap in the fence she could see Darnel circling her brother, and it took every ounce of her determination to stay put, and not storm into the yard. Jack had been flashing the cash about, coming over all good-fellow-well-heeled. And now she knew why. He was being lured into the underworld of Leo Darnel. Evie could hear Darnel's oily tone and it turned her stomach.

'I look at you, and I see myself. I was once a boy like you. I had nothing.' He fingered the shining horse brasses hanging on a nail. 'Look at me now,' he said slipping his fingers inside his hand-made cashmere overcoat, and Evie's body tensed. Judging the way Darnel was talking, it didn't seem likely he knew who Jack was. But why was her brother here, in the haulage yard? The sign over the wooden gates said Skinner and Sons, but was that a cover for Darnel's lawless activities?

Evie's heart raced with fright when she saw Darnel put his hand into the inside pocket of his coat. But her fear turned to anger when, instead of the gun, Darnel produced a wad of white five- pound notes, as thick as the length of her thumb.

'Now I've got all this.' Darnel fanned his face with the money, looking pleased with himself. His demonstration had the desired effect when Jack's jaw dropped. His eyes wide. 'I used my head, see,' Darnel said. 'Kept my mouth shut and my eyes open.'

'Good for you,' Jack said, and Evie was relieved when her brother found his voice. She could tell he was impressed, but his initial astonishment had waned by the shrug of his skinny shoulders.

'My family came to the dockside when I was a just a boy,' Darnel continued. 'Didn't speak the language. Treated like shit. I was nothing. You hear me? Nothing. Like you.'

That's your opinion, Evie thought, but she was glad Jack knew better than to cheek the villain.

'But now it's different. I am somebody. I have my own place, my own business. I have ten handmade suits in my wardrobe...'

'Good for you.' There was no mistaking the sardonic tone in Jack's voice.

'But I don't forget where I came from. The River Mersey flows through my veins... I could use a boy like you.'

'Not interested,' Jack sneered. 'If I need something, I'll get it for myself. I'm in no hurry.'

'You want to kiss the dockside goodbye?' Darnel pushed back the dark fedora, his hand in the pocket of his tailored trousers. 'I can help you brush the dirt of the streets from your feet.' Evie saw Jack hesitate before answering. As if he was mulling over Darnel's offer. Her heart cried out. *Don't listen to him, Jack!*

'Doing what?' Jack's glare was unwavering, and Evie felt the tension, so thick she could slice it and serve it with chips.

'Is there somewhere we can talk?' Darnel asked, 'I don't like to discuss business in the street.'

'I'm fine out here, Mr...?' Jack said, but Darnel did not answer. 'I didn't catch your name, but I never forget a voice... We've met somewhere before.'

'I doubt it,' Darnel said. 'I've been away since...'

'Since?' Jack was not as green as the fields he left behind in Ireland.

'Christmas.' Darnel lit a big fat cigar and flicked the spent match across the yard. 'Business.'

'Doing what?' Jack asked. That voice was unmistakable. And he knew where he had heard it before.

'This and that.' Darnel was giving nothing away, he noticed. 'Can you drive?'

'I can learn.' Jack knew he was not mistaken. He recalled that night on the dock when he was collecting kindling for the fire. He knew the voice. But this fella didn't look like the one with the gun.

'Come around to my yard. Tomorrow. Two o'clock.'

'No thanks,' Jack put his hands in his pocket, and kicked a stone with the side of his foot. 'I'll give it a miss if it's all the same to you.'

Evie's heart beat so fast she could hardly breathe. Her brother was a good lad. He wouldn't get mixed up with the likes of Darnel. He had more sense than that.

'You could earn yourself more money than you've ever seen in your life.'

'I am my own man,' Jack answered, making Evie's heart sing. 'I won't be working for a man like you. I have no masters.'

'Fine words,' Darnel said, 'but you may rue the day you said that.'

'No, he won't,' Evie said, pushing open the wooden gates and confronting them. Jack spun around. She was proud of the way Jack had handled the situation and he wasn't stupid enough to join one of Darnel's dubious get-rich-quick capers. A fleeting spark of gratitude told Evie her brother was glad of the interruption.

'Evie. It's good to see you.' There was a glint of steel in Darnel's smarmy words, but Evie was passed caring. The thug did not scare her anymore. Not when he intended to drag her brother into his seedy world of greed and violence.

The thought of what Darnel was offering stiffened her backbone. Those days were over. Her brother would play no part in shady dealings. Jack would be somebody. The three of them – herself, Jack and Lucy – would hold their heads high, and gain the respect denied them by their mother's antics. It had been ten days since they had dragged her body from the canal.

Murdered, the coroner said. She glared at Darnel. Did he have something to do with her mam's death?

'You go home, Evie. I'll catch you up.' Jack held her determined gaze for a moment and Evie knew he was just as strong-minded as she was. However, she would not let him lose face in front of the spiv. 'I'll explain later.' Jack had something to tell her. He had a mature head on his shoulders. He'd do the right thing. She was sure.

'Don't be long,' she conceded. Understanding Jack's desire to show Darnel he was no pushover. Before she turned to leave, an old man in baggy, brown corduroy trousers, a leather waistcoat and a battered, moth-eaten felt hat appeared from the green wooden shed that had the word 'Office' painted in black on the door. He didn't look like he was in the mood for a chinwag.

'What's going on out here?'

'Who wants to know?' Evie eyed the old man who, she presumed, was one of Darnel's skivvies.

'I could ask the same of you, young lady,' the old man said, 'but I would be much more polite about it.' As he spoke, she noticed Leo Darnel slope from the stable yard and realised she might have made a mistake.

'Evie, go home,' Jack pushed the words through his teeth. 'You will get me the sack!'

'The...?' Evie looked at him, let the information sink into the jumbled thoughts racing through her head. 'How long have you...? Since when...?'

'I knew it was useless to think you would wait until I get home to explain.' Jack took a long deep breath and said, 'I've been helping Mr Skinner with the horses... I worked with horses back in Ireland. He offered me a job, full-time.'

'But what about your education? You have a few months to go.'

Jack nodded. 'Books and learning won't put a meal on the table, Evie. And I can't watch you struggle anymore.'

'But we're doing all right since I started cleaning in the pub,' Evie pleaded.

'Look,' Jack said, 'we can talk about this later. I've still got work to do.'

'You bet your life we will talk later,' Evie said, turning on her heel and heading home.

* * *

'I paid the rent, so there's no need to worry,' Jack said coming into the kitchen with his hands in the air.' Evie looked at her brother and didn't know whether to kiss him or bang his stupid head with the teapot! 'I want an explanation, Jack, and don't tell me not to worry – that makes things worse.' Over the next half hour, he came clean and told her he had no intentions of going back to school when he could earn money to help feed the family.

'But why didn't you say something. I've worried the guts out of myself, thinking you were in cahoots with Darnel.' Jack's eyebrows rose in surprise.

'That little weasel? The scourge of the dock road? The night-mare of the working man?'

'Don't let his stature fool you, Jack – he's five feet eight inches of pure evil.' Evie didn't take her eyes off her brother, her perse-vering glare driving home the intensity of her warning. 'But enough about him for now. Why you didn't tell me you had a job, I'll never know.'

'I thought you'd make me pack it in,' Jack said. 'I know how stubborn and independent you are. You would have struggled on regardless. Do you think those last few weeks in school would have made me the brains of Britain? They wouldn't.'

'But what about your future?' Evie asked. 'I don't want you sacrificing that to keep this family afloat.'

'I love working with the horses,' Jack said, 'it's one of the best jobs in the world. And you're only cleaning the pub until Mrs Harris' leg is better.'

Evie knew he was right. Yesterday, Ada Harris had come into the tavern. Although she was still hobbling on a stick, Mim's best friend did not hesitate to let it be known she would be back in her rightful place in next to no time. Evie knew it would force her to give up the work she and her family depended on so much.

'I wanted to take the worry from your eyes, so I did,' Jack said. Evie wondered how different their lives must have been out in the Irish countryside. He had often told her about the farm, saying that coming back to Liverpool was like walking smack-bang into a wall of noise and smoke and people – hundreds of people! It must have come as a shock, she thought, knowing for the past seven years they had become accustomed to clean air, green grass, and all the vegetables they could eat.

'I missed the routine of the stables when I came back here,' Jack said, breaking into her thoughts. 'But now, I intend to look forward not back. And all because the auld fella, Skinner, had the good sense to hire a first-class worker like me.' He flipped his thumbs into an imaginary waistcoat, wiggled his fingers in the style of Oliver Hardy and winked at Lucy who giggled.

Evie laughed. 'I don't know where you get your modesty from. I really don't. Does old man Skinner go out to the countryside much?' Evie asked, her eyes narrowing. Something occurred to her. If the old man didn't pay Jack for the bits of work he did before he took him on full-time, then how did he pay him? Jack wasn't the lad who would pull his tripe out for no reward. Jack nodded, and the knowing smile that crept over his face told its own story.

'He was the one who left the food parcels?' Evie said when the penny dropped.

'For sure, he delivers animal feed out Thornton way. And, seeing as he can't eat all the farmer's *donations*... Stuff that had gone over, or bruised, like...'

'Those vegetables looked perfect,' Evie cut in, before realising the true nature of the *donations*. The black market thrived not only in the towns and cities, she thought, but the countryside, too.

'He was glad to give it all to a deserving cause, he said,' Jack continued as if he hadn't heard her.

'Well, thank the Lord for Old Man Skinner,' Evie sighed. 'Those food parcels kept us from starvation many a time.' They had been left a couple of times a week of late.

'To be true – they did,' Jack nodded. However, he could not ignore that worm of guilt wriggling away inside him. Old Man Skinner also gave him the odd tanner here and there, and he – not being of the saintly variety – spent every penny on himself. He'd earned it. So why not? Sure, wasn't a man deserving of a treat after a hard day's work? But now he wished he had spent none of it. Evie was doing her best to keep this family together and there he was, spending money that could have taken the worry from her eyes.

'Oh, Jack! Come here...' Evie stood on her tip-toes and gave him a lung-emptying hug. 'You do not know how pleased I am!'

'Behave yourself, woman!' Jack gave an exaggerated gasp to

hide the creeping guilt growing heavy as a hundredweight of spuds, curling his shoulders. In that moment he promised himself that he would not be so grasping in future. His family needed him to be honest, and from now on, Jack decided, that's what he intended to be – God willing. 'So, when you've finished squeezing the living daylights out of me, I'd like to come up for some air.'

'What's happened?' Lucy asked. Her brother and sister were grinning like a pair of Cheshire cats and, for the first time since they had found her mother, everything seemed right with the world.

After tea there was a knock at the door and when Jack went to answer it, they surprised him to see Angus standing on the step. 'Hello, Angus, what brings you here? Come in.'

'I hope I'm not disturbing you; I've brought this back for Lucy.' When they got into the kitchen Angus unwrapped the frame he had promised Lucy. 'It will look nice hanging on the wall.'

'It'll be the first time anything has hung on the wall since Da was killed at sea,' Evie said, knowing her mother had never been partial to pictures or photographs cluttering up the place. But the gesture thrilled Lucy, now her drawing would take pride of place over the mantelpiece.

'That's a fine-looking frame, sir...' Lucy's clear Irish brogue was filled with wonder as she examined the whittled wood admiring Angus' handiwork, which even had real glass to protect her drawing from the smoke belching from the grate when the wind was high. They were so entranced by Angus' gift that nobody noticed Jack's deep-set, worried frown.

This is bad, he thought, seeing Lucy's drawing of her good shepherd for the first time. The face in the picture flashed into his memory but, like a dream he couldn't quite grasp, he needed to think. If he stared at it too much, the fleeting memory would disappear like a snowflake in sunshine. He couldn't look at it again. He *wouldn't* look at it again. The face brought back emotions long buried. Loud voices. Anger. Threats. Danger! Then it dawned on him. The man in the picture was the one who brought him home and dumped him in the freezing snow outside his own front door.

He was the man who shot him!

29

'No! He can't be,' Evie gasped. Lucy had gone to call for Bobby Harris and was well out of earshot. Jack lowered his head, to get a better look in his sister's tear-filled eyes.

'Evie, tell me. Who is he?' Evie took hold of Jack's hand, the way she did all those years ago when he and Lucy left for Ireland. The gesture told him to be strong.

'Lucy was just a babe in arms when he was killed.' Evie had taken little notice of the picture when she first saw it. She had too much on her mind. But now... the face was thinner. The hair sprinkled with flecks of white. The eyes were... The eyes brought back memories she had long since buried.

'Love... is a cold wind that blows nobody any good.' Her voice cracked. 'Those were his last words to me.' There was a lengthy pause when neither of them spoke. She had forgotten much about her father, except his aloof words, which now came back to haunt her.

Ever practical, she pulled a frayed handkerchief from the sleeve of her cardigan, wiped her eyes, blew her nose and said, 'Lucy must have seen a picture, somewhere...'

'Then how can you explain me seeing him?' Jack asked and for a moment, Evie didn't understand what he was talking about. Jack's words dawned on her, and she hoped she was wrong. The dock? The gunshot?

'Maybe after all the upset with Mam, you were mistaken?' She tried to make sense of it all. 'You were half-starved. Frozen to the bone. It was dark!' Her voice rose with each heightened explanation, until it reached a disbelieving squeak. 'How could you see who anybody was?'

'Since they found Mam, I've been trying to make sense of it all. I only managed a quick glimpse of the gunman. But it was enough...' Jack left the explanation hanging in mid-air. He had no wish to upset Evie any more than she had already been. He knew what he saw that night. And nothing or nobody would sway him to believe otherwise.

* * *

Connie was clearing the bar of the last few glasses when she stopped what she was doing.

'You're leaving?' she said simply when Angus came into the bar carrying his suitcase.

'Not yet. Tomorrow. Early,' Angus said. 'I can't say when I'll be back.' He was sitting on the stool Connie thought of as his own. She didn't ask where he was going. That was not fair. Because there were things that had to be kept secret because of his job, and she did not want to put him in the position of refusing to tell her. She always knew this day would come but that didn't make it any easier.

'I'll come back,' Angus said, not his usual chirpy self. Something was troubling him, she could tell. He hadn't said a word all evening. 'Of course you will.' Connie forced a smile. She didn't believe a word. This was their time and it was quickly slipping away.

Before he arrived, she was existing. She knew that now. Going through the motions of work and sleep. Putting up with everything her mother pushed her way and complying without complaint. So much wasted time...

Do this, Connie. Do that. Fetch this Connie. Did you get my wintergreen? Library book? Did you find yourself a life while you were at the shops? Don't find love, Connie! Don't leave me on my own!

She had given all of herself to Angus without a second thought. But now he was so distant. Preoccupied. He had lost interest. She wasn't naïve enough to think theirs would be the all-consuming romance of a lifetime. But she cared for Angus and thought he felt the same way for her. She loved everything about him. His company. His easy charm. He even flattered Mim's insatiable ego and lit up the room just by walking into it. For the first time in years she felt good about herself and gave thanks every day for having him in her life.

What she did not expect, was this creeping dread of the day when he would say goodbye forever. She was not the woman who threw herself at a man. There was a name for women like that. And she wasn't one. Quite the opposite. But Angus had woken something inside her that was more than desire. Optimism. Anticipation. Love. And most of all that inner strength that made anything, and everything, seem possible.

During the war, there were good-time girls. The ones who went for anything in trousers because their men were away so long and moved on to the visiting servicemen when they arrived.

Married or not. The women didn't care. They lived for today, it may be their last. All they wanted was to feel alive.

Connie watched from afar. Not passing judgement when the old women, such as Ada Harris, tut-tutted.

Nurses weren't allowed to wear powder and paint, so Mrs Harris *approved,* not that Connie needed her approval, and certainly never asked for it. But she was Mim's friend and self-styled housekeeper, which made Connie feel less guilty when, the first chance she got, she was posted overseas to nurse the troops.

But it wasn't all bombs and bullets. She had a good time too... *The divil makes work for idle hands, tra-laaa!* But Mim made her feel so guilty for going away and doing her duty. Cementing her into an honourable, soul-destroying situation where her long-suffering hypochondriac of a mother was the most important person in her own world.

Connie accepted her lot without complaint. She would like to think it would horrify Mim if she knew the emotional turmoil that she had foisted upon her. But she knew Mim was far too self-absorbed. And now, Angus, her illumination on a gloomy day, was leaving.

Connie raised her chin. Her days of doing her mother's bidding were numbered, she thought, and without a shadow of doubt, when Angus left here, she was leaving too. She had no intentions of chaining herself to a life behind the bar.

She and Angus slept in the same bed all that night. Connie didn't care if her mother found out. All she wanted was to feel his strong arms around her, holding her, loving her. She lost herself in his lovemaking, savouring every moment. If she could have burrowed under his skin, she would have. Anything to keep him close.

When Connie rose the next morning, Angus was gone. The note propped up on the sugar basin next to his room and board money made her heart constrict. A pain, like nothing she had ever felt before.

Dearest Connie,

Didn't want to disturb you. Catching the 8.45 from Lime Street. See you soon.

Love, Angus xx

She read those brief words a thousand times. He could not have said less. Opening the door of his room Connie stepped inside, closing it behind her. This room *was* Angus. And even though he had been meticulous, she could still see small details of his presence.

The ruche of the bedcover where he had sat, fastening his shoes. Connie stroked the cover and sat where he had sat. The room had a lingering trace of pipe tobacco.

She lifted his pillow, pressing it to her cheek and inhaling the fragrant oil he used to tame the abundance of dark, silver-flecked hair, knowing this was where he lay his head.

Did he ever dream of her, she wondered?

The mocking whine filled her head. It told her she was not good enough to sustain a proper adult relationship and made itself known in moments of overwhelming heartache.

What on God's earth gave you the idea he would stick around? the mocking voice asked. *Throwing yourself at him so, is giving him permission to pick you up and drop you whenever the mood strikes!* Connie swallowed hard, refusing to allow herself the luxury of a good cry. That would be too easy. She had been a fool. And would suffer the consequences...

'Have you fallen asleep up there!' Connie recognised the note of impatience in her mother's voice.

'Coming!' Connie called, stripping the plain white pillowcase from the feather pillow and taking it into her own room, swapping her pillow for his. It was the closest she could get to being close to him now.

She wept tears of love and longing for Angus McCrea.

Talk about up shit creek without a paddle. Her thoughts were a maelstrom of confusion, jumping from one subject to another, and not finding a solution to any of them. It thrilled part of her. But it devastated another part. She was four weeks late. And Connie didn't need her expert medical knowledge to know she would not see her period again for a long, long time.

* * *

The sudden piercing ring of the telephone gave Mim a jolt. They hardly used the contraption except to put an order through to the brewery. She approached it like a time-bomb about to go off. It was ten-thirty in the morning. Nobody ever rang at this hour.

'Good morning. Tram Tavern. Miriam Sharp, landlady. To whom am I speaking?'

'Their money will have run out by the time they get to speak, Mim,' Connie said, heading through to the bar, 'and you're not the landlady – it's my name over the door.' Mim was beginning to irritate her because she didn't get much sleep last night. Mim pulled a face and concentrated on the call.

'May I speak with Angus McCrae please?' Mim heard a voice that had the same crisp, Scottish tone as Angus, except this one was female.

'Mr McCrae is not available at this time of the moment.' Mim had meant to say time of the morning, or moment in time, in her best telephone voice, but the whole thing got jumbled. She did not like answering the telephone at the best of times, the blasted thing made her words come out all wrong.

'I am *Mrs* McCrae. Mrs Eliza McCrae...'

With a pencil poised to take a message, Mim rocked to her fur-lined ankle boots. 'Mrs McCrae...?'

'Would you ask Angus to ring me... on the usual number.'

'Mrs Eliza McCrae?' Mim, awestruck, looked through the

open doorway of the bar where her daughter was talking to Evie, both preparing for opening time. Connie and Angus had become friendly of late, and even though Connie didn't suspect, Mim would have to be blind not to see the way Angus' eyes followed her daughter's every movement.

'I wonder if you would tell him I have found the most marvellous house.' Eliza McCrae broke into her thoughts. 'I want him to see it as soon as possible. He'll be thrilled.'

Mim didn't need to write the message. It was seared into her brain.

'Give him my love and tell him I shall see him on Friday, as usual.'

'I will do that thing.' Mim got the words out before the low purr followed the click on the other end of the line. Still holding the receiver to her ear, Eliza McCrae's words danced through her head. *He'll be thrilled. I'm sure.*

So, Angus wasn't a widower. Mim felt the same all-consuming fury as the day the enemy blew up the two houses at the end of Reckoner's Row, killing all inside. How dare that man treat her daughter like this?

Connie did not wear her heart on her sleeve. She was so particular. But Mim knew her daughter had a particular fondness for the softly spoken Scotsman.

'Well, this is a fine kettle of cod,' she said, replacing the handset. Angus was not the knight in shining armour after all. He was another weak-willed man, out for what he could get! Mim had seen plenty in her time behind the bar. They stood out a mile to the trained eye. But Angus had hoodwinked her good and proper!

'You snake!' Mim said through her teeth as Evie passed through to make the morning pot of tea.

'I beg your pardon!' Evie's eyes widened in surprise. 'Did you say something, Mim?

'I was thinking out loud,' Mim said, flustered, following Evie into the small kitchenette they used as a staff room, to make tea.

'Thinking?' Evie asked, filling the kettle.

'What will Connie say about this latest event of turns,' Mim answered, not wanting to give too much away. 'Maybe it's best I say nothing. What do you think?' Mim answered her own question. 'Yes. That's it. I'll keep it to myself. Say nothing. It's for the best.'

'What's for the best?' Evie asked putting the loose-leaf tea into the pot.

'That phone call,' Mim said nodding to the hallway. 'You'll never guess who that was on the other end? Angus' wife!' Mim nodded again as if to confirm her words and Evie dropped the lid of the teapot into the sink, luckily it didn't break. 'I thought Angus was a widower?'

'Well, that phone call was from *Mrs* McCrea,' Mim said. 'She told me she found them a lovely house, and she wants Angus to see it straight away.' The news was out of her mouth before Mim realised Connie was standing behind her.

Watching the colour drain from Connie's face, Evie felt herself shrink a little. Connie should not have found out that way.

'Excuse me...' Connie put her hand over her mouth, headed for the bar and into the ladies' lavatory.

'Give her a minute,' Mim said, looking contrite. 'I didn't think she'd take it so hard!'

'She's bound to,' Evie said, wishing she had said nothing.

'I'll make myself scarce,' Mim said, 'I'm always putting my foot in my mouth and saying the wrong thing.' Evie watched Mim hurry upstairs, leaving her to face the music and wondered what she could say to Connie when she came back. A short while later, Connie took her usual seat at the small round wooden table in the bar.

'You look a little green around the gills. Is everything all right?' Evie asked, stirring her tea, not in the least bit shocked to see tears running down Connie's face. She had never seen Connie like this. She was the strong one who held everything together. The person everybody depended on in a crisis.

'Not much shocks me anymore, you know,' Evie said pushing back her chair and putting her arms around her friend. 'Come on, you can tell your Aunty Evie.' Her remark had the desired effect when Connie managed a teary smile and she realised, last year the roles had been reversed, and to prove they were both thinking along the same lines Connie sniffed into her hanky.

'The tables have turned,' she said drying her eyes. 'Now I'm crying on your shoulder.'

'Well, I've cried on yours often enough,' Evie said, 'glad to be of service.'

'Mim's news couldn't have come at a worse time,' she said. Evie was dying to ask, but she had no intentions of prying. If Connie wanted to tell her worries, she would do it in her own good time.

'But what did I expect?' Connie said as if talking to herself. 'His wife may have died during the war, but Angus is not a man to remain unattached forever.'

'I'm sure there's a simple explanation,' Evie said. 'He always struck me as the honest sort.'

Connie sighed. 'It's too late to worry about that now.'

Evie wondered if Connie was imagining Angus' neck when she twisted the damp handkerchief in her hands. She was not so naïve she didn't suspect. Connie's morning sickness. Her emotional outbursts.

'Oh Evie,' Connie said. 'I've been such a bloody fool!

30

Angus stepped off the Irish ferry at Gladstone Dock and headed towards the nearest pub, popular with sailors of every nationality. It was their first call as they stepped off their native ships with pockets full of money, which the female clientele were always eager to relieve them of. It surprised him to see Sid Harris behind the bar. Unable to return to the docks, Sid was now a floating barman who did the odd night behind the bar of the Tavern, give Connie the night off, or if she was extra busy.

'It was chocka-bloc that night in the tavern, and a large group of sailors came in,' said Sid as Angus listened. 'It led to good-humoured banter, you know what the locals are like when a new ship comes in.'

'I know,' said Angus, taking mental notes.

'Sometimes you get the odd skirmish, but nothing serious as you know, nothing I can't handle.' Sid grinned when he took a baseball bat from behind the counter and stroked it.

'Quite,' Angus said. He wasn't a disciple of brute force or cracked skulls but agreed that the threat produced an amenable house. 'What happened then...?'

His journey on the Irish ferry had been rough, the first pint didn't touch the sides. He had learned a lot on his trip and hoped he could glean a little more.

* * *

As he headed towards Reckoner's Row the golden glow of the setting sun cast a warm glint over the Mersey and Angus felt like a man who had everything he ever dreamed of. Even, the possibility of an answer to who killed Rene Kilgaren he thought with a satisfied smile. But first he must find out more about Lucy's good shepherd who, as it turned out, could be more than a figment of the child's imagination. And not as saintly as Lucy thought he was.

31

'Angus! I didn't expect you to come back.' Connie's pulse raced when she lifted her head and saw Angus walk into the bar. The sight of him put a giggle in her belly that disturbed her. She thought she had seen the last of him.

'I told you I would come back.' His quizzical expression told Connie she worried for nothing. But she was wrong. She gave the barmaid instructions to take over the bar and motioned for Angus to follow her upstairs.

He had another woman in tow and had the barefaced gall to walk into her pub like there was nothing wrong. Giving herself credit for sizing up a charlatan at first sight, she now knew she had never been more wrong. Angus, like a sailor, may have one – or even two women in every port.

Cool as you like, thought Connie wriggling from his thwarted embrace. Not a word about where he had been, or who he had been with.

'Connie, have I done something wrong?' Angus asked from the far side of the living room.

When she didn't answer, he caught her more skilfully in his arms. Connie could see the troubled look in his eyes.

She should pull away, but she couldn't. The strength she needed failed her. She dared herself to look into his eyes, and in doing so a rush of emotion stormed through her body. Her skin quivered to his touch.

'Connie, please tell me what's wrong?' Angus brushed her cheek, and all the love he ever thought he had experienced disappeared, replaced with a newer, deeper emotion he had not known before now.

'I can't talk here,' she said. She was going to take the rest of the day off. She didn't want Mim to see Angus until they had sorted this thing once and for all. She had intended to go for a walk. Somewhere quiet where she could make sense of it all. Make plans for a future that did not include Reckoner's Row. Or Mim. Or the father of her unborn child...

'Let's go for a drive,' he said, as if reading her thought.

'A drive?' Connie asked. She hadn't been on many of those since she came back from overseas. 'You have a car outside?' He nodded, and she went over to the window and looked down to see a gaggle of awestruck children, headed by Bobby Harris and Lucy Kilgaren, milling around a shiny black Austin, which he had collected from head office in nearby Strand Road.

'We don't get many of these coming into the Row,' Connie said, watching the wide-eyed street imps examining every inch of, what would seem to them, the height of luxury. They stroked and cooed, unable to take their eyes off the beast that took up the front of a house.

'I thought we could go for a countryside drive. I gave Bobby and Lucy threepence to look after the car for me,' Angus had something important to say, and didn't want to discuss it in the confines of the Liverpool backstreet pub.

'Nobody will touch your car, Angus,' Connie answered, a little put out. 'It's safe down there.' He'd had everything he could get from Reckoner's Row, Connie thought. Information. Good leads. And her! Her mind in turmoil she wondered if he had come back for the few belongings he had left behind, and...? What then? A slow drive in his shiny motor, while contemplating a quick good-bye? Never to be seen again. Off to seduce the next gullible woman who would fall for his charm.

'I didn't mean to cause offence,' Angus said, as if she was a customer whose drink he had just spilled, and she raised a cynical, shaped eyebrow. Biting back a sceptical retort.

She had never been as a pushover, as known by the male population of the dock road. Earning the respect of the customers because she knew when to keep shtum or when to speak out. She was competent. On hand when wives went into labour or a kid cut his knee. And, the most important thing of all, Connie thought, she was not dependent on a man for her entire existence! So what the bloody hell was she doing, swooning over a married man who would hightail it out of here before she could say, *last orders, please!*

* * *

Tying a silk headscarf under her chin, Connie slipped into the front seat next to Angus. So close. Yet so far. They travelled in silence until they reached the greenery of the countryside.

'I have got nothing against Reckoner's Row,' Angus said breaking the long silence between them and knew immediately he had said the wrong thing. 'It's friendly – once people accept you, and they've got a heart as big and full as the Mersey.' He was wittering, making no sense, but for the love of all that was sacred, he wished he knew what he had done to upset her so much.

'No, Angus,' Connie said, turning to look right at him as he drove through the countryside, 'this place is grimy, it's peopled with suspicion, and you could live here until you were ninety and never be accepted. Not once they find out you are a bizzy. Reckoner's Row isn't the kind of street a policeman like you would live, given the choice.'

'Connie,' he asked with caution, 'is something wrong? Have I upset you?' He had expected his usual warm welcome, expecting to hold her in his arms, in his bed.

'Upset me?' Connie asked, with a nonchalant wave of her hand.

Why was it so hard to tell him she knew his wife was alive? Gazing out of the car window taking in the thatched cottages and lush pastures, Connie tried to hide her devastation. If she was being honest, somewhere, deep down, she knew the mammoth revelation would spell the end of their relationship, and she wasn't sure she could handle not seeing him again.

He had become the centre of her universe in the short time he had been here, but she was not going to beg him to stay and help raise their beloved, much wanted child. Because when Angus cleared out his room and out of her life. She had plans of her own.

'I like kids,' he said, 'you can learn a lot about yourself from kids – they see things in black and white. No grey areas to muddle everything up. They don't overthink things and decide two and two make twenty-two. It's just four. Plain and simple.'

'The kids around the dockside are a canny bunch, Bobby Harris might look as if butter wouldn't melt, but, like his mother, he can make a penny scream.' She smiled for the first time that day. 'He'll go far, I'm sure.'

'His uncle owns the Carters' yard, I believe?' Angus said, and Connie nodded.

'Aye, Jack Kilgaren works there, too. Old Man Skinner keeps himself to himself, unlike his sister.'

'Ahh, the indomitable Mrs Harris.' Angus was relaxed as they sat in front of a roaring fire in a little country inn. Connie wondered how he could be so blasé knowing he was hiding such a huge lie. Still, she couldn't bring herself to broach the subject of his wife. Angus was taking in the relaxing ambiance, a world away from the Tram Tavern.

'I bet you'd love to run a place like this, Connie?' Connie

shrugged, admiring the inglenook fireplace and horse brasses polished until they gleamed. 'But I'm sure it would be far too quiet for Mim out here.' He looked awkward.

His eyes roaming the snug room instead of looking at Connie as he spoke, and she realised he had brought her here to give her the brush-off, and she wanted to put off the dreaded moment as long as possible.

'You've found all you needed in your investigation?' she asked, determined not to show Angus the turmoil that was making her feel sick. He nodded and picked up his drink, while hers remained untouched.

'I was wondering—' he said, but Connie didn't let him finish when she blurted.

'So, is it Darnel behind the warehouse robberies?'

'Yes, and much more, but—'

'Oh, right,' Connie said, moving on, 'so when do you think you'll be making an arrest?'

'He's as slippery as a wet fish,' Angus said. 'I've got to be certain my evidence is water-tight. And talking of water, we know he didn't kill Rene.' Connie's jaw dropped, and her eyes widened in surprise. 'He didn't?'

'No, he was behind bars the night it happened, drunk and disorderly.' Angus looked around to make sure he wasn't being overheard, and Connie's ears pricked up. She would have laid money on Darnel being Rene's killer.

'Oh, poor Rene!' Connie gasped. She knew the barmaid liked a laugh and enjoyed herself when she could, but she wasn't a woman who would go off with a stranger for no reason.

'We found her shoe near a frozen part of the canal.'

'Blimey!' Connie whispered. Fascinated at the things they could find out with nobody saying a word.

'We also got a perfect imprint of a man's shoe in the frozen mud,' Angus said. 'Not your usual kind of shoe, thank goodness, not common at all.'

'How can you tell?' Connie asked pushing away the gin, the smell making her feel nauseous.

'Size twelve. Brown. Expensive,' Angus answered succinctly.

'How do you know all that?' Connie couldn't help but ask more questions, she found the whole thing fascinating. 'That is amazing.'

'Rene had brown polish on the side of her navy-blue, peep-toe shoes,' Angus said, 'and also on the toe of her nylon stockings. So she got close to whoever she was with.'

'Lots of men wear brown shoes,' Connie said, 'are you going to arrest them all?'

'Wearing brown shoes is not an arrestable offence,' Angus said stretching his legs to reveal his own brown coloured brogues. 'However, the shoemaker's name, Cordwainer and Sons, was stamped into the sole of the male shoe.' Angus looked very pleased indeed. 'Lucky for us the area had been frozen up until we found Rene's body and a quick-thinking bobby managed to gouge the imprint out of the mud.' The shoes were hand made by a family firm in Northampton.

'Handmade?' Connie gave a low whistle, which made Angus frown.

'Average cost, six months' wages of your local docker.'

'Blimey!' Connie's eyes widened as she tried to take in the news. Darnel didn't murder Rene. She didn't drown. And slight of build, she wouldn't stand a chance against a man with size twelve feet! 'Any idea who killed her?'

'Let's not talk about all that now,' Angus said, taking hold of Connie's hand across the table. 'There's something I have to tell you.'

Here goes. Connie hardly dared breathe, deciding whether to let Angus continue before she gave him the news of her own. 'Angus I think I know what you will say, and I want to say... I knew this day would come.' She pulled her hand free, 'and I won't think any less of you, for doing what you say you will do...' She was babbling. She sounded like Mim. *Shut up, woman!*

Angus benevolently let Connie have her moment, knowing she would wind down to a full stop, given time. There was no point butting in, because he doubted he would get a word in edgeways. When Connie stopped, he opened his mouth to speak and she started all over again.

'There's something I've got to tell you, but I don't want you thinking I'm trying to push you into a corner, because I know that's not right, and I wish you'd told me from the off that you had a wife and you're not a widower after all, like you said you—'

'What wife?' Angus looked puzzled. 'I am a widower.'

'But Mrs McCrea telephoned, and she asked Mim to pass on the message about the house you were buying together.' Connie slowed to a stop.

'Well now,' said Angus when she finished. 'First of all, yes I will buy a house.' Connie failed to suppress the small but sharp intake of breath. 'But she is not my wife. I brought you here, so I could show you something. A chocolate-box cottage, some might call it. I want your opinion.'

'Oh,' was all that Connie trusted herself to say.

'Come on, let me show you.' He got up from his chair and went over to the wooden stand to collect Connie's pale coloured duster coat and helped her put it on, before she picked up her handbag and followed him to the car.

They travelled in silence on the short journey to the village, the centre of which was a beautiful lake complete with a small family of swans gliding on the water. Connie stood transfixed.

'They mate for life, you know...' Angus said, following her line of vision.

'They've got more sense than humans, I'd say.' Connie's tone was harsher than she intended. But she was fed up. Why did everything have to be a mystery. It surprised her when he took hold of her hand and led her towards a cottage that, as Angus so rightly said, would not have looked out of place on the lid of a chocolate box. Taking a key from his pocket, he opened the door and led the way.

'Here,' she said when she entered the cosy cottage, 'I hope you haven't brought me all the way out here to have your wicked way.'

'Is that what I do?' he asked with a smile and a glint in his eyes. 'Have my wicked way with you – and here's me thinking I was showing you my undying love.' Connie, looking out of the window, turned and looked at Angus. Really looked.

'You are full of surprises today, that's for sure,' she said trying to keep her voice steady as an all-encompassing heat rose from her neck to her cheeks. Angus had never told her about his undying love before.

'See this woman,' he said picking up a framed photograph from the mantelpiece, 'she is Mrs McCrae, but not the one you think she is.' He handed Connie the picture frame. 'This Mrs McCrae is my brother's wife...'

'Your brother who was...'

'Killed at Dunkirk, yes.' His lips stretched into a straight line. 'This is Liza, his wife who with my help has been putting her affairs in order, so she can move back to Scotland.'

'Oh, Angus.' Connie felt very foolish.

'But that isn't the reason I brought you here, I'm buying this cottage and I wanted to know what you think.'

'Why does it matter what I think?' It wasn't like she would visit.

'Is it the type of place you would ever consider living in?' Angus asked when she didn't offer an opinion.

'I think it's beautiful. Perfect. Like something you see in books or on the pictures. I'm not sure Mim would like to live here though.'

'That's good,' said Angus with a cheeky grin, 'because I wasn't thinking of asking Mim to live here... I only want you.' This time Connie didn't even try to stop her mouth from gaping.

'You mean you want me to...'

'Would you do me the honour of becoming my wife, Connie?' Angus had hardly got the words out before she stood on the tip of her toes and flung her arms around his neck. Connie could feel the warm flush of happiness radiating through her whole body as tears of elation ran freely down her cheeks. She could not be happier.

'Yes Angus, yes, yes, yes.' This day had turned from one of her worst to the best ever.

'You know when you said you only wanted me to live here with you,' Connie said a little breathlessly and Angus nodded. 'Would it be a problem if somebody else came along, too, do you think?'

'You're not thinking of kidnapping young Bobby Harris, are you?' Angus laughed, knowing how fond she was of the young whippersnapper. But he was not laughing when Connie told him her news. He couldn't. His heart was too full of love and pride at this miracle they had created together.

'A baby!' Angus repeated the words over and over, worrying Connie with his quiet astonishment.

'I won't pressurise you, Angus... You don't have to marry me. I didn't think I could have children but...' Connie's voice failed her, and silence hung like a curtain between them. Angus tried to make sense of what she told him.

'I'll be a father?' A slow smile creased the corners of his sparkling eyes. 'My love, you could never give me a more precious gift.' Angus calmed a little, took her in his arms and held her so very close. Moments later, in a muffled voice Connie said, 'Angus, I really would like to live long enough to give birth to this child.'

'I am so sorry my darling, but it's the shock – I never thought I would be a father.'

'Me neither,' Connie answered. 'A mother, I mean.'

'I know what you mean. Here sit down. I'll make you a cup of tea. Do you want something to eat – you're eating for...'

'No thank you, Angus.' Connie said firmly. 'I am not eating for two. I'll share, until she's born.'

'A girl? How do you know?' he asked, and Connie laughed.

'I don't know, but let's call it women's intuition.' She liked the thought of raising her child here, in this beautiful village where swans sailed outside their very own window. It was a long way from sooty Reckoner's Row. She had only one worry...

* * *

'Married?' Mim whooped with delight when Connie told her later. 'Married! I thought you would never give me an excuse to buy a new hat!'

'Don't you mind me leaving here?' Connie said, to which Mim replied.

'Mind? I've prayed for it... Now I can have my beloved tavern back again.' It was Sunday and they were having afternoon tea of ham sandwiches, jam scones, and homemade shortbread biscuits courtesy of Angus' sister-in-law.

Angus bit back the question of where the jam had come from, knowing Mim had put on a nice spread and didn't intend to spoil the happy atmosphere with *officialdom*. The old girl had taken the news well. He knew how clingy she was where Connie was concerned.

She was up to something. He could tell.

* * *

It was Friday afternoon and the dockworkers had all been paid the night before, so the bar was hectic this dinnertime, keeping Connie so busy she did not give her mother's dying duck act a second thought.

'It was good of you to stay on and help me out behind the bar, Evie,' Connie said as they cleared out the last of the stragglers at three o'clock. 'I don't know what I'd have done without you.'

'I'm sure Mrs Harris would have helped,' Evie said, re-filling the sink and washing the remainder of the glasses and ashtrays that only moments earlier had littered the tables.

'You wouldn't catch Ada serving, she thinks it's the divil's stomping ground behind this bar. She went upstairs to see Mim a few minutes ago and – oh, look out, here she comes.' Connie noted that Mrs Harris looked none too pleased either.

'Call yourself a nurse?' Ada Harris asked Connie, prodding the bar with her forefinger. 'Call yourself a good daughter?'

'What are you waffling on about, Ada?' Connie asked, flicking a damp bar towel and putting it across two pumps. But her concern hit the roof when she saw Ada's anxious expression.

'You'd better go upstairs and have a look at your mother, she's not well!'

'Mim's a good actress, you know, Ada,' Connie said, 'but I'll give her the onceover. Put her mind at rest.' Heading to the stairs, Connie wondered how long it would be before Mim started her old tricks. The best form of Mim's defence was her ailments, they could get her anything she wanted. But not anymore, Connie thought. She would not, could not, cancel her wedding to Angus, in three weeks' time. If Mim didn't like the idea, then she shouldn't pretend she did and then feign another illness.

'Don't be coming the old soldier with me, Mim!' Connie said when she took her mother a cup of tea. Mim was sitting up in bed, resplendent in a crocheted bed jacket, her hair still in pin-curls and a hair net at this hour. Connie found it unusual, because no matter how ill her mother pretended to be, she still made sure her immaculate, S-shaped waves were in place.

'I think I'm running a fever,' Mim said when Connie popped a thermometer into her mouth.

'Don't talk,' Connie said, suspecting the four hot-water bottles secreted about the bed had a lot to do with her mother's high temperature. Connie shook the thermometer and looked at Mim. She looked pale, but so did everybody these days – and without her lippy, Mim always looked insipid.

'You have that nice cup of tea, and I'll be back when I've cleaned the bar,' Connie said, satisfied her mother would not toddle off her mortal coil just yet.

When she went up later with another cup of tea and a couple of aspirins, Connie went straight her mother's bedroom. Maybe she would fancy something to eat? Or sit in the living room and listen to the wireless for a...

'Mim?' Connie felt her heartbeat quicken, horrified when she saw her mother slumped, face-down across the bed. *Don't panic. You're a trained nurse!*

'Mim... Mim are you all right?' There was a perceptible wobble in her voice as she approached the huge double bed her mother had slept in since the day she married dear old Dad.

Dressed in a plaid, woollen dressing-gown, Mim had one slipper on her foot and one slipper had fallen to the floor. If she was pretending to be sick, then she was doing a fine job, Connie thought. Her parched lips sticking to her teeth.

'Mim. Answer me!' Her voice rose when she turned her mother over and saw immediately. Mim was not putting on an act. Her translucent skin was devoid of colour and her eyes were closed. *Jesus, Mary and Joseph!* Connie prayed, *don't let her die.* She lifted her mother's limp hand and she felt her wrist for a pulse. Mim stirred and Connie breathed a short sigh of relief. But not for long.

'Get me the doctor,' Mim groaned, 'I need something for this pain...' Then she closed her eyes again. Connie rushed to the top of the stairs, shouting over the bannister.

'Evie! Ada! Someone... Call an ambulance!'

* * *

'So I wasn't even worth the half a crown for a doctor?' Drowsiness slurred Mim's words as they transported her to the cream-coloured ambulance waiting outside the tavern. Connie patted her hand, accompanying her in the back of the ambulance while Evie finished the cleaning and locked up the pub.

Within half an hour she was sitting with Connie on a wooden bench in the corridor of Stanley Hospital. When they saw the doctor approach, Connie jumped up and went to find out what was happening.

'We will have to open her up,' the doctor said. 'I'm thinking it is a strangulated hiatus hernia. Your mother would have been in a lot of pain. We're taking her into theatre immediately to repair the damage.'

'It's my fault,' Connie cried, 'I should have listened.' Her throat tightened. 'I should have stayed with her.'

'These things happen so quickly, it is difficult. Please don't blame yourself,' said Doctor Walsh. 'We will do everything we can.'

'She doesn't even know... about the baby...' Connie told Evie, letting her tears flow unchecked. For the next few hours Connie paced the corridor outside the operating theatre. She knew what was going on behind the closed door. She knew the staff were doing their best.

'I'm sure she'll be fine,' Angus said. His arm around Connie's shoulder, he hoped Mim would be back to her usual chirpy self in no time. 'I'll go and get you a nice cup of tea from the WVS canteen,' Angus said, feeling a little guilty. He wanted Mim up and about as soon as possible because he and Connie had a wedding to go to.

When Mim came back from theatre, Connie hurried to meet her dazed mother and was allowed onto the ward to see her for a few minutes, on the understanding she was not to get upset again.

'Oh Mim, I am so sorry,' Connie cried, 'I should have known you weren't well.'

'Don't fret, love...' Mim said, still groggy from the anaesthetic. 'I will be fine... The doctor said I had a hated hyena... and he strangled it...'

Connie looked to Evie, and Evie looked back. They both held in a giggle – relieved that Mim was her old befuddled self. Moments later Angus came through the door, and Connie burst into tears.

33

'I was thinking...' Angus said, three weeks later, striking a match and putting a light under the kettle while Connie got the cups and saucers from the cupboard. 'About the cottage... I received a letter this morning asking if I would go to the solicitor's to sign the final documents.'

Mim was out of hospital and more or less back to her robust self, but Connie was still unable to tell her mother she was not only moving out of the pub, but moving out of Liverpool altogether. Now, Angus was about to tell her that today was the day when the sale of the cottage was being finalised. After that, there would be no turning back.

She would lose her precious tavern, not just the only true home she had ever known but also her livelihood, her independence. And what about Mim? She had been so poorly, and she would have to fend for herself, alone, and run the pub...

'Angus... I... I...' Connie's heart was sinking. How could she tell Mim she was moving out? And how could she tell Angus she didn't want to live in the quiet countryside.

'What I was thinking,' Angus interrupted, 'is that we're not cut out for the quiet life right now, you and me.' His words were slow and measured and Connie felt the blood in her veins grow cold. Had he changed his mind about wanting to make an honest woman of her? She opened her mouth to speak, but no words came. What could she say?

'So, I was thinking... what if we stay on here in the tavern? I'll still buy the cottage – it's the only thing I have left of my brother.' Connie nodded, of course. 'But we don't have to live there permanently. It could be our very own bolt-hole when Mim wants a bit of peace.'

'You would do that for me, Angus?' Connie asked, and Angus nodded his head.

'You know I would,' he said, his arms around her waist, his words full of love. 'Anything that makes you happy, my darling.'

'Would you give up detective work and help me run the tavern?' Or was she being greedy, asking him to give up the work he loved, wanting the moon, the stars and the sun-shiny sky?

'It's time I settled down,' Angus said. 'Always being on duty took its toll on my first marriage, I don't want that to happen again with you. I want to watch my son grow...'

Connie raised her eyebrows. 'Your son? We will have to wait and see.' She nestled in the security of his loving arms, sure that this all-consuming happiness came around only once in a lifetime.

Angus gave a contented sigh. Giving up his job would be a bit of a wrench, but it was worth it. Although, he would probably keep his hand in somewhere along the line. However, at thirty-seven, he knew he wasn't too old to start a new way of life with the woman he adored.

34

Connie woke very early on the morning of her wedding three weeks later, and looked out of her bedroom window, the semi-circular bay giving her a birds-eye view of the dock road and the Liverpool waterfront.

Even at this early hour, the bustle and the busyness was a regular sight. The overhead railway carrying workers along the seven miles of docks, and the ships lying like huge child-bearing mothers, sustaining not only the city but the country as a whole.

The golden glint of sunshine dappled the murky waters of the Mersey, as if dressing it up for her special day and Connie smiled to herself. This view would remain with her for the rest of her life.

She could hear her mother noisily rattling cups in the kitchen, and when she padded barefoot to the living room, she saw Mim, resplendent in her red plaid dressing gown and dark hairnet, was already pouring tea.

'I'll do that, Mim,' Connie said, knowing her irrepressible mother wasn't going to let something as insignificant as a brush with death stop her making a cup of tea on the morning of her only daughter's wedding.

'And why would I let you do that?' Mim asked. 'It's not as if I'm incarcerated.' She had lost all interest in the wedding when Connie told her initially that she would be moving away from Reckoner's Row.

'I think you mean incapacitated, Mim.' Connie smiled. Mim resisted all urges to organise her wedding day and had looked on in silent censure, not wanting anything to do with the whole debacle, and said so in no uncertain terms – Connie was thrilled. Nothing was going to spoil her big day.

'I know what I mean,' Mim said, pushing Connie's cup and saucer across the table.

'Mim,' Connie said, thinking this was the best time to let her mother know she was staying.

'You don't mind if Angus and I stay on here after our honeymoon in the country, do you?' She knew her mother dreaded being left on her own since her father died and found the last few years of the war a particular trial. Mim's eyes lit up momentarily, but she was giving nothing away.

'What about that fancy cottage? You said it was the best place you'd ever seen.'

'I know,' Connie replied, 'but it's so far away. You'd have to get a train and two buses if you wanted to come and visit.'

'Me? Visit?' Mim said, buttering her toast with as much care as Michelangelo must have done when painting the ceiling of the Sistine Chapel. 'I'll be far too busy running this place alone to visit anybody.'

'That's what I thought,' Connie explained, 'and you only get one mam...' The events of the last weeks and months had taught her that much.

'Oh well, if you feel you can't manage without me,' Mim

sighed, issuing an off-hand wave, 'I'll just have to get used to the idea.'

'I thought you'd say that.' Connie knew the news was a relief, when Mim suddenly sprung up and went to fetch her new wine-coloured cavalier hat.

'What do you think?' Mim asked, stroking the lustrous, irides-cent side feathers that curved from the velvet brim to the magiste-rial tilt of her chin. Suddenly she radiated a new vibrancy, wanting to go over the table arrangements, the seating plans. Connie knew she had done the right thing keeping her good news from her mother up 'til now, given Mim's startling burst of unfettered enthusiasm.

Let Mim have this, she thought, nothing could go wrong now. She had organised everything just the way she and Angus wanted their day. Even the weather was accommodating. The indulgent sky was brightest blue, the sun was shining and there was nothing that could possibly mar her perfect day...

* * *

'I do,' Connie said gazing up into Angus' deep blue eyes. She wore an elegant pale blue calf-length skirt and matching fitted jacket with a nipped-in waist that showed her curvaceous figure and brought a special glint to the eyes of her husband-to-be.

The so-called New Look costume was all the rage – if you had the money and the coupons to buy the sophisticated outfit that showed Connie's flawless complexion and dazzling eyes to perfection. On her head she wore a pale blue beret with matching lace that covered her bride-flushed face.

Lucy was a delightful flower girl, and maid of honour Evie caused Danny Harris' heart to skip a beat when he saw her follow Connie into the church. Jack, resplendent in a brand-new suit, walked the bride up the aisle of Saint Patrick's church to stand beside Angus and his best man, Birdy Finch, while Mim dabbed her happy powder-puffed eyes.

When the ceremony was over, they trailed out of the church into the Saturday morning sunshine, heading to Old Man Skinner's shire horse standing ready to pull a painted cart dressed in white ribbons, even though Connie asked Jack not to make a fuss.

'If I can't make a fuss of the woman who saved my life, then who can I make a fuss of,' Jack said, swelling with pride in his navy-blue three-piece suit, complete with his very own matching waistcoat – he had not been so well dressed since he made his first holy communion – except, this time he would not allow his finery to go straight into Uncle Bill's pawnshop!

Angus helped his new bride up the wooden steps and seated her on the bench that had been constructed and they waved to the residents who had come from all over Bootle to see the happy couple and share in their fabulous day.

'Oh, it was a lovely service,' a neighbour said. 'Little Lucy looked like a little ballerina in her frothy yellow dress. But it's Evie I feel so sorry for, she has it all to do now her mother's not here.'

'I heard she's as happy as they come,' another neighbour said.

Connie raised an ecstatic eyebrow. The tide had turned regarding how the residents of Reckoner's Row felt about Evie and at last, they saw her not as the daughter of Rene Kilgaren who was no better than she ought to be, but as the stoic young woman who was bringing up her siblings as best she could under the circumstances.

And it did Connie's heart the power of good to know most people could only see the good in the girl these days. Ada Harris was another matter altogether. That woman had a swinging brick instead of a heart where Evie was concerned.

* * *

'May I be so bold?' Danny Harris said to Evie, encouraging her to link his arm, then turning to Lucy he nodded for her to take the other arm and they neared the second carriage with Jack.

'Why, thank you, kind sir.' Lucy looked to her older sister and smiled. Evie's face had turned a lovely shade of pink and, determined not to look at anybody, stared straight ahead. Lucy looked to Danny, who winked and gave her a little nudge with his elbow.

Lucy felt they had shared an unspoken secret. He had his eye on their Evie and their Evie knew it. That's why she refused to look at him. Lucy smiled. It would be lovely if Evie accepted Danny's invitation to go to the pictures with him one night.

Swelling with pride in her borrowed bridesmaid dress of lemon-dyed parachute silk with a white tulle overskirt, Lucy felt like Cinderella about to go to the ball when Danny helped her onto the carriage. She noticed he saved the seat next to himself for Evie.

'The bride looks nice,' Danny said, and Evie nodded, her face growing an even deeper shade of pink. 'It's been a lovely day so far, the sun came out at just the right time,' he continued, and Evie nodded again. He turned to Lucy and smiling he asked: 'Did you notice when it went missing?'

'What went missing?' she asked, her eyes wide.

'Evie's voice, she seems to have lost it.'

Lucy giggled and lowered her eyes when Evie gave her a silent caution. But Danny was a little bolder. Dressed in all his finery, Lucy thought he looked dapper in his navy blue, double-breasted, pinstriped jacket and matching trousers. The turn-ups had a crease so sharp you could do yourself an injury if you touched it.

'I expect she'll find it lying around somewhere.' Danny

cupped his lips to Lucy's ear and stage-whispered loud enough for Evie to hear, 'And then we'll never hear the last of it.'

Lucy couldn't help herself; Danny was funny, she threw her head back and laughed. Evie couldn't help but smile.

'You two are impossible,' Evie said, looking over Jack's shoulder opposite, not trusting herself to look at Danny, who was... impossible.

They headed back to the tavern where tables, magnificent in best white tablecloths, glittering crystal glasses and gleaming silverware graced the T-formation tables in the best part of the Tram Tavern where Mim had no hesitation in giving the guests a privileged viewing of a three-tiered spectacular, sitting in all its white-icing glory at the top table.

Connie, greeting her guests, was thrilled when she saw Angus talking to Jack and Danny. He had slotted into Reckoner's Row like the missing piece of a jigsaw puzzle and made her life complete.

Connie hadn't realised up 'til now how much she would miss this place and its people if she left for good. The tavern. Mim... most of all, Mim. The Kilgarens. The gossip. The laughs. The joys and tribulations that went into the making of her everyday life. Things she took for granted. She would have missed it with all her heart, and she was glad that Angus agreed to stay on here.

Anyway, she thought, what would she have done when Angus was working all day? She didn't need to work any longer. But she liked working. It made her feel vibrant, and so much a part of this higgledy-piggledy community of diverse characters, who filled each day with pleasure and frustration in equal measure. She was sure she could join the village women in their various guilds and associations? But...

Connie knew she was more accustomed to hauling drunks out of the bar at closing time than flower arranging in the village hall. She had nothing in common with those refined ladies of the church committee.

A small tinkle of silver on crystal told her that Angus was about to start his speech, and as Connie sat looking up at her wonderful husband, her heart filled with love and pride.

'Ladies and Gentlemen,' Angus began to a roomful of cheers. He gave a small laugh and turned to look at Connie, who shook her head and smiled. He thanked everybody for coming, gave Evie a pair of gold earrings, which he and Connie had chosen together and gave Lucy a gold bangle which made her squeal with joy. To Jack he gave a wrapped gift, which Angus asked him not to open until later. Jack thanked him and looked confused, but something told him to leave it unopened on the table.

Evie felt her heart pound against her ribs when Mim told her that Danny Harris had eyes for her alone.

'He's courting,' Evie said, her cheeks glowing.

'When you walked up the aisle behind our Connie,' Mim said, 'everybody noticed, even Susie Blackthorn. I heard her telling him to stop gawping... She didn't sound thrilled neither.'

'Oh, Mim, don't say things like that.' Evie would have loved it if Danny had been looking at her, but quite rightly, it was Connie who held everybody's attention.

'I can hear the music starting, and I know how much you young ones love to dance.'

Dance?! Evie told Mim she hadn't given the matter a thought. She didn't know how to dance, and, anyway, she would feel more comfortable helping in the kitchen, re-filling plates and washing teacups.

'Not in your maid of honour dress, you won't!' Mim said, pushing her towards the dance floor. As they reached it she saw Susie Blackthorn, who looked as if her eyes would pop right out of her head.

'I like your frock,' Susie simpered, possessively linking her arm through Danny's. 'Isn't Evie's frock nice, Danny? Do you think I'd suit a frock like that? But I wouldn't wear that colour – not many can, it is so draining.'

Evie lifted her chin as she crossed the room. She felt fabulous in her maid-of-honour dress, despite what Susie Blackthorn had to say.

'She's got above herself,' Evie heard Susie say, and realised the comment held no fear for her anymore. She didn't feel like an outsider. And, smiling at the gathered throng, she wasn't treated like one either. She couldn't think what Danny saw in Susie, who never saw the good in anybody. If he had courted someone kinder, more cheerful, like he was, someone who had time for everybody. Then she could have understood. But Susie Blackthorn!

Without warning, she felt her throat tighten and her eyes stung with unshed tears. She must get out of here. Cigarette smoke was making her eyes water. She must find Lucy. If she was playing outside in the bridesmaid dress, the little madam was in for a good talking-to.

35

Something troubled Evie. She hadn't expected to see Danny with another girl. Nor did she anticipate how it would make her feel. Approaching her own house, Evie noticed the parlour curtains were closed.

She had opened them before leaving for the wedding, surely? But, with all the excitement and trying to calm Lucy, she might be mistaken.

People didn't shut their front door until bedtime in Reckoner's Row, and there was nothing unusual in seeing the Kilgaren door open these days. Although, knowing they would be out all day, she knew Jack made sure it was locked. Lucy must have been home and left it ajar.

When Evie entered the house, it was quiet. Too quiet. Listening for any sound of the wireless, which she *knew* she had left on this morning, all was silent.

The house was usually full of noise and bustle with Jack and Lucy coming and going, bickering about everything and nothing. Evie, very gently, closed the vestibule door. She shivered. In the dusk of the spring evening she felt like she did when she entered the local church. Tiptoeing across the polished linoleum, towards the parlour door. Evie didn't know why she felt like this. But there was certainly something wrong.

The house was so still. Passing the closed parlour door, she ventured into the kitchen. Opening the door, her eyes grew wide and her jaw dropped. Lucy was sitting in the chair by the fireside, still in all her finery.

'Are you all right, Lucy?' Evie asked in hushed tones from the door. She knew the day had been full of excitement for her young sister. Maybe she needed peace and quiet?

Then she noticed the sideboard doors were wide open and the floor littered with domestic debris, ransacked drawers, broken china. What had been going on while she was out!

'Lucy?' Evie deliberately kept her voice low. Lucy looked very pale. 'It looks like a bomb's hit the place.' Her heart pounded in her chest as her eyes scanned the once-tidy room. 'Tell me, Luce.' Her voice deepened, terror giving it a hard edge. The child silently pointed to the parlour, and Evie heard a thudding noise on the other side of the wall.

Evie hurried towards the door. But Lucy, who had a surprisingly strong grip for a child stopped her. She looked to Evie and put her finger to her lips.

'Lucy,' Evie hissed, 'what's going on?' She was going into the front room to see what was happening in there. Lucy looked terrified, and Evie noticed she was trembling. Putting her arm around her young sister, Evie convinced her that everything was going to be fine.

'He said he's come back for what belongs to him, and he's not leaving without it.'

Evie didn't ask what Darnel had come back for. As far as she was concerned, he had stripped the place of everything he had contributed when her mother lived here.

'Go out the back way, fetch Jack!' Fear made Evie's mouth dry. If Darnel dared raise his hand to her again, she would go for him. By God she would. Picking up the poker from the hearth, she walked towards the lobby.

'Don't go in the parlour.' Lucy tried to pull her from the door. Her eyes were wide with fear.

'I'm not scared of him, Lucy,' Evie said. Her words cut short when she saw Lucy crying.

'Who?' Lucy sniffed, holding her skirt like Jack had done all those years ago, encouraging her to forget her own trepidation. She had a family who she intended to look out for and protect.

'Leo Darnel?' Evie's eyebrows pleated in confusion as Lucy shook her head. 'You know who he is, don't you?' Lucy nodded. She had seen a picture of him in the newspaper in connection with a dockside robbery.

'The man in the parlour,' Lucy said, 'is the shepherd.' Her lips screwed into a little knot of anger. 'But he's not good no more. He shouted at me. Told me to sit down and behave.'

'Did he, now?' Evie said, determination coursing through her veins. 'We'll soon see about that!' Feeling sick, she remembered what real fear felt like, but did her best to hide her dread from Lucy. Those days were gone. 'What happened, Lucy?' Evie asked. 'Tell me what went on?'

'He said Mam hid his money in there.' Lucy's voice quivered as tears rolled down her face.

'What money? We've got no money.' Evie took a deep shuddering breath, trying to calm herself. Now she knew what Darnel meant when he said they were in danger. Evie thought they were in danger from him. But she was wrong. He was warning her about a man who was much more dangerous.

'Go now! Fetch Angus!' Lucy raced out of the back door in a cloud of yellow tulle and down the yard. Evie saw her drag open the gate and in the blink of an eye her young sister was gone. Safe.

Within minutes Angus came through the front door, which Evie had left ajar, with Danny following close behind. Angus motioned for Jack to move forward, putting his fingers to his lips.

'Lucy's good shepherd?' Evie informed Jack in hushed tones.

'He's in this house?' He asked. She nodded. Yes.

Angus, at his most commanding, gestured for Jack to take a position at the side of the parlour door. This was his wedding day. He should be dancing with his new bride.

'He may be armed,' Jack said in a low whisper, taking his position. 'He was the last time I saw him.' His large hand splayed behind him to stop Evie overtaking and getting into the parlour.

'Lucy?' Evie whispered, looking around the kitchen, her eyes desperate. The child was gone.

Moving with panther-like grace and calm, Angus closed the vestibule door. He covered all angles. The front door was ajar. He moved to stand at the foot of the stairs. Evie clutched her dress in her clammy hands.

'This man has no compunction about killing a woman, we know that,' Angus told Evie, 'but we don't know about children.' Evie's insides turned to water. Unsure what he was capable of.

'Stay back,' Angus whispered when there was no sound from the parlour, and the quick exit they had been expecting did not happen. They listened more. Not a peep. Angus nodded to Danny, before he shoulder barged his way into the parlour door. It opened with a terrific crash and hit the parlour wall.

* * *

The high-pitched clang of the police car bell vied with the ring of the ambulance before both vehicles screeched to a halt. After a moment Angus came out, his face devoid of expression. He held Evie back and, looking to the police constables, he said, 'You'd better come and see this.'

* * *

'Something's happened!' Ada Harris said needlessly, elbowing her way to the front of the huge crowd of neighbours who had left the wedding party in the Tram Tavern and gathered outside.

'D'ya think?' Susie Blackthorn's cynical reply went amiss as she moved closer.

'Well, a police car and an ambulance don't turn up for nothing,' Ada said, ignoring her sarcasm. Everybody in Reckoner's Row milled around the Kilgarens' front door. Kids had stopped their games to watch uniformed men race into the house.

'I'm going to find out what's going on!' Ada said, never behind the door where news was concerned. While, in defeat after breaking its tether, the jacket of her two-piece flapped wildly in the weak spring sunshine. Susie followed at a lick now, too. They reached the house just as a policeman in a gaberdine mackintosh and homburg hat came out of the house and stood guarding it. The parlour curtains were shut tight.

'What's happened? What's the matter?' Ada asked. 'Is it Connie? Jesus, Mary and Joseph!' She made the sign of the cross.

'I'm afraid I can't say anything.' The policeman looked very solemn.

'And I'm afraid you'll have to,' Susie demanded, irritated beyond reason.

'I'm so sorry, love,' he said. 'There's blood and brains all over the show.'

'My Danny's in there!' Susie screamed, and Ada poked her in

the back with her index finger. 'Please let me in, we're as good as family. You've got to tell me what happened!'

'I bet it's that Darnel's gone berserk' Ada said. 'Finished them off good and proper!'

'Don't be stupid.' Susie set off a chain of murmurs that quickly went around the curious crowd. Darnel's name was mentioned frequently.

'Done Lucy in,' neighbours said behind their hands. When the front door opened again, the waiting crowd got their patient reward. However, they were relieved to see the body on the stretcher was not that of the child. It was the unconscious body of Leo Darnel, being stretchered into a waiting ambulance.

36

Evie took in the terrible scene through the open parlour door. With her back hard up against the narrow lobby wall, she stared slack-jawed and wide-eyed at the bare room, devoid of furniture. Blood-spattered cardboard boxes scattered across the linoleum floor, and a breathless man was doubled over, holding on to the marble fireplace her mam loved so much.

Evie needed to run, to scream, but her body had turned to petrified stone as he gasped for breath from his earlier exertions of beating the living daylights out of Leo Darnel. She should be glad, and grateful, but she felt neither.

Lifting his head, blood and sputum suspended from his cut lip, he glared at Evie. Her blood turned to ice when she saw recognition glint in his cold grey eyes. The ghost of her past stood before her, but this one was not dead.

'Get Lucy out of here!' His ragged words rang through her head like a cymbal crash as globules of foamy saliva spurted vehemently from his lips in that familiar Irish rasp. His livid command bringing back terrifying, long-buried memories.

Fingernails digging deeply into the palm of her hand, Evie

knew she must be strong. Stronger than her mother. She must not show fear. That was Mam's biggest mistake, she was cowed by this man's tyrannical outrages. His children were the pawns Frank Kilgaren used to control his wife, and the biggest weapon in his arsenal.

The floodgate of memories opened. He'd threatened to take Jack and Lucy from her mam. But the war did that when they were evacuated. Evie watched uniformed bobbies hold back her *long dead* father and secure him in handcuffs.

'Frank Kilgaren, I am arresting you for the murder of your wife, Rene Kilgaren, and for the attempted murder of your son, Jack Kilgaren...'

'I didn't know it was him. It was dark. I just wanted to scare him off!' Frank Kilgaren protested, obviously ignoring the magnitude of his many misdemeanors.

'We thought you were dead!' Evie gasped.

'... Washed up on the Irish coast, unconscious for days, picked up by a sheep farmer.' He was detached, emotionless. His words slotting everything into place.

'Lucy's good shepherd.' Angus quietly informed Evie, and her heart sank. Over the years she had invented a perfect father. So too, young Lucy. A more loving, more compassionate man who would cherish and care for them.

'Mam only knew peace when you were dead...' Evie stretched her back to its full height and lifted her chin. This man had terrified the woman he promised to love and to cherish. The biggest threat to the children he swore to protect. She hugged Lucy close and Jack, resplendent in his new suit, stood head and shoulders above the two of them.

'I recognise that voice. You brought me back home on the night I was shot!' Jack realised he had just called Reckoner's Row, *home*.

Evie, feeling safe now, recalled a distant thought. Words her mother spoke to her on that Sunday before she left Reckoner's Row. *Evie,* she said, *if anything ever happens to me, just remember, I could not burden you with the ugly truth.* Like a warning, her mother's words echoed inside her head and now made sense.

'Rene knew you were alive,' Angus said to Frank. 'And you had her children?'

'I kept them in Ireland, paid my sister to look after them, hoping Rene would follow,' her father said, and Evie let out a small rush of air as two policemen bundled him out of the parlour door.

'Lucy was too young to recognise who you were...'

'I worked on a neighbouring sheep farm. Jack never saw me.'

Standing aside Evie said, 'so it was you who wouldn't allow them to come home – not Mam!' Her mother was trying to protect her, even though she could not say anything at that time.

'She had another man here. In my place.' Frank Kilgaren struggled but the burly constables were too strong. 'Nobody could blame a dead man for murder.'

'She threw Darnel out,' Evie sobbed. 'You didn't have to kill her.'

'I brought the kids home, but she wouldn't take me back.'

'You thought you'd teach her one final lesson.' The tears that flowed down Evie's cheeks were tears of anger, and from that anger she gained courage.

'She wasn't your possession. She was your wife. The mother of your children. Locked in a loveless marriage. You don't know how to love!'

'Love is a cold wind that blows no good,' Frank Kilgaren said as he was led outside to a jeering crowd of onlookers and Evie shuddered as her father was bundled into a police car. His dark eyes, staring into nothing, were devoid of warmth, of love. The bogeyman had been captured.

'One thing I vow,' Evie whispered, watching Susie Blackthorn clinging possessively to Danny's arm, 'I will chase my dream of a happy family life, and I will never allow anyone to make me feel worthless again.' Her mother had taught her that much, at least.

ACKNOWLEDGMENTS

Thank you to my amazing, enthusiastic agent extraordinaire, Felicity Trew at the Caroline Sheldon Literary Agency, who restored my faith when I needed it most.

Thank you also to my fabulous editor Nia Beynon and all the team at Boldwood, whose professional experience, attention to detail and publishing expertise is second to none!

MORE FROM SHEILA RILEY

We hope you enjoyed reading *The Mersey Orphan*. If you did, please leave a review.

If you'd like to gift a copy, this book is also available as an ebook, digital audio download and audiobook CD.

Sign up to Sheila Riley's mailing list for news, competitions and updates on future books.

http://bit.ly/SheilaRileyNewsletter

Continue the story on Reckoner's Row with *The Mersey Girls*, available to order now.

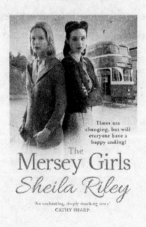

ABOUT THE AUTHOR

Sheila Riley wrote four #1 bestselling novels under the pseudonym Annie Groves and is now writing a saga trilogy under her own name. She has set it around the River Mersey and its docklands near to where she spent her early years. She still lives in Liverpool.

Visit Sheila's website: http://my-writing-ladder.blogspot.com/

Follow Sheila on social media:

facebook.com/SheilaRileyAuthor
twitter.com/1sheilariley
instagram.com/sheilarileynovelist
bookbub.com/authors/sheila-riley

ABOUT BOLDWOOD BOOKS

Boldwood Books is a fiction publishing company seeking out the best stories from around the world.

Find out more at www.boldwoodbooks.com

Sign up to the Book and Tonic newsletter for news, offers and competitions from Boldwood Books!

http://www.bit.ly/bookandtonic

We'd love to hear from you, follow us on social media:

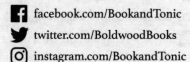

facebook.com/BookandTonic

twitter.com/BoldwoodBooks

instagram.com/BookandTonic